THE DEVIL'S PARTY

Borgo Press Books by BRIAN STABLEFORD

Algebraic Fantasies and Realistic Romances: More Masters of Science Fiction
Beyond the Colors of Darkness and Other Exotica
Changelings and Other Metamorphic Tales
A Clash of Symbols: The Triumph of James Blish
The Cosmic Perspective and Other Black Comedies
The Cure for Love and Other Tales of the Biotech Revolution
The Devil's Party: A Brief History of Satanic Abuse
The Dragon Man: A Novel of the Future
Firefly: A Novel of the Far Future
The Gardens of Tantalus and Other Delusions
Glorious Perversity: The Decline and Fall of Literary Decadence
Gothic Grotesques: Essays on Fantastic Literature
The Haunted Bookshop and Other Apparitions
Heterocosms: Science Fiction in Context and Practice
In the Flesh and Other Tales of the Biotech Revolution
The Innsmouth Heritage and Other Sequels
Jaunting on the Scoriac Tempests and Other Essays on Fantastic Literature
The Moment of Truth: A Novel of the Future
News of the Black Feast and Other Random Reviews
An Oasis of Horror: Decadent Tales and Contes Cruels
Opening Minds: Essays on Fantastic Literature
Outside the Human Aquarium: Masters of Science Fiction, Second Edition
The Path of Progress and Other Black Melodramas
Slaves of the Death Spiders and Other Essays on Fantastic Literature
The Sociology of Science Fiction
Space, Time, and Infinity: Essays on Fantastic Literature
The Tree of Life and Other Tales of the Biotech Revolution
Yesterday's Bestsellers: A Voyage Through Literary History

THE DEVIL'S PARTY

A BRIEF HISTORY OF SATANIC ABUSE

by

Brian Stableford

THE BORGO PRESS

An Imprint of Wildside Press LLC

MMIX

Copyright © 2009 by Brian Stableford

All rights reserved.
No part of this book may be reproduced in any
form without the expressed written consent of the
publisher. Printed in the United States of America.

www.wildsidepress.com

FIRST EDITION

CONTENTS

About the Author 7

Introduction 9

1. The Evolution of Satan
   The Old Testament 19
   Magic in the Old Testament 23
   The War in Heaven 26
   The Crisis of Faith 29
   The Early Evolution of Christianity 32
   Gnosticism and the Occult Tradition 35
   The Millennium and the Anti-Christ 39

2. The Politics of Persecution
   The Logic of Persecution 43
   Persecution and the Early Christian Church 47
   The Evolution of the Inquisition 54
   The Destruction of the Knights Templar 58
   Further Politically-Motivated Sorcery Trials 61

3. Satan's Harlots
   Witch-Beliefs and the Early Church 66
   Pacts with the Devil 71
   Early Treatises on Satanic Witchcraft 74
   The Hammer of the Witches 77
   The Documentation of the Great Witch-Hunt 82
   The First Phase of the Witch-Panic 85
   The Lull Before the Storm 87
   The Second Phase of the Witch-Panic 91
   The Conduct of Witch-Trials 93
   The Confessions of Accused Witches 95
   The Decline of Witch-Hunting 100

4. The War Between Skepticism and Belief
   The Problems of Skepticism 103
   The Backlash of Belief 108

    A New Kind of Skepticism 110
    The Royal Expert 115
    Memoirs of Witch-Hunting Men 121
    The Spread of Skepticism 127
    The Last Large-Scale Witch-Trials 132

5. Literary Fantasies
    Early Literary Treatments of Witchcraft and Black Magic .. 139
    The Literary History of Satan and the Diabolical Pact 145
    The Effects of the Panic on the Literary Image of the
        Witch 151
    Satan and Satanism in Modern Horror Fiction 157

6. Scholarly Fantasies
    Reinterpretations of the History of Satanic Abuse 160
    The Spin-Off of the Occult Revival 163
    The Progeny of Michelet's Sorceress 168
    An Apology for Witch-Hunters 175
    The Continued Proliferation of Scholarly Fantasies 179

7. Lifestyle Fantasies
    The Attraction of Fantasized Lifestyles 182
    Class Divisions in Magical Lifestyle Fantasy 185
    Aristocratic Lifestyle Fantasies and the Occult Revival 189
    Revisionist Witchcraft 193
    The Material Rewards of Magical Lifestyle Fantasy 197

8. The Resurgence of Satanic Abuse
    Domestication and Demonization 204
    The Extension of the Moral Panic 209
    Satanism in Modern Confessional Literature 213
    The Reliability of Child Witnesses 218

Selected Bibliography 223
Index 229

ABOUT THE AUTHOR

BRIAN STABLEFORD was born in Yorkshire in 1948. He taught at the University of Reading for several years, but is now a full-time writer. He has written many science fiction and fantasy novels, including: *The Empire of Fear, The Werewolves of London, Year Zero, The Curse of the Coral Bride*, and *The Stones of Camelot*. Collections of his short stories include: *Sexual Chemistry: Sardonic Tales of the Genetic Revolution, Designer Genes: Tales of the Biotech Revolution*, and *Sheena and Other Gothic Tales*. He has written numerous nonfiction books, including *Scientific Romance in Britain, 1890-1950, Glorious Perversity: The Decline and Fall of Literary Decadence*, and *Science Fact and Science Fiction: An Encyclopedia*. He has contributed hundreds of biographical and critical entries to reference books, including both editions of *The Encyclopedia of Science Fiction* and several editions of the library guide, *Anatomy of Wonder*. He has also translated numerous novels from the French language, including several by the feuilletonist Paul Féval.

INTRODUCTION

The phrase "Satanic abuse" acquired a certain fashionability in the final two decades of the twentieth century as a result of a series of episodes in the USA, Canada and Britain in which allegations were made that groups of adults had sexually molested young children in the context of arcane rituals. Some commentators concluded that these rites were "black masses" conducted by Satan-worshippers.

Allegations of this kind were made, apparently spontaneously, by children in widely-separate places. Some were subsequently corroborated by other children named by the initial accusers. Despite their apparently-fantastic content, these stories were believed by at least some of the adults to whom they were told. As a result, there emerged a population of "believers", who felt that the weight of the evidence emerging from so many disparate sources was entirely adequate to prove that there really were considerable numbers of Satanist pedophiles banded together in more-or-less organized groups. These believers began to fear that the police, the social services and the courts were failing to protect children from this kind of collective molestation by virtue of their unwillingness to accept that such things could possibly be happening in the modern world.

Many people who found some of the allegations believable remained dubious about the precise interpretation which should be put on them. In particular, they hesitated over the question of whether the primary motive for the founding of these alleged groups was pedophilic—in which case the ritual elements of their practices were merely theatrical devices for intimidating their child-victims—or whether the primary motive was to practice Satanism, child molestation merely being one of the things that practicing Satanists routinely do. One might think that this is a distinction without a difference, but the matter is more complicated than that, because explicit accusations of Satanism often include further crimes, particularly the murder of babies by way of sacrifice.

THE DEVIL'S PARTY, BY BRIAN STABLEFORD

The references to human sacrifice made by some of the children involved in cases of alleged ritual abuse put off many observers who could have found the more modest notion of "theatrical pedophilia" credible. There was, therefore, a substantial group of commentators who felt that there must be *something* behind the allegations made by the children, but felt that the more fanciful aspects of the allegations must be disregarded if people were ever to find out what was really going on.

The more wholehearted believers, who were ready to accept the allegations of human sacrifice because they felt that the remainder of the children's stories could be trusted, were inevitably led towards the conclusion that covert Satanist cults of a particularly vicious kind were widespread in both Britain and North America. The arguments put forward by some of the believers in ritual child molestation thus found common ground with those of various Christian groups which had long attempted to secure the commitment of their existing members and to seek new converts by stressing the everpresent menace of active evil. Certain Christian groups that had already been issuing warnings about the dangers of modern Satanism and witchcraft were quick to involve themselves in the debate about ritual child molestation, and to construe the allegations of the children involved as proof that their warnings should have been taken more seriously.

The paragraphs above employ the past tense because the moral panic associated with "Satanic child abuse" was relatively short-lived, as was a similar but less significant moral panic regarding the influence of Satanist "black metal" rock music. This is not so say, however, that no believers in Satanic child abuse remain in the early years of the twenty-first century, and certainly not to say that belief in the existence of Satanists has waned, Indeed, the number of individuals willing to describe themselves as "Satanists" has probably continued to increase, although people who call themselves Satanists vehemently deny that they are involved in child molestation or human sacrifice, and claim that they are, in fact, the ones who are being abused by such vile accusations.

Accusations of Satanism have a long history, and such accusations were, for many centuries, the ultimate form of abuse within Christendom. Accusations of that sort were used as a justification for persecution of various kinds and degrees, whose most extreme forms include all manner of torture and murder—most famously, or notoriously, the practice of extorting confessions from alleged witches, who were then executed by burning. Many of the multitudinous branches of the Christian faith eventually came to the conclusion, along with secular rationalists, that all such accusations made in the past had, in fact, been groundless, and that "witch-hunting" as a general practice is a hideous mistake, generated when moral panic oversteps its ordinary boundaries to become moral insanity. However, that change of mind by the majority has not prevented various minorities from continuing to employ accusations of Satanism as and a psychological and social weapon.

Ironically, the recent emergence of individuals willing to describe themselves as "Satanists" or "witches", and to adopt certain "Satanist" or "pagan" rites and practices, is a reaction to and reflection of the continued willingness of Christians to resort to such injurious abuse. There was a time when Christians made moral capital out of being the victims of unjust persecution, and made martyrdom into a kind of psychological and social currency. Now that Christianity is an orthodox belief-system in Western civilization, while lacking sufficient political power to exact the same penalties for heresy that were routinely exacted in the sixteenth and seventeenth centuries, it has generated its own opposition-in-kind, prompting some of its own dissenters to bid for the moral capital of unjust persecution and the psychological wealth of martyrdom.

The growth of skepticism has robbed abusive accusations of Satanism of the greater part of their injurious force, but it has not resulted in the extinction of such accusations. In reducing their effect, however, it has enabled an opposition to materialize, which has attempted to turn the thrust of the abuse back on itself, deliberately confusing and recomplicating its terminology. There is a sense, therefore, in which the more recent moral panics regarding the activity of "Satanists" have been an attempt to reclaim a privilege of abuse that had not only been almost lost but almost inverted. The condemnation of "Satanic child abuse" was a backlash against a backlash: an attempt to redeem the lost virtue of "witch-hunting" by proving that there was, indeed, something that was worthy of pursuit and persecution, and which needed to be pursued and persecuted.

Perhaps that brief and relatively impotent panic was the reflexive twitch of a dying credo, but there is little reason to think so, given that the first years of the twenty-first century have seen a spectacular increase in attempts by Islamicists to stigmatize the West in general, and the USA in particular, as a "Great Satan", and to encourage an unprecedentedly dramatic inflation in the psychological and social currency of "martyrdom". The evidence suggests that the social utility of Satanic abuse—in the broader sense of the term that refers to the use of accusations of Satanism as a form of abuse—is far too great to allow its abandonment, and that its decline in some social, sectors will merely result into its displacement into others. If this is so, it implies that hatred and paranoia are, and always have been, more powerful motivational forces in human affairs than affection and the pursuit of happiness—but if history teaches us anything, that is surely the first and foremost conclusion that rises to its surface.

* * * * * * *

The moral panic associated with "Satanic child abuse" served to illustrate some further corollaries of the particular kinds of paranoia that lead some members of society to suspect that there are Satanists luring in the community and others to worry that "witch-hunting" its itself a dangerous evil. Skeptical commentators often suggest that child witnesses must have been led by questioners anxious to elicit particular replies, and that much of what the makers and corroborators of the allegations said might—or must—have been "put into their mouths" by interrogators seeking to justify their own beliefs. The fact that children who have been abused are often very reluctant to talk about it helped to increase the difficulty of evaluating the accuracy and spontaneity of evidence emerging from interrogation.

Another common recourse of non-believers was to suggest that the more lurid aspects of the children's evidence might—or must—have been derived from horror films they had seen, probably by means of video-tapes, and that reality and fantasy had become confused. This argument was connected to another ongoing moral panic about the potential effects of sexual and violent material in films, to which many young children had recently gained access by virtue of living in households with VCRs.

Just as the moral panics themselves had a long history behind them, so these corollaries extrapolated long-standing arguments about the reliability of evidence obtained by interrogation and the likely effects of various kinds of fiction on naive minds. The uncertainties associated with these factors had very different effects on institutional observers of the moral panic.

Because of the plausibility of dismissive moves of the kinds outlined above there was an understandable tendency among legal prosecutors wishing to proceed with cases involving alleged sexual molestation to tone down allegations about "rituals" lest judges or juries conclude that the evidence of sexual molestation was thereby tainted and rendered unreliable. Most of the cases of alleged ritual abuse that actually reached the courts, foundered in exactly this fashion.

By contrast, the sensational aspects of these kinds of allegations made them very newsworthy, equipping them to function as "stories" of much the same kind as those from which the ideas might have been borrowed in the first place. The fierce arguments raging between believers and non-believers served to increase that newsworthiness even further. This kind of "feedback" effect between accusations of Satanic abuse and representations of "Satanism" and "witchcraft" in fiction and news stories is a key factor in the maintenance and elaboration of the entire network of ideas.

These kinds of confusion infect the entire history of accusations of Satanism, and provide an awkward context for any attempt to carry that history forward.

All of our knowledge of the past is, of course, imperfect and imperfectible, no matter how conscientiously we may strive to perfect it, because all such knowledge is based on relics that have survived into the present; such relics inevitably produce an image that is selective and open to distortion.

We are well aware of the incompleteness of the images that we have of prehistoric cultures, which have to be inferred from the lingering traces of buildings and tools. Modern archaeology has acquired an awesome expertise in discovering and interpreting tiny fragments of the distant past, and in making brilliant deductions from the long-buried wreckage of ancient kitchen-middens and rubbish-heaps, but everything we know about cultures that did not use writing is based on the (sometimes highly speculative) analysis of their hardware. We can know very little about the "software" of such cultures: their customs, their beliefs, their myths and their tales.

The privilege of having *historical* information—information derived from the writings of past cultures—is such a dramatic advantage in helping to build up a fuller picture that we sometimes forget its disadvantages. Documents do indeed give us a priceless insight into the software of the cultures which produced them, because writing provides a medium in which people can preserve at least some of their ideas and beliefs, and can record at least some of the events of their lives. Unfortunately, documents are produced for a wide variety of reasons, most of which have nothing at all to do with the convenience of historians to come, or with supplying the answers to questions that such historians might want to ask. Even when documents are produced explicitly for the benefit of "posterity" they will not necessarily be scrupulously objective and painstakingly accurate—indeed, they may well be subject to all kinds of distortions *because* their writers have an image to project and a case to plead.

We are apt to think of "history" as a set of hard facts, which merely require to be ascertained—and there are, indeed, a good many hard facts of history, which can be established beyond reasonable doubt, including most of the dates that comprise the popular image of what history is all about. A great many of the documentary sources that historians use do, however, require subtle processes of interpretation, and are routinely open to interpretation in widely different ways. Even those documents that are supposed to be objective records of events—birth-certificates, financial accounts, official minutes, and so on—are occasionally forged or deliberately distorted. In spite of half-hearted protestations to the contrary, the contents of the average daily newspaper are subject to many kinds of deliberate and accidental misrepresentation, and the average history text-book is only slightly better. Most documents, of course, do not even pretend to be objective records, or maintain pretences that are so shallow as to be immediately rejectable.

Although it is less selective than the evidence of prehistoric relics, all documentary evidence is nevertheless highly selective. Even in an abundantly-documented society like ours there are very many events that are "invisible" to history. There are many kinds of events whose recording is actively avoided by their participants, whether because they are illegal or socially stigmatized, or merely considered to be private and personal. All these phenomena are, from the viewpoint of the historian, visible only in vague and probably-distorted mirrors.

Most of what we know about the perpetrators of crimes, in our own society as well as those of the past, is derived from examples of their failure—from the successful exploits of the police and the courts. A successful crime is an undetected crime, and can only be visible to history as a mystery; the most successful crimes of all are those that are unidentified as crimes, and which therefore succeed in hiding from history. Such secret activities are not undocumented, but they are documented entirely by means of recorded rumor—and everything we know about the way rumors spread through our own society inclines us to the view that a history based on rumor is a very unreliable thing indeed. The problem is further compounded by the fact that rumors dealing with successfully-hidden crime find it just as easy—far easier, in fact—to deal with imaginary crimes than real ones.

The Devil's Party, by Brian Stableford

The history of Satanism and witchcraft—including contemporary newspaper reportage of "Satanic child abuse"—is almost entirely composed of rumors and their repetition. Sometimes, the repetitions are contrived to perpetuate the rumors, sometimes they are contrived to oppose and dismiss them, but the unreliability remains. There is only one way to refine such a history in a rational fashion, and that is to eliminate the impossible. When that is done, there is, alas—with due respect to Sherlock Holmes—no guarantee that what is left will be true, but at least the field of play will have been considerably reduced.

It is in this respect that the historian of Satanism and witchcraft has his only advantage, for most of what has been alleged about Satanists and witches is manifestly impossible, and can therefore be confidently proclaimed to consist of lies. Indeed, so much of what has been claimed is manifestly impossible that one is strongly tempted to take the opposite view to Sherlock Holmes and assume that the rest is lies too, even though the lies in question exercise a certain amount of plausible restraint. (Given the nature and purpose of Satanic abuse, plausible restraint is understandably rare, but it is not entirely unknown.)

Some previous "historians" working in this area have failed to make this initial methodological step, but they have usually been dedicated to the purpose of attempting to redefine the perceived boundaries of the impossible. Even attempts to write histories of Satanism and witchcraft that do attempt to rule out the impossible *a priori*, however, often compromise that assumption by adopting as their primary aim the mission of trying to fathom out what, if anything, "really happened" to provoke accusations. This is probably a pointless task, and is, in any case, a speculative one.

* * * * * * *

In observing that the history of Satanic abuse is as extensively polluted by rumor and speculation as it is possible for history to be. It is also necessary to observe that the rumors have almost all been generated, at least in the first instance, as aspects of that abuse.

The vast majority of documents making any reference to Satan or to supposed worshippers of Satan, have been written by anxious Christians whose primary purpose was to distance themselves from and express their virtuous loathing for the kinds of evil that Satan and his followers represented. Most of the (relatively rare) documents that represent themselves as the work of actual Satanists are no exception to this rule, being deliberately faked as "black propaganda"; the tiny minority produced by twentieth-century individuals who have adopted Satanism as a lifestyle fantasy are primarily devoted to denying that traditional accusations have any truth in them, and asserting that "true" Satanists not only have nothing to be ashamed of, but are actually morally superior to their superstitious accusers. Many "histories" related to this area of this research are merely participants in an ongoing process of mythologization.

It is for this reason that the notion of a "history of Satanism"—unlike a history of Satanic abuse—is something of a contradiction in terms. Historians who take books of supposed black magic and the confessions of accused witches as objects for speculative interpretation, like the pseudohistorians who take them at face value, always run the risk of becoming builders of elaborate scholarly fantasies, as many of them actually have.

There is also a significant productive process that works in the opposite direction; everyone who has ever aspired to be a magician, of whatever sort and for whatever reason, had to accept as axiomatic the notion that there is an arcane body of wisdom, covertly handed down from time immemorial, into which they could be initiated. All would-be magicians are, therefore, committed to pose as historians, either perpetuating or (more often than not) inventing a pseudohistory to shore up their imposture. Far from claiming the credit for any innovations they may add to inherited pseudohistory, they are highly likely to attribute them to sources far more prestigious than themselves, preferably even more ancient than the equally-apocryphal texts they inherited. Out of this kind of activity there has grown up over the centuries a kind of "alternative history" of magic, including multitudinous accounts of rituals and conjurations.

The advent of modern skepticism has not inhibited the production of these alternative histories in the least. Indeed, it has had the opposite effect; such works proliferated very considerably in the twentieth century. The fact that posing as a magician is no longer likely to lead to the gallows, the stake or to jail, or even to social ostracism, has opened a significant window of opportunity for such poseurs, who often have much to gain by impostures of that sort. There are enough people who are interested in magic and its possible workability to have created a lively sellers' market for the supportive apparatus sustaining such poses, including many different alternative histories—some of which are richly embellished with accounts of Satanist Sabbats, black masses and the like. Various aspects of these credulous alternative histories are still widely believed, and the desire to believe in them is given considerable support by the fact that they tend to be far more melodramatic, and hence far more interesting, than the drier, duller and more tentative history that has been pieced together by the best efforts of scrupulous historians.

Not all these imaginary histories of occult affairs assume that people accused of being Satanists really were doing what their accusers charged them with doing. Indeed, some of the more elaborate scholarly fantasies that have been constructed from the confessions of alleged witches and sorcerers have gone to extraordinary lengths to argue that the people accused of attending Satanist Sabbats in the sixteenth and seventeenth centuries must have been conducting rituals of a very different and much more benignly-intended sort. Many different versions of alternative history have been used as resources by modern "lifestyle fantasists" who pose as emphatically non-Satanist witches. The already-confused litany of Satanic abuse that arose from the great witch-panic has been further complicated by the abuse that these more recent groups have directed at one another and at the orthodox historians who deny their alternative histories—and, of course, by the abuse they have received in their turn from skeptics who think that their poses are ridiculous, or evil, or both.

The intrinsic appeal of melodrama is not the only factor involved in maintaining support for alternative histories of magic. Unorthodoxy always offers more scope for innovation than orthodoxy—which, simply because it *is* orthodox, tends to seem settled and complete. People ambitious to be original, and to seem clever, are always likely to dissent from orthodoxy as a matter of policy, and such individuals must always be prepared to pour scorn on rival opinions, no matter how authoritative they appear; thus, the more orthodox skepticism becomes, the more opposition it generates.

In an ideal world, it might be easier to separate fact from fantasy than it is in our imperfect one, and the business of writing history might be more straightforward. In the world in which we live, however, fact and fantasy are very intricately entwined—even in private thought and action, let alone in the testimony we are called upon to give when we are required to explain and justify our actions to others—and the business of writing history is not at all straightforward. This makes it all the more necessary that we should attempt to do it as scrupulously as we can, and to have as clear an idea as we can of what it is that we are trying to do.

What this book will attempt to do, as a matter of central policy, is to look at accusations of Satanism and witchcraft *as accusations*, emphasizing the manner in which they took form and were negotiated rather than the simple question of whether or not they had any kind of truth in them. It will concentrate on such matters as the reasons why people wanted, and still want, to abuse one another in this extreme fashion; the manner in which they derived or selected the particular terms of their abuse; and the manner in which the abuse generated and reflected imaginative notions contained in works of acknowledged fiction, news, popular legends, adventures in pseudo-scholarship and fantastic embellishments of actual behavior.

This is not to say that the argument contained in the text will suspend judgment on the question of whether there is any substance to past or present accusations of Satanism; quite the opposite. The text will take it for granted that there is no substance whatsoever in such abuse, and that none of it ever has ever been, is now, or ever will be empirically or morally justifiable. That is, however, a starting-point rather than a conclusion to be reached or proved. The primary purpose of the text is to go on from there to examine the details of the abuse and its rhetorical mechanisms, in the hope of finding more interesting observations to make than the simple truth that conscious and active worshippers of evil are extremely rare—if any ever existed at all—and are certainly not responsible for any significant fraction of the abundant evil that actually exists in the world.

I.

THE EVOLUTION OF SATAN

The Old Testament

Of all the documents used in the West in the attempt to understand its cultural history, none illustrates the inevitable problems of interpretation that are bound to arise in such a quest better than the Bible. It is full of puzzles and contradictions, and generates much confusion if it is assumed that it attempts to tell a single coherent story. That confusion is particularly intense with respect to its contribution to and support for beliefs regarding Satan and Satanism.

Satan is such an important figure in the New Testament that it is easy to forget or overlook his virtual absence from the Old Testament, but the modern impression that Satan was involved in the Biblical story of man in its earliest stages is mostly the product of Christian hindsight. The religion of the Hebrews, as embodied in the Old Testament, seems to be rigidly monotheistic; it recognizes no anti-god opposed to Jehovah. In the older documents, at least, all misfortunes are unhesitatingly attributed to the will of God. *Isaiah* 45:6-7 has Jehovah proclaim: "I am the Lord, and there is none else. I form the light, and create darkness: I make peace, and create evil: I the Lord do all these things." Christianity is fundamentally at odds with Judaism on this point, and in its entire philosophy of evil.

The Old Testament roots of the Christian anti-god, and of the name "Satan", are essentially two-fold. On the one hand, there is the use of the common noun *satan*—which means adversary—on several occasions, most notably in the story of Job. On the other hand, there is the story of the serpent in Eden told in *Genesis*.

The *satan* of *Job* is clearly no anti-god. He is, in fact, one of the "sons of God" who poses the question of whether Job's perfection might be attributable to good fortune rather than to indestructible faith and love. In response to the question God conducts an experiment, whose outcome tests Job's endurance in the face of all the misfortune that can be heaped upon him—a test that he ultimately survives, though not without difficulty. The rendering of "Satan" as a proper noun in the English translations of the story is misleading, but even if it is accepted, there is no indication in the text that Jehovah and Satan are on unfriendly terms.

The only Old Testament passage in which the original Hebrew uses Satan as a proper noun is I *Chronicles* 21:1, where we read that "Satan stood up against Israel and provoked David to number Israel". This is, however, the more recent of two Biblical accounts of this particular incident, the earlier version being in II *Samuel* 24:1, where the passage reads: "And again the anger of the Lord was kindled against Israel, and he moved David against them to say, Go, number Israel and Judah." What appears to have happened in between the two writings is a change in the fashion of thought. The second writer is presumably trying to stress God's transcendence of mundane events by introducing a mediator. There is still no suggestion, however, that this Satan is evil. The census in question is followed by a plague sent as punishment, but both II *Samuel* and I *Chronicles* say unequivocally that "the Lord sent pestilence upon Israel".

The translation of *Satan* into *diabolos* in a pre-Christian translation of various Old Testament books into Greek, known as the Septuagint, added a new concept to the term, presumably by accident; *diabolos* means not merely "adversary" but also "slanderer". It is the adaptation of *diabolos* into English that produced the word *devil*. In *The Wisdom of Solomon*, which is known only *via* the Septuagint and is considered apocryphal, we read (2:24) that: "God created man to be immortal, and made him to be an image of His own eternity. Nevertheless through envy of the devil came death into the world." The *diabolos* to whom the reference is intended is probably Cain, the first murderer, but some readers preferred to construe it as a reference to the serpent in Eden, and the reference to the devil's envy thus became a key element in subsequent accounts of the Devil's motivation.

Even if the latter were the case, the quote would not necessarily attribute any supernatural quality to the serpent, but the general assumption among Christian commentators has always been that the serpent must have been a diabolical spiritual being in disguise. Inspection of the original story, however, suggests that this interpretation is highly dubious. When God speaks to the serpent in *Genesis*

3:13, saying "Because thou hast done this, thou art cursed above all cattle and above every beast of the field; upon thy belly shalt thou go, and dust shalt thou eat all the days of thy life," He certainly seems to be addressing the creature itself rather than any spiritual being in disguise. Why punish serpent-kind if the guilty party was only pretending to be a serpent?

Although there is no unambiguous trace of an anti-god in the Old Testament, there are various cryptic passages that seem to refer to lesser demons. None of these references is explicit, and it seems probable that they refer to obsolete beliefs that were in the process of being rigorously discarded by the Hebrews as they adopted the fervent monotheism of Judaism. Although virtually eliminated from the Torah, such demons are much more elaborately featured in the Talmud, where they feature in numerous folktales, including the symbolic tale of their banishment from the world, imprisoned in bottles, by Solomon. The references that survive in the Old Testament are further confused by English translators, most of whom followed examples set by William Tyndale and other contributors to the "Authorized Version" compiled in the reign of James I.

The *seraphim* or "fiery serpents" referred to in Numbers 21:6-8 and *Deuteronomy* 8:15 seem, in those contexts, to be demons of the wilderness, but they were later represented as angels in *Isaiah* 6. The *se'irim* or "hairy ones" (sometimes translated as "he-goats" or "satyrs") referred to in *Leviticus* 17:7, II *Kings* 23:8, *Isaiah* 13:21 and *Isaiah* 34:14 were presumably animal demons of some kind. There are several other references in the book of *Isaiah* which probably refer to demons who had been demoted to mere metaphors; these are the *ziyyim* (translated as "wild beasts", the *'ochim* (translated as "doleful creatures"), the *benoth ya'anah* (translated as "ostriches", though the term means "daughters of greed" and the Septuagint renders it as "syrens"), and the *iyyim* (which comes from a word meaning "screech" and presumably refers to a bird of prey, though it is sometimes rendered as "wolves").

The most important reference to a named demon that survives in the Old Testament is to Azazel—reckoned in the Talmud to be the king of the demons—in a passage in *Leviticus* 16:7-28, which relates to the casting of lots for two goats, one of which is sent into the wilderness for Azazel (usually translated as "for the scapegoat", although this term ought to refer to the goat itself). Azazel was presumably a demon of the wilderness to be propitiated by this rite. Another named demon is Lilith, referred to in *Isaiah* 34:11-15; the name is generally translated as "screech-owl" or "night-monster".

Judaic folklore sometimes links the two names together, some tales suggesting that Lilith was, or became, Azazel's wife. Lilith was also linked with Adam, represented as his first wife—presumably as a result of writers attempting to reconcile *Genesis* 1:27, which states "So God created man in His own image...male and female created he them", with *Genesis* 2:15-21, where we find Adam alone before the creation of Eve.

    The virtual erasure of these demons from the scriptures obviously did not prevent their survival in the folklore of the Hebrews, and they were to enjoy something of a resurgence in the extraordinarily elaborate apocryphal and pseudoepigraphical writings that were produced in the two centuries before the birth of Christ—a tradition from which the New Testament borrowed several ideas, most notably the story of the War in Heaven, whose most extravagant description is in the book of *Enoch*. Azazel is featured there, but merely as one of the rebel angels, rather than their leader. To what extent the continual Old Testament warnings against the worshipping of idols refer to older Jewish mythology rather than the alien faiths of neighboring peoples we can only speculate. As we shall see in later chapters, though, ideas do not need to retain the status of beliefs to be sustained, and their demotion to items of folklore and fiction does not prevent their occasional repromotion to items of faith. The idea that all folktales and legends must have some essential kernel of truth is remarkably stubborn, even in an era when the manufacture of folklore is an industry fully committed to the ideals of mass-production. Nevertheless, in the Old Testament itself, the determination to clear away such obsolete beliefs, and to establish an authentic monotheism in their place, is very obvious.

    One of the most striking attributes of Judaic monotheism, as described and constituted in the Old Testament, is that it leaves so little room for the attribution of blame for misfortune to anyone or anything but God. The notion of evil demons had been all-but-abandoned, and there is little evidence that the writers of the scriptures were much preoccupied by the actions of evil magicians. The Jews accepted the burden of guilt for all their misfortunes upon their own shoulders, considering it the legacy of the sins of their fathers, who had failed to honor their contracts with Jehovah. This notion has evident affinities with the Christian doctrine of original sin but is quite distinct; the contracts between Jehovah and the Jewish people emphasize the *collective* identity of the Jews, but Christian doctrine focuses much more narrowly on the individual and his particular record of sin and salvation, so that original sin is a kind of "initial debit" shown on every account.

The harsh judgment which the Jews passed upon themselves—the acceptance of collective responsibility for the vicissitudes of chance—is connected both with a strong sense of cultural identity and with a certain fatalism of outlook. The fatalism was, however, counterbalanced by the hope of eventual reconciliation and reward: the myth of the Promised Land, which would ultimately be won by obedience to the dictates of the covenant. The astonishing resilience of the Jewish world-view under appalling pressure, and the continued power of the myth of the promised land, are still very evident in the history of the twentieth century, especially the creation of the state of Israel in the wake of the Holocaust.

The early Christians retained the hope of a better state to come, either by admittance to Heaven on an individual basis or by a miraculous transformation of the world following the return of Christ to Earth, but in Christian tradition, this reward—whether individual or collective—became much more dubious, because its attainment required far more than mere patient endurance of whatever misfortunes history happened to throw up. In the Christian world-view, the path to eventual salvation was made far more problematic and difficult of attainment, by virtue of the existence of a force of active evil forever engaged in the business of tempting men away from it: Satan, and the legion of demons which he commanded.

Magic in the Old Testament

Before continuing the story of the specific evolution of the idea of Satan, it is useful to look at the Old Testament's attitude to magic. Within Christian tradition, the orthodox view has always been that magic is evil, and therefore Satanic; in the late Middle Ages this was extrapolated by scholastic philosophers into the notion that people who practice magic—witches and sorcerers—must, whether knowingly or unknowingly, have made a tacit or explicit pact with Satan. There has, however, always been a parallel tradition that regards magic as something morally neutral and potentially virtuous, quite unconnected with Satan.

There is no doubt that the Old Testament disapproves of magic, regardless of its source; the Jews were strictly forbidden to practice it. The Authorized Version of *Deuteronomy* 18:10-12 states that:

"There shall not be found among you *any one* that maketh his son or daughter to pass through the fire, *or* that useth divination, *or* an observer of times, or an enchanter, or a witch.

"Or a charmer, or a consulter with familiar spirits, or a wizard, or a necromancer.

"For all that do these things *are* an abomination unto the Lord: and because of these abominations the Lord thy God doth drive them out from before thee."

Chapters 19 and 20 of *Leviticus* offer the following warnings:

"Ye shall not eat *any thing* with the blood: neither shall ye use enchantment, nor observe times.

"Regard not them that have familiar spirits, neither seek after wizards, to be defiled by them: I *am* the Lord your God.

"And the soul that turneth after such as have familiar spirits, and after wizards, to go a whoring after them, I will even set my face against that soul, and will cut him off from among his people.

"A man also or a woman that hath a familiar spirit, or that is a wizard, shall surely be put to death: they shall stone them with stones: their blood *shall be* upon them."

The most celebrated and most succinct of all such passages to be found in the Authorized Version is *Exodus* 22:18, which simply says: "Thou shalt not suffer a witch to live."

It must be remembered, however, that these passages come from a translation of the Bible that was made while witch-hunting in Britain was still going on. The words used reflect, to some extent, the beliefs and the preoccupations of the translators rather than those of the Hebrews themselves.

The appearance of the word "witch" in English versions of the Old Testament was one of the principal warrants of the British witchfinders, and a powerful argument in favor of belief in witchcraft—so powerful, in fact, that John Wesley was led to comment that "Giving up witchcraft means, in effect, giving up the Bible"— but the word could not possibly have referred to the same kind of "witch" that Wesley believed in, because the Christians supposed witches to be worshipers of Satan and there is no Satan in the earlier books of the Old Testament. The skeptic Reginald Scot alleged in his *Discoverie of Witchcraft* (1584) that the original Hebrew word translated as "witch" in *Exodus* meant "poisoner" and had nothing to do with the supernatural. (Although the action of poisons was understood no better than the action of disease in Biblical times or seventeenth-century Britain, and could have considered as a form of magic, the common opinion always was that it was a natural phenomenon.)

If one sets aside the interventions of translators, it can easily be observed that the unambiguous and stern disapproval of magic recorded by the original writers of the Old Testament was not reflected in any significant fear of magicians. Indeed, the Old Testament prophets were fully convinced that Jehovah could and would protect them from the threats of evil magic. There are no Old Testament accounts of witch-hunting, and no passages referring to the threat of maleficent magic as a danger to the social order. In *Exodus* 7 and 8 Aaron is required to compete with the magicians of Pharaoh's court, but, because he has the power of the Lord to draw on, he needs no magic of his own to win the competition; a few small miracles easily put the Egyptian magicians to shame. In *Numbers* 22 the magician Balaam is asked by Balak, king of the Moabites, to curse the Children of Israel (who were invading his land), but the intervention of the Lord causes Balaam to bless the invaders instead of cursing them; again the implication is that magic could not prevail against the Israelites, because they were protected by Jehovah.

The most important reference to magic in the Old Testament is perhaps the story in I *Samuel* 28:3-25, in which Saul visits the individual known to English readers as "witch of Endor". The word "witch" is not used in the actual text, which refers to "a woman that hath a familiar spirit", but it does occur in the gloss that was added to the head of the page in many reprints of the Authorized Version. The story tells how Saul, who has previously expelled from his domain "those that had familiar spirits and wizards", wishes to know the outcome of an impending clash with the Philistines. He goes (in disguise) to a female necromancer, who calls up the spirit of Samuel. The spirit reveals that the Lord has deserted Saul and will deliver Israel into the hands of the Philistines as a punishment for disobedience.

In spite of the enthusiasm of Christian witchfinders for this example of Biblical witchcraft there is no implication in this passage that the woman who summons the spirit is an evil person. After Saul's interview she comforts him, and even kills a fatted calf so that he may eat before returning home. This suggests that the Old Testament condemnation of magical practices was *not* based on the assumption that magic was considered to be the sole prerogative of evil persons, but was an aspect of the total monotheistic commitment of the Jews—an acceptance of the fact that any benefits that they might enjoy ought to be the gifts of God. The Jews were not afraid of magic, because they considered themselves to be protected from it, except insofar as the Lord should feel disposed to allow them to be harmed; nor did they allow themselves to use magic—but they did not consider people who did use magic to be intrinsically evil or necessarily malevolent.

For some time, at least, most Christians seem to have adopted a similar attitude. At the very least, Christian anxiety about evil magic and demons—including Satan himself—was counterbalanced by their trust in God's protection. Anxiety regarding magic and magicians seems to have remained at a relatively low pitch throughout the first thousand years of Christendom, in spite of a number of localized and temporary panics. In the second millennium of the Christian calendar, however, there was a dramatic and drastic attitudinal change, one of whose consequences was the unprecedentedly widespread, sustained and violent witch-panic of the sixteenth and seventeenth centuries. That change of attitude was, in part if not in essence, a drastic failure of trust in the willingness of God to protect his worshippers, and a despairing acceptance of the fact that He allowed the Devil far more license to tempt witches and to injure innocent people than had previously been supposed.

The War in Heaven

There is no very obvious link between the Old Testament uses of the word *satan*, or the story of the serpent in Eden, and the rich demonology characteristic of Jewish apocalyptic writing and early Christian documents. The story of the War in Heaven and the subsequent fate of the fallen angels told in the most celebrated of the apocryphal documents, the book of *Enoch*—which probably dates from the second century BC—might, however, be derived from two rather enigmatic comments in *Genesis* 6:1-4:

"And it came to pass, when men began to multiply on the face of the earth, and daughters were born unto them,

"That the sons of God saw the daughters of men that they *were* fair; and they took them wives of all which they chose....

"There were giants in the earth in those days; and also after that, when the sons of God came in unto the daughters of men, and they bare *children* to them, the same *became* mighty men which *were* of old, men of renown."

The significance of these verses is obscure, and there is no explicit suggestion that the "sons of God" to which they refer are angels, but *Enoch* takes that view, expanding the story considerably to form the beginning of a melodramatic account of miscegenation between angels and men (the giants being the offspring of the unnatural union), which eventually leads to a war in Heaven. Jehovah then commands the archangel Michael to take punitive action against the "defiled" angels, whose leader is named Semiazaz. It is required that they be bound in caverns beneath the earth for seventy generations, until the day of judgment, when they can be confined in "the abyss of fire" along with all other beings so condemned. It is worth noting that in *Enoch*, as in Genesis, these events take place long after the expulsion of Adam and Eve from Eden, and there is no connection between this version of the fall of the angels and the luckless serpent.

Other apocalyptic writings extend or alter the tale told by *Enoch*. The book of *Jubilees* does not confine all the fallen angels to a prison beneath the earth, but allows some to remain on the surface, wreaking destruction and tempting men to sin. These demons are said to be under the leadership of Mastema. The idea of temptation and of competition between God and the demons to win the allegiance of individual men is further developed in the *Testaments of the Twelve Patriarchs*, where the demons—here under the leadership of Belial—make strenuous attempts to alienate men from God. In these documents, which presumably revive and reconstruct old demonological beliefs, we see the modification of a strand of unorthodox Jewish thought with a dualistic world-view in which Jehovah is still opposed by a host of demons, whose variously-named leader was the "ancestor" of the Christian Satan.

These ideas were undoubtedly taken up by new sects. Some of the so-called Dead Sea scrolls found in caves near the ruins of the community of Qumran during 1947-56—which include most of the books of the Old Testament as well as these apocryphal books—feature liturgical curses directed against the leader of the fallen angels, who is called by various names, including *Mekilresha'* ("My king is wickedness") and—for the first time—Satan. These documents probably antedate the birth of Christ by a few decades, although the actual time of origin of the prescriptions for prayer that they contain is uncertain. The attitude embodied in these curses is, however, strikingly different from the world-view of the Old Testament books and has much more in common with Christian mythology.

The New Testament writers and the founding fathers of the Christian faith reinterpreted many references in the Old Testament according to their own views, and thereby "discovered" many more fallen angels, or alternative names by which Satan might be known. *Matthew* 12:24 explicitly identifies the god of the Phoenicians, Beelzebub (or Baal) with Satan. A reference in the Authorized Version of *Isaiah* 14:22 to Lucifer—the Latin for "light-bearer" employed as a translation of the Hebrew *hillel*, meaning "morning star"—whose original use was probably a metaphorical reference the King of Babylon, was also construed by the Church fathers as a reference to the leader of the fallen angels, and Lucifer became one of the most common substitutes for Satan.

The principal substance and purpose of Jewish apocalyptic literature is not the construction of a retrospective mythology relating to the origin of the forces of evil, but rather the anticipation of a coming battle in which those forces would be annihilated. This coming settlement—the Apocalypse—is the real core of the renewed mythology. In this respect, Jewish apocalyptic thought has obvious affinities with other contemporary systems of dualistic thought, especially the Zoroastrian mythology that apparently thrived in Persia before its invasion from the East, whose details were eventually written down in the *Zend-Avestra*. In Zoroastrian dualism, the work of a hierarchy of benign divinities head by Ahura Mazda is opposed by that of an equally powerful troop of malevolent deities, led by Ahriman. Apocalyptic mythology of the Enochian variety might be regarded as a syncretic incorporation of Zoroastrian ideas into the Mosaic myth of the Promised Land and the ultimate reconciliation of the God of the Covenant and his Chosen People.

In the orthodox Jewish philosophy the Promised Land was to be an earthly reward, and so it remained in most of the apocalyptic literature. By associating the notion with a vast conflict of spiritual beings, however, the apocalyptic writers did confuse the issue somewhat, preparing the way for a new interpretation of the reward of virtue as a purely spiritual matter. The earthly reward, of course, involved the entire Jewish people, and was the inevitable end to history, but the eventual substitution of the notion of a purely spiritual reward and the consequent de-historicization of salvation facilitated the growth of the notion that it might be a purely personal reward, potentially deliverable to each individual immediately after death. Jewish ideas were gradually confused, and eventually dramatically transformed, by this line of thought, so that a rigid monotheism gave birth to a rather different kind of religion.

The history of the Christian world-view is, in one sense, the history of a retreat from the wholehearted acceptance of the burden of collective moral responsibility for misfortune. The Christians, like other Jewish sects of the same period, invented an anti-god on whom all misfortune might be blamed, and gave him a legion of evil demons to assist in the work of temptation. Eventually, they were also to give him a similar legion of earthly minions, in the form of worshipful witches. By this means, the followers of Christ mustered all the convenient scapegoats who might be appointed to take the blame for evil circumstance into a single system. The reasons urging them to follow this ideative path were undoubtedly complex, but they obviously felt the necessity very deeply indeed. It is difficult to imagine that the early proto-Christians suffered more or worse misfortune than other Jews, but they found an alternative method of coming to terms with that misfortune, which proved just as forceful and just as durable.

The Crisis of Faith

The historical causes of the crisis of faith that produced the Jewish apocalyptic writings of the second and first centuries BC are as vague as most historical causes, but the character of the apocalyptic writings themselves, and the pattern of events in which the Jews were involved during those two centuries, provide several important clues. It is worth considering this question in detail because there might have been significant similarities between this crisis and the later one that produced the witch-panics of the sixteenth and seventeenth centuries; it might even be possible to find parallels with the causes of twentieth-century anxieties about Satanism.

The Jewish myth of the Promised Land is basically an optimistic one, Utopian in character. It imagines that, at the end of a long and difficult struggle, the Hebrews could redeem themselves in the eyes of God and be rewarded under the Covenant. Prominent among the virtues emphasized by this myth is patience; the Covenant is essentially a long-term contract. Apocalyptic mythology, on the other hand, sees the end as imminent; its optimism is much more extravagant and much more fervent. Such fervent optimism is, however, inevitably counterbalanced by an equally fervent anxiety.

Jewish apocalyptic writings feature extremely severe criticism of those who have failed, and are failing, to keep the faith. There is a heavy emphasis in such writings on the sorting out of the worthy from the unworthy, the separation of those who deserve the anticipated reward from those who do not. *Enoch* 91:7-8 says:

And when sin and unrighteousness and blasphemy

> And violence in all kinds of deeds increase,
> And apostasy and transgression and uncleanness increase,
> A great chastisement shall come from heaven upon all these,
> And the holy Lord will come forth with wrath and chastisement
> To execute judgment upon the earth.
> In those days violence shall be cut off from its roots,
> And the roots of unrighteousness together with deceit,
> And they shall be destroyed from under heaven.

Even in today's world we are used to hearing would-be prophets cry that the end of the world is nigh; we know that such cries are commonly associated with a deep sense of the irredeemable corruption of the world, and the notion that wickedness has gained the upper hand in the fight against good. The appearance within Jewish apocalyptic mythology of a complex mythology of active evil suggests that something similar was involved in the emergence of the apocalyptic writings and such sects as that associated with the Qumran community.

There were two crucial events in Jewish history during the two centuries before Christ which can be readily associated with the growth of this new mythology. The first was a liberation, the second a new loss of liberty.

For several centuries before the middle of the second century BC the Jews had been subject to foreign rule—first by the Babylonians, then by the Persians and finally by the Syrian Seleucids. In 142 BC, however, the Jews successfully revolted against the Seleucids and recovered the long-lost independence of Judea. They began to extend their new empire, and ultimately recovered most of the lands that had once been governed by David and Solomon. It was presumably this change in the historical fortunes of the people that generated a new sense of the imminence of the fulfillment of the Covenant. This process must have seemed to many people to be the recovery of the promised land; it is understandable that they found grounds for hoping that the moment of reward could not be far away.

The new-found enthusiasm brought anxieties as well as a sense of triumph, though. It heightened the awareness of some would-be religious leaders to the faults of their fellow men. Once having been awakened to the possibility of imminent reward, some people apparently became worried by the prospect that it might be snatched from their grasp (as they believed it to have been in the past) as a result of the wickedness of a few. The upsurge of religious fervor is probably explicable in these terms; this pattern of conjecture allows us to see how certain aspects of the apocalyptic mythology came into being.

The independence of Judea lasted for less than a century. In 65 BC the Roman general Pompey stormed Jerusalem in the climax of his Middle-Eastern campaigns. The Roman Empire continued to expand its bounds thereafter, bringing much of Europe, Asia Minor and North Africa together into a single political entity. The Jews became, once again, a subject people, within the grip of an empire much more powerful, if somewhat less oppressive, than the Babylonian and Egyptian empires that had previously enslaved them. They reacted more fervently and more violently against this new subjection than their ancestors in Babylon and Egypt, but their efforts failed dismally. A series of revolts eventually led to the Emperor Titus sacking Jerusalem in 66-70 AD and destroying the Temple. In 132-135, after a further rebellion, Jerusalem was deliberately obliterated, as a harsh lesson to other would-be revolutionaries against the empire, whose long decline was already under way and generating considerable anxieties.

The loss of Judea's independence did not altogether destroy the expectations that had grown up among the Jews. What it appears to have done was, on the one hand, to confirm and inflame the anxiety regarding the possibility that the reward might be snatched away again because of the wickedness of the few, and, on the other hand, to transform the mythology itself. The basically Utopian character of the myth of the Promised Land was, in some versions of the new apocalyptic mythology, altered into a transcendent mythology. The price of keeping the expectation of imminent reward was, at least for some, a change in the kind of the reward they could expect.

For many generations the Jews had cherished the myth of a messiah who was to lead them to the Promised Land. After 142 BC they came to believe that his arrival was imminent, but after 65 BC they found themselves on the horns of a dilemma. Either they had to change their minds and recover their fatalistic patience, or they had to look for a new kind of messiah offering a new kind of reward. Perhaps inevitably, some chose one course and some the other; the Jewish faith was riven by schisms. Those schisms were subjected to further stress by the events of 70 AD and 135 AD, in which the Temple, and Jerusalem itself, were destroyed. The effects of that stress produced two distinct and very different strands of faith. On the one hand there was a resurgence of the old orthodoxy; on the other, there was the birth of a new messianic religion: Christianity.

The Early Evolution of Christianity

The older books of the Old Testament represent Jehovah as the god of the Jews, and no more than that. The Covenant united the tribes of Israel as one party in the contract with Jehovah, so that every Israelite accepted the burden of responsibility for past and future generations as well as his own. This acceptance of responsibility, however, had a tendency to grow. The latter part of the book of Isaiah extends this notion to imply that the Israelites are suffering for the sins of *all* mankind. The Day of Judgment here seems to be a universal process or event, although only the Jews are to be redeemed as a result, and the suffering of the Jews is construed as a peculiar testament to their eventual redemption. This notion is implicit in all the later apocalyptic writings.

Jesus and his disciples constituted a Jewish sect, and Jesus addressed his early teaching exclusively to the Jews, but, according to *The Acts of the Apostles,* the sect soon developed the notion of a universal commission to convert the Jews and gentiles alike to their new faith, thus making possible the redemption of *all* mankind at the Day of Judgment. Christianity thus became a crusade for universal salvation, which took as its basic assumption the credo that all men could be won from the worship of whatever false and demonic gods they had adopted in error, thus becoming eligible for reward instead of punishment at the Day of Judgment. This was not established as a basic feature of the new faith without conflict, its eventual success being largely due to the writings by or attributed to Saint Paul, but it was eventually elevated to the status of a central orthodoxy. One corollary of the mission was an acceptance of the fact that Satan was a very powerful individual, who already had most of the world's people under his deceptive dominion, and would not easily surrender them to the worship of the true God.

The historical success of Christianity as a world religion was, of course, dependent upon and intimately bound up with its hunger for converts and its determination to absorb all other cultures and faiths. Faiths that do not actively seek converts cannot establish empires of belief; there is a logic of "cultural selection" akin to that of Darwinian natural selection, which favors the emergence and evolution of convert-hungry religions; Islam subsequently followed a similar historical trajectory, with similar success. The darker aspect of this avidity for converts is, of course, an uncompromising intolerance of rival faiths, which inevitably come to be seen as demonic. The early Christians began to see proof of Satan's activities in every barrier that was erected against their crusade for converts; the natural reluctance of followers of other faiths to abandon their traditions was construed as a stubborn commitment to the paths of evil. The difficulties and anxieties experienced by Christians in search of converts increased the fervor of their determination to take up arms against Satan and redeem the world from his dominion.

Previous cultures that had believed in evil demons or anti-gods had tended to be far more concerned with their propitiation than with active opposition to them. There had been substantial movements in other religious cultures—including those of Egypt and Persia—toward the notion that the only gods who merited worship were the good ones, and that the propitiation of evil gods was therefore evil, but these movements remained internal to the cultures concerned. The early Christians decided, however, that the only good God was their own and that all men who worshipped other gods—no matter how benign those gods might seem—had to be rescued from their folly by whatever means came to hand, no matter how reluctant they might be to be rescued.

In the service of this aim, the Christians developed a new mythology of the war between good and evil, which, although it evolved out of the Enochian myth of the fallen angels, altered it in several significant ways. First of all, it projected the War in Heaven back in time so that the serpent in Eden could become a consequent manifestation of the leader of the fallen angels. Secondly, it represented the actions of the angels who were tempted to sin as no mere fall from grace but as an actual rebellious uprising. The leader of the fallen angels was, in this view, no longer a miserable creature who had lapsed from the standards expected of him, but a prideful individual whose ambition had been—and still was—to usurp the throne of God. *Enoch*'s rebel angels were imprisoned within the Earth to await the Day of Judgment sadly, but in Christian mythology their imprisonment was modified by a license to make the earth into a battleground, with the souls of men the prizes in an everlasting contest.

Virtually all the books of the New Testament are still in accord with *Enoch* on the matter of the fall of the angels and their fate, although a few passages can also be read in the context of the new mythology. The new mythology appears unequivocally only in *The Revelation of St. John the Divine*, and even this book seems slightly inconsistent in its attitudes. *Revelation* 7:7-9 tells the story of the war in Heaven in the following terms:

"And there was war in heaven: Michael and his angels fought against the dragon; and the dragon fought and his angels,

"And prevailed not; neither was their place found any more in heaven.

"And the great dragon was cast out, that old serpent, called the Devil, and Satan, which deceiveth the whole world: he was cast out into the earth, and his angels were cast out with him."

The reference to the serpent here might tempt unwary readers to link the passage with the Eden myth, but the word seems to be used simply as an alternative to "dragon" for purely metaphorical purposes. The link between Satan and the serpent that tempted Eve was not decisively forged until the writings of the second century Christian apologist Justin Martyr; Justin's case was based primarily on the above-quoted passage, although he also co-opted as "evidence" a reference in *Isaiah* 27:1 to "the piercing serpent" Leviathan. Justin also lent strong support to the notion (which originated with Paul) that all the gods of the pagans were members of Satan's host of devils. Justin was the first writer to represent Christianity explicitly as a kind of "liberation movement" to free men from their subjection to Satan, and he addressed himself largely to a non-Jewish audience.

There remained one vital difference, however, between the War against Satan as it was conceived by the early Christians and the war as it later came to be conceived by the Medieval Church. In the days of Justin Martyr, and for several centuries afterwards, Satan was seen as an *external* enemy. Through his demons he ruled the pagans, and it was as their ruler that he was to be fought, but those already converted to Christianity were, *ipso facto*, free of his dominion. Early Christian writers like Iranaeus and Tertullian were agreed upon this point, and Origen opined that the power of Satan was on the wane because of the success of the Christians in winning converts.

While Christianity was still expanding its sphere of influence this continued to be the way that Christians saw the fight that was their mission—but once they had triumphed, and established a Holy Empire in Europe, the situation changed. Once the Christians had converted the people whom they saw as the due recipients of their teaching—or had failed after several attempts, as with the Moslems who held the Holy Land—they gradually became more and more preoccupied with the idea of Satan as an enemy *within*, whose demons constituted an internal menace to the realm of Christendom. This preoccupation evolved by degrees into a virtual obsession, and was one of the most important factors involved in the great witch-panic of the sixteenth and seventeenth centuries.

Gnosticism and the Occult Tradition

When Christianity emerged as a system of thought in the declining Roman Empire, the predominant intellectual tradition was inherited from Greek philosophers, especially the works of Aristotle. Aristotle had begun his career as a student at Plato's Academy, but had subsequently founded his own rival school, the Lyceum. In establishing his own intellectual independence, he had made something of a policy of disagreeing with Plato on virtually every major point of philosophy. This rivalry was maintained in the Roman Empire, where several schools of thought attempting to preserve or renew older philosophical traditions—including those describing themselves as neo-Pythagorean and neo-Platonic—survived or were renewed.

The neo-Pythagoreans and neo-Platonists defended aspects of the older philosophies that Aristotle had discarded or de-emphasized, particularly the Pythagorean notion that there was a fundamental natural harmony describable in terms of numerical mysticism and reflected in a complex series of analogies between different aspects of experience. Plato had also been somewhat preoccupied with patterns of this sort, so neo-Pythagoreanism and neo-Platonism were both essentially "holistic", asserting that everything in the universe is connected, and that the connections form a complex pattern of analogical relationships. One corollary of this notion as that all belief-systems are, in fact, merely different versions of an underlying truth, and that all of them have some merit—a notion that fitted in quite well with the Roman Empire's initial religious tolerance, but contrasted sharply with the exclusivity of the Christian world-view, causing a keener rivalry to develop between Christians and the anti-Aristotelian schools than had previous existed between those schools and Aristotelians.

The most important neo-Platonic philosopher was Plotinus, whose *Enneads* were assembled by his disciple Porphyry. The holism of Plotinus' thought was embodied in the notion that the intelligibility of the world had to be attained by a threefold path—integrating the routes to understanding followed by the Musician, the Lover and the Philosopher—and a key analogy likening and linking the microcosm of the human soul to the macrocosmic motions the heavens. Porphyry's chief successor, Iamblichus, explicitly attempted to reconcile all forms of religion within a single syncretic system—but he felt forced to expel Christianity from the scheme in response to the Christians' own determined exclusivity.

This move permanently colored Christian attitudes to neo-Platonist ideas. It was still causing problems in the Renaissance for philosophers who wanted to recover the legacy of neo-Platonism along with other Classical learning, but the problems began much earlier, when various early Christian groups attempted to take aboard aspects of neo-Platonic thought. Some such doctrines were encountered by St. Paul among the Corinthians, where there had apparently arisen a "spiritual aristocracy" whose members believed themselves to be possessed of a more profound wisdom, and capable of deeper mystical experiences, than their fellow Christians. They embraced a special kind of dualism, arguing that the spiritual soul of man was the sole concern of God and that the material body—perhaps even the whole material world—was either irrelevant or a creation of Satan; their notion of the primacy and immortality of the soul was firmly neo-Platonic, but in the context of Christian thought they became known as Gnostics—believers in the existence of an esoteric body of wisdom, the *gnosis*, forming a supplement to the gospels and their New Testament addenda.

Contests between St. Paul and his followers and various rival groups take up much of *The Acts of the Apostles* and are a major preoccupation of the Epistles, but those dealing with the apparent pollution of Christian doctrine by Gnostic neo-Platonism are the most mysterious as well as the most fervent. As a defensive move, Gnostics tended to dress up any neo-Platonic ideas they adopted with careful layers of mysticism—an obfuscatory strategy that confused the entire subsequent history of Christian alchemy, astrology and medicine, to the extent that Mysticism became a significant topic in its own right, sprawling across the boundaries of church doctrine.

The history of Gnosticism is clouded in mystery, most of the surviving references occurring in texts written by writers anxious to condemn Gnostics as heretics. The most important documentary relic of a Gnostic sect is a Coptic codex of the fifth or sixth century called the *Pistis Sophia*, which condemns magic and venerates Christ, but the Gnostic quest to elevate the minds (or souls) of members of their élites to heights of knowledge and experience to which common people could not aspire was anathema to Christians, who were much more narrowly focused on the gospels. The supposedly-elevated souls of the Gnostic élites tended to regard the material world as rather vulgar, unimportant to the divine plan and purpose, and this resulted in the occasional adoption of extreme attitudes to the life of the body. Although extreme asceticism was probably more common, it was extreme licentiousness that called forth bitter condemnation from others. The brief epistle of *Jude* apparently preaches against such a sect; verses 4 and 7-8 read:

"For there are certain men crept in unawares, who were before of old ordained to this condemnation, ungodly men, turning the grace of our God into lasciviousness....

"Even as Sodom and Gomorrah, and the cities about them in like manner, giving themselves over to fornication, and going after strange flesh, are set forth for an example, suffering the vengeance of eternal fire,

"Likewise also these *filthy* dreamers defile the flesh, despise dominion, and speak evil of dignities."

The idea that Gnostics were prone to sexual license and other indulgences was to crop up again and again, and became an accusation leveled at all heretical sects, regardless of their actual creeds; it became a core element of the abuse which Christians leveled at all kinds of "Satanists".

Although many of the Gnostic sects were Christian in the sense that they attributed to Christ the role of redeemer, some apparently denied him any real importance and some adopted alternative redeemers; one of these was Simon Magus, whose fate is described in *Acts*. The sect that flourished in the name of Simon Magus was obviously short-lived, but it attracted some particularly vitriolic attacks from Christian writers, and the accusations which were leveled against its members are significant in terms of later ideas of Satanist practices. Simon was charged with being a magician who used menstrual blood and semen in his magic, and was said to call upon the aid of demons, thus becoming a proto-Satanist. He was not alone. *Acts* also includes an encounter with "Elymas the sorcerer", and the list of magicians was further swelled when some neo-Pythagoreans and neo-Platonists fought back against the loud advertisement of Christ's miracles by inventing their own rival miracle-workers. The neo-Platonist philosopher Apollonius of Tyana was posthumously promoted as a rival miracle-worker in a fictionalized biography written by Philostratus in the third century AD. In Philostratus' account, Apollonius is hailed as a benign and virtuous miracle-worker, but in the eyes of the Christians he immediately became an evil magician.

One of the most influential of the rival sects that Paul's followers had to combat was founded by Mani in the third century. In Mani's Persian homeland Mithraism had recently displaced the old religion of the Zoroastrian Magi and the Christians' determination to win converts brought them into sharp conflict with the new creed. Mani seems to have designed his new system in an attempt to harmonize the faiths and the situation. He drew heavily on the older tradition of Zoroastrianism, which had strong affinities with both the rival systems and could therefore provide a bridge between them. He also imported some beliefs from Buddhism, with the explicit aim of providing a religious system acceptable to all peoples of the known world. Inevitably, though, his system was attacked from all sides as a heresy.

Mani's scheme represented Good and Evil as equal powers, man's body being the product of Satan while his soul was the creation of God. Mani offered himself as the last in a line of prophets, which had included Noah, Abraham, Zoroaster and Buddha, but which conceded Christ only a minor role. The Manichean élite was to practice rigorous asceticism but the inferior order of "hearers" had only to follow a set of simple moral precepts in the hope that they might eventually deserve reincarnation as members of the Elect, with the consequent opportunity of finally delivering their souls from the prison of matter. The religious ceremonies of the Elect were secretive.

Mani was crucified in Persia in 276 AD, but Manicheism spread through much of Europe. The Christian Roman emperors after Julian the Apostate drove the sect underground and it is not known how long it persisted in secret. In Africa, though, it was left alone and was still flourishing at the end of the fourth century. St. Augustine was a Manichean hearer before his conversion to Christianity in 386, and, as with most converts, he was loud and persistent in his condemnation of the faith he had renounced. Pseudo-Manichean dualism was to emerge several times more in the Christian world, in the form of sects that were suppressed with increasing vigor by the ever-more-powerful Church. Christian attacks alleged that some such dualistic sects, believing the material world to be the creation of an evil principle or "demiurge", took to worshipping this principle instead of God, thus becoming explicit rather than tacit Satanists; supplementary charges of working evil magic with demonic aid were common corollaries.

This pattern of continual re-emergence and suppression continued into the Renaissance, when the revivification and further Rémystification of the neo-Pythagorean and neo-Platonic traditions revived and extended the argument. The syncretizing efforts of Iamblichus were renewed by the addition to the mix of another holistic and mystical tradition that similarly claimed descent from remote antiquity: the Kabbalah.

Despite the determination with which orthodox Jews had clung to the Mosaic law and their "official" scriptures, the oral tradition that existed alongside their written doctrine, and was mingled with it in the Talmud, always retained a certain submerged force and authority. The demonological beliefs that resurfaced in the apocalyptic writings, and the magical lore that was also condemned by the official doctrine, were more generously accommodated within an alternative "secret wisdom" broadly similar in its inclinations to the mystical holism of neo-Pythagoreanism and neo-Platonism. By the second or third century AD this secret wisdom had come to be known as the Kabbalah, and in the course of a further thousand years it acquired a considerable reputation as a repository of esoteric knowledge. The Kabbalah assumed written form in the thirteenth century, when its lore was incorporated into two key texts: the *Sefer Yetzirah* or "Book of Creation" and the *Zohar* or "Book of Splendor".

The holistic synthesis of residual Gnosticism, recomplicated Mysticism and rediscovered neo-Platonism with the Kabbalah was often called "the Hermetic tradition", representing itself as having originated in the (long lost) works of the legendary Hermes Trismegistus—an appropriately mysterious figure, to whom an appropriately enigmatic passing reference had been made by St. Augustine in *De Civitate Dei* [The City of God]. Its more common title was, however, "the occult tradition", the word *occult* being derived from a Latin word meaning "hidden". The term "occult science" became commonplace in the Renaissance, when such disciplines as alchemy and astrology were defended against the corrosions of modern science by means of the logic of neo-Platonic holism. The occult tradition survived and thrived in opposition to both orthodox Christianity and modern science, overlapping to a considerable extent with both but also providing each of them with a significant alternative world-view.

The Millennium and the Anti-Christ

The confidence of early Christians that converts to their faith could easily resist the blandishments of Satan by prayer or by the pronunciation of Christ's name gradually waned as experience took its toll. The apocalyptic enthusiasm of the early Christians was frustrated, and the longer that frustration lasted, the more they had to adopt their philosophy. The early preachers of the gospel undoubtedly hoped to see Christ return to earth within their lifetimes, to begin a promised thousand-year reign—the Millennium—over a world from which evil had been banished. When the world obstinately refused to end and the early Christians' hopes of immediate reward went unfulfilled, many of them felt that the postponement of the hoped-for end must have much to do with the fact that Christendom remained obstinately corrupted by sin.

The inevitable corollary of this frustrated apocalyptic fervor was a steadily increasing emphasis in Christian writing on the role of Satan as the seducer of men and the wrecker of God's plan. Pope Gregory I, who ascended to the Papal throne in 590, waxed lyrical on this subject. He never tired of describing Satan as the most cunning of enemies, always ready to surprise the unwary, to exploit weakness, to masquerade as an angel of light in order to trick the credulous, to make extravagant promises, to inspire vanity and to stimulate desire. The man who persisted in virtue, according to Gregory, was not let alone by Satan, but rather became the object of redoubled efforts and ever more sophisticated temptations. By this means, the endurance of sin, even when people seemed to be making sincere efforts to avoid it, was easily explained. The image of man and his plight advanced by this explanation is that of a victim of unusual malice, who needs not only the will to be virtuous but immense skill in virtue also. It is a peculiarly contorted image, which concedes the fallibility of all men without admitting the essential naturalness of sin.

The early Christian writers had imagined the power of Satan to be waning as the conversion of the Roman Empire reduced the number of his minions vastly. Pope Gregory and his successors, by contrast, feared that Satanic power was on the increase. Optimism was regenerated when Charlemagne defeated the Saxons at the end of the eighth century and brought them into the Christian fold, but was eroded again by the bitter disappointments of the crusades of the eleventh, twelfth and thirteenth centuries, whose failure slowly obliterated the hope that Christian armies might conquer and convert the whole of the known world.

When the Moslems succeeded in setting a firm limit to the expansion Christendom, the Christian world was forced to become more introspective. From the thirteenth century on it was difficult for any Christian writer to assert confidently that the war against evil was being won and that Satan's power was on the wane. Indeed, a common refuge of despairing writers was that evil was proliferating so rapidly that the faithful must fight a desperate rearguard action, until the (imminent) Day of Judgment condemned the guilty to perdition.

These anxieties can clearly be seen in the continual recurrence, throughout Christian history, of breakaway sects whose charismatic leaders asserted that the end of the world was nigh and that the Millennium was imminent. Such Millenarian cults frequently sought to elaborate and re-melodramatize the Christian mythology of evil in various ways. One of their most frequent recourses was to the idea of the Anti-Christ, which provided Christ with an opposing counterpart in parallel with God the Father's opposition to Satan.

The main Biblical warrant for belief in the Anti-Christ is taken from *Revelation*, though the term is not used there. *Revelation* refers to a "Beast" cryptically identified by the number 666. This may be a coded reference to the emperor Nero, but numerological cryptography is flexible enough to allow almost any other interpretation a would-be decoder wants to find. The term "anti-christ" is, however, used several times in the first epistle of John, the main reference being *I John* 2:18: "Little children, it is the last time: and as ye have heard that anti-christ shall come, even now are there many anti-christs; whereby we know it is the last time." Here the connection of the notion of Anti-Christ with the imminent Day of Judgment is clear enough, but the word seems to be used metaphorically to refer to lapsed Christians or non-Christians. Whether the myth of a *particular* Anti-Christ, who would appear as the Day of Judgment approached and attempt to woo mankind away from God, was established at the time of this writing is not altogether clear, but the notion certainly became well-entrenched in later Christian popular tradition.

The emperor Nero had been a natural candidate for the role of the evil counterpart to Christ when *Revelation* was written, and the author of that text had apparently taken Nero's death to be the signal that the end was nigh. Because the end had not come by the time *Revelation* was incorporated into the New Testament, the apocalypse described there had to be reinterpreted to refer to events yet to take place, and Nero's role thus became available for attribution to any convenient Earthly figure held in contempt. The prophecy was invoked time and time again by writers whose work tended to pass into oblivion when their expectations of the imminent beginning of the Millennium proved false.

Millenarianism was discouraged by St. Augustine in *De Civitate Dei*, which construed *Revelation* as a spiritual allegory and contended that the Millennium had already begun with the birth of Christianity, but Augustine's opinion was continually opposed by writers determined to take *Revelation*'s anticipations literally. The Anti-Christ became a key figure in such writings, as a figure who would carry the great Satanic plot into a new phase when the end of the world materialized, and who was therefore to be feared and welcomed in equal proportions—feared because of the danger he would pose, but welcomed because his advent would be proof that the long-anticipated end had arrived at last. It was taken for granted that his Satanic affiliations would be heavily disguised, so that he could lull the unwary into becoming his followers, and hence doom them to damnation. All powerful individuals were suspect; any influential figure was likely to be accused by someone of being not only *a* minion of Satan but *the* minion of Satan—including many popes as well as schismatics and skeptics.

The main contribution to the Christian mythology of evil made by the myth of the Anti-Christ was that it required men not only to be on their guard against the subtle spiritual temptations of Satan himself, but also to beware of the cunning seductions of men who might be Satan's secret agents. It helped to establish a context of thought in which paranoia about *human* instruments of Satan became deeply entrenched. This encouraged the blurring of the distinction between accusations of heresy and accusations of Satanism, so that the two eventually became essentially the same.

Thus was the complex evolution of the Devil completed. The Old Testament satans who served God loyally gave way to a supremely cunning and menacing anti-god, who not only commanded a vast legion of demons but also established an elaborate empire of human servants. This was a way of seeing the world which, once formulated, could not easily be abandoned, least of all before the corrosive assaults of rationalist skepticism—for the growth of skepticism itself could easily be seen as further evidence of the subtle and ever-increasing power of Satan.

II.

THE POLITICS OF PERSECUTION

The Logic of Persecution

The historical success of such world religions as Christianity and Islam is intimately connected with their heavy emphasis on the use of any and all means to secure converts. The lengths to which adherents of such religions are prepared to go in persuading non-believers to convert are graphically illustrated by the wars of conquest that Christian armies fought as they attempted to colonize the entire globe. Many militant Christians considered the end of universal salvation so important that it justified all manner of means. It is for this reason that Christians, and the adherents of other religions made in Christianity's image, became the world's foremost experts in the business of persecution.

All societies, of course, tend to express their official value-system by persecuting groups that dissent from it, and sometimes by stigmatizing certain groups that actually endorse it. The way in which social groups are selected for stigmatization and persecution vary according to the situation, depending on the kinds of groups that have the power and the determination to try and force society as a whole to conform to their way of thinking. While Christianity remained the religion of a minority within the Roman Empire, Christians had no opportunity to persecute others, and they suffered persecution themselves. Once Christianity became the established religion of the declining Roman Empire, however, the way became clear for the development of an Empire of Faith more ruthless and tyrannical than any which the world had previously seen. Those groups within the borders of the Empire which resisted conversion were harried relentlessly.

Inevitably, the faith that proved most resilient to this pressure was one that had steadfastly withstood the temptations of apocalyptic thought during the previous five centuries: the orthodox Judaism that was now the faith of small colonies of refugees displaced—not for the first time—from their homeland. The Jews bore the brunt of Christian prejudice and persecution for nearly two thousand years, but they did not bear it alone, and the fiercest purges of all were carried out against dissident groups within the Christian fold. The Jews were subjected to all kinds of libels, the most infamous being the "blood libel" by which they were said to use the blood of Christian infants in the baking of unleavened Passover bread, but they were rarely accused of being wholehearted Satanists. That dubious privilege was mostly reserved for secret heretics allegedly at work within the body of the Church.

In order to root out these secret heretics, the Christian persecutors eventually developed a special method of inquiry, and a special army of inquisitors, whose name ultimately became a byword for merciless cruelty. It is the fact that these methods could "discover" and display enemies, even where none existed, which gave birth to the modern notion of "witch-hunting"—which has, of course been applied by analogy to situations where political elites attempt to root out hidden enemies. Thus, communists have been "witch-hunted" in capitalist countries, while "deviationists" have been the object of similar persecutions in communist states. Other standard candidates for institutionalized persecution are immigrants, particularly if they have a different skin-color.

Persecution always begins with vilification. A mythology grows up describing the supposed activities of the stigmatized group, usually referring to "disgusting" habits and often to clandestine criminal activity. In extreme cases the victims of persecution are held to be undermining the fabric of society, posing a threat to morality as well as to the actual political power-structure. Some kind of actual conspiracy threatening public order is a common element in such persecutory mythologies.

In ordinary circumstances, persecution remains at the level of rumor, discrimination and petty hatred, smoldering without ever breaking out into large-scale violence, but it always has the potential to flare up. When vilification moves into a higher gear, the stigmatized groups tend to be charged with a whole set of stereotyped behavioral traits, which are as extremely antisocial as the persecutors can imagine; inevitably, these include sexual perversion, cannibalism, and deliberate violation of the most sacred taboos of the dominant creed. Violence is often prefaced by the vocalization of these vilifying fantasies; they have the power to generate a kind of mob rage, which—however uncoordinated it may be—may easily lead to murder.

When persecution becomes "official", and government agencies of one kind or another take over the reins of public outrage, members of the stigmatized group may be subjected to "show trials". These are not really legal procedures designed to determine guilt or innocence, although that is what they pretend to be. Their real function is to serve as collective ritual expressions of opposition to certain sets of values or ways of life. Show trials are never "fair" in the sense that defendants have a reasonable chance to demonstrate their innocence or argue their case; in order that the ritual may serve its expressive purpose, the accused have to be guilty.

It is extremely convenient for the purpose of show trials if the defendants can be persuaded to confess their guilt, and even more convenient if they can be persuaded to repent publicly of their crime. Obtaining confessions is often easy, provided that vilificatory fantasies are not included in the actual indictment, because many persecuted groups are persecuted for holding beliefs and values that they sincerely hold. Persuading the accused individuals to repent, however, is often—for the same reason—very difficult. Wherever officially-sanctioned persecutors find difficulties, whether in extorting confessions or in demanding repentance, they do not hesitate to unleash all the powers of persuasion they can command: torture, false promises, and the more subtle techniques of persuasion that are nowadays grouped under the heading of "brainwashing".

It would be a mistake to view the persecutors' use of torture to extract confessions merely as a means to the end of discovering guilt. There is a more important sense in which the confession *is* the end, and the legal procedure that invokes it merely the means. The determination of guilt or innocence is not in any real sense at issue—accused persons *have* to be guilty to justify the whole ritual, and torture is simply an efficient means of assuring that the accused will play their parts properly. If the accused persons are required to admit to the kinds of anti-social and anti-human actions described by vilificatory fantasies, pressure of some kind will almost certainly have to be brought to bear, and often is.

Ordinary trials may, of course, occasionally take on some of the attributes of show trials, especially where public outrage has been aroused by a particularly heinous crime. The tendency of the police and the judiciary to slip into a show trial mode when confronted with cases of terrorist violence or child-murder was graphically illustrated in late twentieth-century Britain by a number of cases in which innocent people convicted mainly on the evidence of coerced or trumped-up confessions were released on appeal.

The elaborate nature of the confessions extorted by the Christian heresy-hunters who annihilated the Albigensian Cathars and later turned their hand to literal witch-hunting—which are far richer in detail than could possibly be needed for the simple purpose of securing convictions in court—have puzzled some modern commentators. The sheer mass of bizarre detail has persuaded some readers and commentators that they must be taken seriously as reflections (however distorted) of real events. If we recognize, though, that the confessions were the real aim of the procedure we shall more easily appreciate the contribution that their fullness, complexity and vivid imagination must have made to the theatricality of the ensuing show trials.

The elaborateness of such confessions is, from the point of view of their extractors, a kind of testament to the moral justification of the whole process. Those who were tortured were, in essence, being persuaded to play their part, and it must be remembered that many of them shared the same interest in the affirmation of a particular moral stance as their accusers. Once having accepted their part in the play, some at least threw themselves into it wholeheartedly. Some members of the Soviet Communist Party "purged" by Stalin in the 1930s were similarly persuaded to co-operate fully in their own persecution by an appeal to their loyalty to the faith that was being affirmed and protected.

Persecution may be regarded as a kind of "social catharsis", discharging pent-up tensions; this helps to explain why it tends to be a sporadic phenomenon. Short bursts of frenzied persecutory activity are often followed by periods of calm, until their purgative effect wears off and tension begins to build once more. In most societies at most times, persecution is present at a low level, with no more than the occasional flare-up of small-scale violence. It is difficult to analyze exactly what kind of combination of circumstances is necessary and sufficient to cause escalation to the level of a literal or metaphorical witch-hunt, but natural catastrophes always tend to encourage such flare-ups. Thus, for instance, when the Black Death reached Europe in 1348 there was a desperate search for scapegoats who might be charged with poisoning the water-supply; the Jews were eventually drafted into that role and were slaughtered in their thousands. Not every great catastrophe, however, is associated with a flare-up of persecution, nor every persecution panic with a great catastrophe. The escalation of persecution is one of a number of possible responses to a number of different historical situations which resemble one another only vaguely.

This is, of course, a thoroughly (but not undeservedly) cynical analysis of the business of persecution. Persecution itself is rarely as cynical, in that most persecutors really do believe in the vilificatory rumors that they spread, and in the moral propriety of extracting confessions by whatever means are at hand. Many fervent persecutors remain convinced until their dying day that they never did anything wrong, and that all the people they tortured and killed deserved to die. Hindsight usually shows them up in a different light. Those who fully understand the business of persecution, however, sometimes can and do use its apparatus entirely cynically, for their own commercial and political ends, and this should not be forgotten either.

The difficulties with which historians interpreting the documents of past persecutions have to cope are considerable. The problem of trying to assess the honesty of confessions offered in such a context is further compounded by the problem of trying to judge the sincerity of the agents of persecution. Very different alternative histories can be drawn out of the surviving documents, according to the judgments that are made.

At least some of the episodes described in later sections of this chapter might conceivably have been sincerely motivated on the part of the persecutors involved, but the weight of evidence does suggest that most of them were utterly cynical, motivated by greed and malice. Given the importance that these cases had as exemplars for later witchfinders, and still have for modern believers in diabolism, there is a certain terrible irony in the fact that they probably grew out of a series of slanders.

Persecution and the Early Christian Church

The early Christians learned the logic of persecution the hard way. As a newly-emergent religious group they were a ready-made target for persecution. They also manifested a contempt for other religious systems that went beyond Jewish exclusivity in becoming—by virtue of its emphasis on salvation by conversion—unusually arrogant and unusually assertive. The fact that Christ himself had advocated behavioral humility and behavioral meekness did little to diminish this arrogance and assertiveness in matters of faith.

THE DEVIL'S PARTY, BY BRIAN STABLEFORD

The Romans found Christianity something of a challenge to their customary "live and let live" attitude to religious observance, and it is not surprising that several of their emperors—including some who subsequently became paradigm examples of overweening arrogance—became unusually truculent in their opposition to it.

Several second century apologists for Christianity, including Tertullian and Minucius Felix, found it necessary to reply to persecutory vilification, thus leaving a record of the accusations employed. They followed the usual stereotyped pattern: Christians were rumored to be cannibals, and their clandestine rites were said to involve drinking the blood and eating the flesh of infants, as well as promiscuous indulgence in sexual perversions.

Some historians have attempted to "explain" these accusations as a series of misunderstandings of what happened at the Christian *agape* or "love-feast" and of the doctrine of transubstantiation (which holds that bread and wine used in communion become the body and blood of Christ), but such explanations are quite superfluous. These particular insults would have been used anyhow, simply because they were the worst insults the rumor-mongers could think of.

Fantastic allegations of this kind were used as excuses whenever Christians were oppressed. The persecution of the Christians of Lyons in 177, in the reign of Marcus Aurelius, was a full-scale affair; many of the victims were privately tortured in prison and publicly tortured in the amphitheatre in order to induce them to confess to various inhuman practices. Such documentary evidence as we have claims that such was the strength of their faith that none actually did confess, but the documents were written by Christians.

The Christians were not the only groups to suffer organized persecutions in the Roman Empire—the troublesome Jews were similarly vilified, and political plotters were occasionally charged with having made dreadful oaths involving the blood of innocent victims—but as the faith spread it became the main focal point of Roman persecution. The further Christianity extended its influence, however, the less practical the persecution of its adherents became—and when the Christians crossed the vital threshold of establishing theirs as the dominant creed within the Empire they ceased to be potential victims of persecution, and became instead potential persecutors. Opinions differ as to whether they were more or less enthusiastic in the business of persecution than those who had earlier persecuted them; actual documentary accounts inevitably reflect the prejudices of the writers rather than the results of objective fact-finding.

There is no reason to be surprised that the Christians, once having gained power, immediately adopted the strategies of persecution of which they had been victims; it would be astonishing if they had not. Nor is the unprecedented intensity of some Christian campaigns of persecution surprising, given that (in spite of what Jesus actually preached) the fundamental nature of the faith was intolerant. Ironically, the affectation of meekness and charity derived from the veneration of Christ, far from cooling persecutory fervor, could be used to enhance it, by providing a protective armor of hypocrisy. However paradoxical it may seem, faith in Christ could encourage and promote cruelty, at least in certain stressful circumstances, because the orthodox Church's emphasis on the soul and salvation allowed persecutors to salve their consciences with the conviction that they were being extremely cruel only to be kind, assaulting the flesh in order to save that which was all that really mattered: the soul.

A similar conviction allowed the triumphant Church to rejoice masochistically in its own history of persecution, celebrating the horrible fates of its martyrs in a prideful and gloating fashion. The central motif of the Christian faith was the cross on which Christ had been crucified: a device of torture and execution, which the Church had made into a symbol of redemption from sin. This made room within the faith for a particular kind of callousness, which denied any sympathy to the sufferings of ordinary people on the grounds that Christ had suffered far worse *for them*. The conspicuously nasty and agonizing ways in which martyrs met their deaths became a guarantee of their holiness; other devout Christians in search of inspiration and saintliness were perfectly prepared to mortify themselves by means of all kinds of self-denial and, in some cases, self-flagellation.

The fact that Christians could revel so delightedly in their own one-time persecution is not unconnected with the furiousness of their own persecutions; it also had a curious effect on the attitudes of some of the victims of Christian persecution, who also likened themselves to martyrs and found in the extremity of their persecution evidence of their own holiness. An ironic extrapolation of this philosophy can be seen in the posture adopted by some of the modern lifestyle fantasists who find the idea of being "witches" or "Satanists" attractive precisely because it invites persecutory vilification from the devout.

THE DEVIL'S PARTY, BY BRIAN STABLEFORD

The change in fortune that was crucial to the Christian Church's emergence as the dominant religion of Europe came in 337 A.D., when the emperor Constantine was baptized on his deathbed. Constantine had become emperor in 313 and had immediately put a stop to the persecution of the Christians, courting their support for purely political reasons. His own beliefs appear to have been rather confused, combining Christian notions with a form of sun-worship, but the attractions of Christian ideas of spiritual salvation to a man nearing death are obvious enough, and his eventual conversion was presumably wholehearted.

By the time of his conversion, Constantine had already given a great deal of money to the Church in return for the political support of its members, financing the copying of the Bible and the building of churches to aid in the program of conversion. He had called the Council of Nicaea—the first "ecumenical" council of the Church, which achieved a good deal in terms of unifying doctrine and liturgical practice, although internal conflicts regarding such matters continued to cause strife for centuries.

The example of Constantine's baptism did much to aid the Church in its ambition of converting the whole Roman Empire, and it grew rapidly in power. It suffered a setback when the emperor Julian came to power in 361—he had rebelled against Christian teaching in his youth and turned to a neo-Platonic pagan belief system—but Julian's attempts to resume persecution of the now-powerful Church were half-hearted and relatively ineffectual. In 363 he was fatally wounded during a campaign against the Persians; a Christian emperor (Jovian) succeeded him, and, with the accession of Theodosius in 379, the victory of Christianity was sealed by its adoption as the official religion of the state.

Before 379 the Church had been limited because it existed within a power-structure defined by secular authorities, but it was now able to begin remodeling the social order, remaking the law and reorganizing the government. The fall of the city of Rome in 410 came too late to be of overwhelming importance, so far as the history of the Church was concerned; a burgeoning network of local bishops was in place by then, and relatively secure in spite of the initial antipathy of the Goths who had conquered Rome. The conversion of the Goths and subsequent pagan invaders became a key target of the new empire of Christendom, which rose to each challenge in turn and continued to thrive—albeit in a relatively modest fashion—for several centuries more. During this period of growth, its persecution of the Jews and other dissenting groups was persistent, but such was the confidence of the expanding Church that such persecutions remained at a relatively low level, rarely flaring up into large-scale violence.

Christendom was by no means the wealthiest or most progressive part of the world during the first few centuries of its dominion. Western Europe was thinly populated, with no towns of more than a few thousand inhabitants; the Eastern remnant of the old Roman Empire was considerably more powerful and wealthy, as was the Islamic world, which included the islands of the Mediterranean and most of Spain. This relative poverty helped the Church to establish an empire of faith in which worldly considerations were subordinated to spiritual ones; Christianity's glorification of humility and suffering undoubtedly acted as a palliative against the harshness of everyday existence (Karl Marx was not being spiteful when he later referred to the religion as "the opium of the people").

The Greek Church that was established in Eastern Europe was also Christian, but it never acquired the same total control over society that the western Church achieved, because secular political and social institutions retained their inherent strength and were not absorbed. The power of these secular institutions was based in the relative wealth of their supporters. It was only in the poverty-stricken West that Christian ideas came to dominate and control the entire social order—and that absolute dominance was not to last forever.

The relative poverty of Western Europe lasted until the eleventh century. After 1100 the region began to emerge from its long economic depression, partly because of climatic changes and partly because of progress in agricultural methods and mechanical technology. Prosperity brought a dramatic increase in population, and opened up a wealth of new possibilities and ambitions. The Church was possessed by the new ambitiousness and became, for a while, even more confident—but the attitudes and values of the faith were better geared to the consolation of the poor than to the discipline of the wealthy. New wealth created new power, which the Church could not entirely harness and control.

Inevitably, pressure for political change began to build up, and a slow re-secularization of government began. The Church was gradually forced to redefine its role and its hierarchy. The Papal system of government remained the chief unifying and coordinating force within Christendom, but it gradually lost its influence over individual kings and nations. Great institutions of learning were established, whose members set out to recover the lost knowledge of the ancient world and to begin by building anew on that foundation: a project that represented itself as the Renaissance.

The knowledge recovered from manuscripts reimported to the Western Empire from its ailing Eastern counterpart was, of course, incorporated into the Christian belief-system—an accommodation achieved by means of the great synthesis completed by Thomas Aquinas in the late thirteenth century—but the Christian faith's monopoly of authority over the ideas of men was lost nevertheless. The Renaissance of the fourteenth and fifteenth centuries was a rebirth of original thought as well as a recovery of lost information. As the Church's political authority was eroded, so too was its authority as the sole arbiter of knowledge, reason and belief.

The Church's representatives could not, of course, perceive what was happening as a kind of progress. Nor could they respond by simply accepting a change of role. From their point of view, it mattered not at all that the changes that were overtaking Europe were the results of increasing material wealth and better standards of living. To the Churchmen, the changes constituted a loss of authority, a diminution of the perfect and coherent order of Christendom. They constituted a deadly threat to the project of universal salvation—and hence to *the world*.

It is hardly surprising, when the situation is seen in this light, that the Church's response to prosperity and progress was to go to war, not so much against men as against ideas. Unfortunately, the Church could only attack the ideas by attacking the people that owned them, or by attacking people who could be stigmatized and thus made to take scapegoat-like responsibility for the Church's own sense of crisis. The long war against heresy, which had already honed the Church's persecutory skills almost to perfection, heated up dramatically. This was to be the era in which Satanic abuse came of age.

The patterns of vilification associated with organized persecution were already evident in eleventh century Christendom. In 1022 the members of a sect that had grown up around Orleans were interrogated before the king and the local bishops. They had rejected many of the dogmas of the Church in favor of a simplified creed based on mystical experience, and they readily confessed to their heresy, believing themselves to be under the direct protection of the Holy Spirit. They were burned in droves, and the burnings were justified by lurid accounts of nocturnal orgies. These orgies were not only said to have been inspired by Satan; it was claimed that Satan had attended them in person.

THE DEVIL'S PARTY, BY BRIAN STABLEFORD

The actual presence of Satan at these alleged orgies was a wholly natural elaboration of the basic pattern of persecutory vilification, given the world-view of the Church. Devil-worship, even more than cannibalism, infanticide and maleficent magic, was for Christians the epitome of anti-social and anti-human behavior, and heresy—turning away from the true way of God—was, by definition, turning *to* Satan. The sin of heresy was the worst sin imaginable, because it was directly opposed to the Church's mission of salvation by conversion. Seducing men into heresy was not merely Satan's most powerful weapon in the ongoing struggle but in practical terms his *only* powerful weapon. All the other sins that he might persuade men to commit—even murder—could be confessed, and, provided that the sinner's repentance was sincere, absolution from them could be obtained. Heresy could be repented too, in theory, but it was so deep-rooted that protestations of repentance were routinely mistrusted.

Because no sin except heresy actually removed the sinner from the protective power of the Church, it was universally accepted within the Church that every effort had to be made to save heretics from their error. Reconciliation to the Church was essential, if it were possible, at any price. Torture, employed to such an end, seemed to its users to be entirely virtuous. The prudent suggestion that even repentant heretics might still be burned to death immediately after their confession, lest they fall once more into the ways of error—although it was more usual for them to be given heavy penances to perform—seemed virtuous too. Unrepentant heretics were an affront to Church and society, having placed themselves beyond the pale of civilization; they *had* to be exiled or destroyed, and, as the Church became more accustomed to the habits of persecution, it leaned more and more to the latter course. The Church itself took no part in the burning—the formal involvement of its ministers ended with the failure of the heretic to repent, and once all methods of persuasion had failed the unfortunate was given to the secular authorities, who completed the task—but the Church instigated and licensed the executions.

The episode at Orleans became the beginning of a trend, but the numbers involved in violent anti-heretical persecutions remained fairly small during the eleventh and twelfth centuries. It was not until 1184 that the principle of persecution was formalized in law. In that year Pope Lucius III and Emperor Frederick I confirmed that heretics must be excommunicated, and that those who failed to recant must be punished by the secular authority. The punishment remained unspecified until 1215, when a considerable degree of uniformity was attained, by the agreement of several rulers, that the death penalty was appropriate. This was formally decreed by Pope and Emperor in 1231.

As the law was clarified and tightened, so was the apparatus by which it was to be enforced. The thirteenth century saw the development of a remarkable legal machinery whose name has become a synonym for injustice and inhuman cruelty: the Inquisition.

The Evolution of the Inquisition

In Medieval times there were three common forms of criminal prosecution: the accusatory, the denunciatory and the inquisitorial. These were adapted to different types of case.

In the accusatory procedure, one man would charge another with having committed an offence against his person or property, and would attempt to prove it. He would call witnesses and produce material evidence. He was required under the principle of talion to equate his risk with that of the accused—if he lost the case, whatever penalty would have been exacted on the accused was imposed upon him. This principle was a considerable deterrent to legal actions that could not readily be proved. Under this form of legal procedure, it was extremely unlikely that anyone would dare to charge his neighbor with practicing black magic or consorting with Satan, because proof would be impossible and the penalty for failure severe.

In the denunciatory procedure, a public officer of some sort was empowered to summon a court to deal with any offences that came within his official knowledge. This procedure was limited in application, pertaining almost entirely to crimes overtly committed in public. Heresy could be, and often was, denounced by officials of the Church, but this could only be done once it was made manifest in word and deed. This kind of procedure was usually associated with cases where the facts were not in dispute, and proving the charges was therefore not an issue.

The inquisitorial procedure, as it existed during the Middle Ages, was effectively an extension of the denunciatory procedure to cases where there *was* a dispute over the actual allegations of crime. Under this procedure a public official could summon a suspect, using arrest and imprisonment if necessary. The indictment would be presented to the accused person, who would be interrogated regarding its substance. If no admission of guilt was forthcoming, the official could separately examine witnesses and then communicate their testimony to the accused person. The accused could summon his own witnesses and be represented by an advocate. Because of the uncertainties involved in the procedure, the penalties attendant upon a conviction were generally lighter than those determined by the other procedures.

In the case of prosecution for heresy, the inquisitorial procedure was the only one appropriate to disputed cases. But heresy, as the most serious of crimes, demanded the most serious of penalties, and therefore demanded that there should be no evident doubt as to the guilt of the accused person. In consequence, when inquisitorial procedure was adapted to the specific task of persecuting heresy, it underwent certain modifications. The procedure was "tightened up" to eliminate the chance of the suspect escaping through the loopholes of the system. The right of the accused person to a proper defense was eroded and eventually denied, and the efforts of the interrogators to obtain a confession were escalated, in order that uncertainty could be eliminated.

The transfer of responsibility for the prosecution of heretics to a special body of inquisitors was a slow one. In 1233 Gregory IX issued two bills making the investigation of heresy the special function of the Dominican Order (later it came to be shared by the Franciscans) but the influence of this decree was slow to permeate the whole of Christendom. Many local authorities resented the invasion of their jurisdiction and actively opposed the Dominicans. Some countries—notably Britain and the Scandinavian nations—never did cede responsibility for prosecuting heresy to the Inquisition, although the local authorities often used the methods of the inquisitors to prosecute their own cases. There is a considerable body of documents consisting of complaints by Dominicans that they were being hindered in their holy work by unwilling bishops and secular authorities, and a continual stream of papal bulls demanding cooperation issued forth from Rome.

There were various reasons for this resistance to the Dominicans. In some cases, the bishops were protecting their own people against outsiders, or jealously guarding their own prerogatives. Another reason, often quoted with relish by more cynical commentators, was the matter of the penances extracted from repentant heretics. These often involved heavy fines and confiscation of property, and local authorities were very reluctant to let the Dominicans reap such rewards if they could reserve them for themselves. The friction between bishops and itinerant friars was further exacerbated by the expectation of the itinerant friars that the bishops should support them in their work by paying all their expenses. Gradually, however, the Inquisition established itself more-or-less permanently in most of the major towns and cities of continental Europe.

The situation regarding the division of money and property received through penances was clarified by a bull known as *Ad extirpanda*, issued by Innocent IV in 1252. The same bull approved and advocated the use of torture by inquisitors, and provided a virtual *carte blanche* for inquisitorial persecution. The rights of local legislators to enact laws obstructing or modifying the power of inquisitors were removed by a bull issued by Urban IV in 1265. Even where the Inquisition's power was limited by covert opposition, and in those places where it was never established, its methods and its aims were gradually adopted.

The power of the Inquisition waned with the power of the Roman Church, and when heresy burst the shackles that the Roman Church had tried so hard to impose upon it—during the period which we now call the Reformation—it disappeared as an institution from many nations. The Protestants, however, were quick to begin their own persecution of heretics—their heretics, of course, including adherents to the old orthodoxy as well as new sects arising in their midst—and the methods of the Inquisition survived it.

The decline of the Inquisition was anything but uniform, and it retained its power in some places long after its disappearance from others. The Spanish Inquisition clung to its power jealously, having reached the height of its influence under the legendary Tomas de Torquemada in 1481-98, and it was still very important in Spanish politics in the seventeenth century; although Napoleon suppressed it between 1808 and 1814 it was not finally abolished until 1834. The Inquisition in Italy never really died, but merely faded away to the shadow of its former self known as the Holy Office, which functioned in the twentieth century largely as a censor of books and as a disciplinary court whose most severe available penalty—excommunication—had lost its teeth.

The first major persecution instigated by a specially-appointed inquisitor was launched by Conrad of Marburg in Germany between 1231 and 1233. Conrad, like many later Inquisitors, required convicted heretics to denounce other heretics before they could be reconciled to the Church, thus ensuring a never-ending supply of denunciations. These were often vindictive or purely random, but Conrad was able to follow up any he found plausible or convenient, and he proceeded to initiate a reign of terror in a whole series of Rhineland towns. The local clergy opposed him and began to set aside his verdicts, and the ensuing confrontation was cut short when Conrad was assassinated and his principal associates murdered or executed—a series of incidents that enraged the reigning pope, Gregory IX, who was wholly convinced of the merits of Conrad's cause. The sect that Conrad had been trying to root out and annihilate were the Waldensians, who seem to have been ascetic Christians practicing voluntary poverty and occasionally preaching against the wealth of the Church and the corruption attendant upon it. Another large-scale persecutory crusade was launched against the Waldensians in Austria in 1311-15.

While Conrad was active in Germany, special inquisitors were set to work in France to eliminate the last traces of a heretical movement known as the Cathars or Albigenses. Members of this sect had already been the victims of an armed "crusade" earlier in the century, which had been ended by the Treaty of Paris in 1229, and the Inquisition's involvement was virtually a "mopping-up" expedition. There was not much to mop up, because the crusaders had shown as much vigor as their counterparts in the Holy Land. The crusade's leader, Simon de Montfort, ensured that his name would be remembered when the inhabitants of a besieged town surrendered and he issued an order that all the heretics should be killed; when his lieutenant asked how the heretics were to be identified, he is reputed to have replied: "Kill them all; God will know his own."

So completely were the Cathars destroyed that little is known of their beliefs, but some Catharist writings do survive, revealing that they were Manichean dualists whose elite—the *perfecti*—were extreme ascetics who forsook sexual intercourse and refused to eat meat. The Catholic writers who condemned them, however, justified their actions by reference to the usual vilifications. Alain de Lille, called upon to explain their name in a tract of 1202, gave both the correct derivation (from the Greek *katharoi*, "the pure ones") and a rather imaginative supplementary suggestion that they were so-called because the Devil appeared to them at their orgiastic ceremonies in the form of a cat.

The Catharist heresy had not been so very difficult to root out, given Simon de Montfort's thoroughness and the fact that the *perfecti*, at least, were easy to identify. The Waldensians were not so easily identifiable. Their doctrines were much closer to those of orthodox Catholicism and their affectation of voluntary poverty hardly made them obvious in an age where involuntary poverty was still—in spite of increasing prosperity—the norm. For exactly this reason, the heresy flourished in areas which were irredeemably poor. Persecution of Waldensians and suspected Waldensians persisted in France until the final years of the fifteenth century.

Another sect subject to inquisitorial persecution was the Fraticelli, a heretical splinter-group of the Franciscan order who considered that the order, in becoming powerful throughout Europe (partly by virtue of taking up the role of inquisitors), had betrayed the spirit of St. Francis. The Fraticelli were associated with a Millenarian movement whose members regarded the Church of Rome as the Whore of Babylon referred to in *Revelation*; they never thrived, but there were enough of them left in the mid-fifteenth century to warrant a vitriolic attack in 1466, which resulted in a show trial of several of its members.

These persecutions and others like them were the "legitimate" functions of the special inquisitors. In all cases, the charges laid against the victims included the usual absurdly nasty-minded vilificatory fantasies, but the actual charges of heresy had some substance. Once the methods and strategies of the Inquisition were established, though, they were available to be used in the service of more cynical ends—and so, eventually, they were.

The Destruction of the Knights Templar

The first major instance of the Inquisition's methods being cynically deployed was rather remarkable, in that it involved their use against one of the Church's own institutions. This was the attack upon the Knights Templar made by Philippe IV of France—nicknamed Philippe le Bel [Philip the Fair]—in the first decade of the fourteenth century.

The Templars were an order of warrior-monks founded in the early twelfth century to give protection to the pilgrims who flocked to the Holy Land following the temporary capture of Jerusalem in 1099. The early headquarters of the order were near to the site of the Temple, and thus the order acquired its name. The Templars supported a standing army engaged in perpetual war against the forces of Islam and was lavishly financed for this purpose. The order grew very rich, acquiring land throughout Europe by taking over the property of its members and receiving liberal gifts from its supporters. The Templars also began functioning as a banking organization, accepting deposits from pilgrims to the Holy Land and issuing letters of credit that were honored throughout Christendom. This banking business thrived as the order devised ways to circumvent the Church's condemnation of taking interest on loans.

In 1291 the Christians were finally expelled from the Holy Land for the last time, and the Templars lost their ostensible function. The order had always aroused some jealousy because of its wealth and power, and because its members regarded themselves as an élite corps of pious heroes. They were responsible only to the Pope, and hence effectively above the secular law. Once their original function was lost, resentment against them was aggravated and given freer rein; the time was ripe for anyone who could effectively attack the Templars to take advantage of public sympathy.

At this time the throne of France was inherited by a particularly ruthless opportunist in Philippe le Bel. The national treasury was virtually bankrupt, and Philippe—who seems to have nursed ambitions beyond kingship—was desperate for money. In 1294 and 1296 he imposed tithes on the Church, thus reversing the traditional means by which the Church derived financial support from the laity. He forbade the export of gold, and began to appropriate all the gold in the kingdom in order to mint coins. He imposed levies on property and trade, and continually debased the currency that he issued. These measures proved so unpopular that he was forced to seek refuge in the Paris Temple for three days, only a year before he turned his rapacious attentions to the Temple itself.

On the 13th of October 1307, Templars throughout France were arrested, charged with heresy, and tortured by crown inquisitors in order to obtain quick confessions. The charges brought against them included the denial of Christ, the worship of an idol in the form of a man's head, and sodomy. The confessions elicited by torture contained admissions of guilt on all three charges, although there was a remarkable lack of agreement as to the form of the idol, some remembering it as a single head, others as a multiple head and yet others as a skull. Some gave it horns, and one conferred upon it the name Baphomet.

These charges and confessions were believed for some 500 years; because it was the first scandal of its type, they were taken at face value. Even contemporary writers are sometimes inclined to concede some substance to the accusations, if only on the grounds that any order of monks is likely to include a few practicing homosexuals, but there is no meaningful evidence of any actual heresy or Satanism. In any case, Philippe's attack on the Templars was certainly not the result of the exaggeration and misinterpretation of rumors; his motives were clearly political and pecuniary. He knew all about the uses and abuses of inquisitorial procedure—he had complained about the abuses of the Inquisition in letters written to the seneschal of Carcassonne in 1291—and was well aware of the kind of vilifications that would have to be used in order to compel the pope to support him in his "crusade". The fact that the reigning pope, Clement V, was a Frenchman living in France and dependent upon Philippe's good will made things even easier.

The campaign was marvelously successful; the Franciscans and the Dominicans were quite ready to participate in the campaign of slander; they carried the persecution of the Templars throughout France and beyond. The Templars rallied under this pressure, and tried to present a defense to the Papal authorities in 1308 and 1309, but the obdurate were burned and those who wished to save themselves from execution had first to confess and then to augment the case for the prosecution. In 1311 Clement decreed the universal suppression of the order and the annexation of all its property and wealth.

Philippe's action provoked a series of significant echoes. His strategy was employed for a second time by Guillaume de Nogaret, who had been Philip's chief instrument in pressing the attack on the Temple. Nogaret's own target was Pope Boniface VIII, who had opposed Philip in 1296 over the matter of taxing the clergy of France. At that time, Nogaret had seized Boniface and imprisoned him; although the populace had secured his release, the pope had died within the month. The next pope, Benedict XI, had excommunicated Nogaret before being succeeded by Clement V, and Nogaret wanted this excommunication revoked. In order to achieve this he had to justify his attack on Boniface, and he did so by bringing posthumous charges of Satanism against the pope. All the charges leveled against the Templars were brought forth against Boniface, and a number of witnesses were produced to testify as to Boniface's familiarity with demons and his sorcerous activities. Clement revoked the excommunication, and annulled the bulls that Boniface had issued against Philip's taxation of the clergy.

The strategy was used for a third time by Philip's servants against Guichard, Bishop of Troyes, this time in connection with a very minor dispute. Again Clement gave in to Philip's pressure, though Guichard ultimately escaped death. A pattern had been established, and it soon inspired others to similar action.

THE DEVIL'S PARTY, BY BRIAN STABLEFORD

Further Politically-Motivated Sorcery Trials

It is not always as easy to detect cynical political motives behind accusations of sorcery as it is in the case of Philippe le Bel's savaging of the Templars, but there are several cases that leave little room for doubt. One s a trial that took place in Kilkenny, Ireland, in 1324-25, only a few generations after the Norman conquest of Ireland, while resentments regarding the reallocation of its lands were still seething.

Lady Alice Kyteler was a rich woman who had grown richer through marriages to four husbands, and whose house had been adapted into a successful inn. The first of her husbands, named William Utlagh (Outlaw), had been a banker and moneylender, and so was their son of the same name. Lady Alice favored her own son so extensively that the disinherited sons and daughters of her three subsequent husbands (all by earlier marriages) became extremely annoyed. These various families extended through several important political factions in the diocese of Ossory. It is hardly surprising that intolerable tensions grew up in this tangled web of relationships and that these tensions should bring forth spiteful accusations. These crystallized into a set of charges, the principal one being that Lady Alice had procured the death of at least some of her husbands by poison and sorcery. These accusations were taken up as the basis for a formal inquiry conducted by the bishop of Ossory, Richard de Ledrede.

In all, ten people were accused of homicide via sorcery, and with assorted heresies. Various apparatus supposedly used in sorcery was produced in evidence and many witnesses (including the disinherited children of her later husbands) gave evidence. Reference was made to potions concocted out of such ingredients as worms, the fingernails of corpses and the swaddling-cloths of unbaptized children. The skull of a decapitated robber was said to have been used as a mixing-bowl and the sorcerous proceedings were alleged to have been illuminated by candles made of human fat. Lady Alice, it was said, had a familiar demon who could appear in the form of a cat, a black dog or a negro, and who copulated with her; his name was given as Robin Artisson. The list of charges was substantiated by a confession extorted one of the accused, Petronilla of Meath—a serving-maid in Lady Alice's inn—by means of a series of floggings. Many of the more lurid parts of the account seem to have been her own inventions.

61

THE DEVIL'S PARTY, BY BRIAN STABLEFORD

Bishop Ledrede presented an account of the findings of his enquiry to the Lord Chancellor, but this was Roger Utlagh, Lady Alice's brother-in-law and William the younger's uncle. He declined to take any action. The bishop attempted to proceed on his own, but was stopped by the Seneschal of Kilkenny (a relative of Lady Alice's fourth husband), who threw him into prison. Ledrede then excommunicated Lady Alice, and was promptly sued for defamation—but when he appeared before the parliament in Dublin he persuaded them that he was in the right. With the parliament behind him he was at last able to take action, and some of the accused—including Petronilla of Meath—were burned; others were excommunicated and exiled. William Utlagh got away with a term of imprisonment and Lady Alice herself was apparently allowed to escape to England.

Ledrede was an Englishman, but he was also a Franciscan and he was in France during the years immediately after the suppression of the Templars and the accusations made against Pope Boniface and Bishop Guichard. He was not the instigator of the Kilkenny affair, but once he became involved he pursued his cause with dogged determination. After achieving his immediate aim he began to pursue the seneschal who had imprisoned him, and managed to have him excommunicated and imprisoned, but his own tactics were later turned against him and he had to flee from prosecution on miscellaneous charges. He returned to Avignon and tried to persuade the pope that all Ireland was pervaded with heresy. When he returned, after nine years of exile, he immediately charged the Archbishop of Dublin with heresy.

Richard de Ledrede's activities hardly compare with those of Philippe le Bel and Guillaume de Nogaret, but he was not in a position of such power that he could fully exploit their tactics. He seems to have been moved by a vengeful temper, which he probably saw as zeal in prosecuting heresy and defending the true faith; the depth of his sincerity is, however, irrelevant to the main issue, as is the question of whether Lady Alice Kyteler really was a mixer of potions and a murderer of husbands. The crucial point is that, once he was moved to attack, Ledrede was quick to use a *modus operandi* whose effectiveness had been proved in France, and which was eventually to become vulgarized as a common weapon of slander throughout Europe. Accusations of sorcery became a viable weapon in spiteful disputes of all kinds, and where they had once been stifled by the implications of the principle of talion, there were now legal institutions that not only permitted them but facilitated them.

THE DEVIL'S PARTY, BY BRIAN STABLEFORD

A more obviously political trial—but one where the accusations were rather more modest—was the trial in 1431 of Jeanne d'Arc [Joan of Arc], the peasant girl who was inspired by supposedly-saintly "voices" to lead the French army to a momentous victory against English invaders at Orleans. She later lent her aid to the citizens of Compiègne when the Duke of Burgundy laid siege to their town, and she was captured by the Burgundians. The Duke subsequently handed her over to the Bishop of Beauvais in return for a payment of 10,000 francs, so that she could be put on trial by the English. The prosecutors, who were determined to blacken her name and wreck her reputation in order to justify her execution, charged her with heresy, blasphemy, and witchcraft. She was severely pressured, though not actually tortured, but never confessed her guilt and was eventually burnt as a "relapsed heretic".

In this instance the slanders failed to take historical root—unsurprisingly in view of the involvement of a hated foreign power. The verdict and sentence passed on Jeanne d'Arc were annulled within twenty years; she was eventually promoted to the rank of saint and martyr, and was formally canonized in 1920. Her closest friend and sternest defender was not so lucky.

If Jeanne d'Arc's trial is, in the eyes of posterity, the most obviously political of all show trials involving charges of heresy and sorcery, the trial of Gilles de Rais might easily be reckoned the least obviously political. Jeanne is today a saint, while Gilles de Rais is still widely believed to have been a practitioner of black magic and a mass-murderer. He established a key archetype of the Satanist magician, and his name remains legendary as that of an arch-villain and probable inspirer of the folktale of Bluebeard. The elaborate documentation of his trial, and the fact that he ultimately confessed the charges leveled against him, have long been taken as proof of his guilt, but it would be unwise to overlook the fact that his accusers had strong vested interests in obtaining proof of his guilt, but had not the power to authorize his torture until his guilt had been proven.

The early part of Gilles de Rais' career was unambiguously heroic. He had already distinguished himself in battle against the English before being assigned to Jeanne d'Arc's guard; he fought by her side and it was his forces that won "her" victories. His reward was to be made Marshal of France. After Jeanne's capture Gilles retired to his estates in Brittany and married a rich heiress. There he kept a more lavish and luxurious court than the king, and he became an extravagant patron of the arts. In 1435, however, members of his own and his wife's families, fearful for their inheritance, secured a decree from the king restraining him from selling or mortgaging any more of his property to finance his munificent lifestyle.

According to the popular account, Gilles then turned to alchemy, in the hope of repairing his fortunes by discovering a means of transmuting lead into gold. Alchemy was one of many fields of scientific inquiry that had been revitalized by the Renaissance, and was not generally considered to be disreputable. It was, however, linked via the occult tradition with practices that were much more suspect in the eyes of the Church. There were many would-be magicians whose reputations remained uncompromised by dabbling in various forms of conjuration, but it was always a risky business. It was alleged that Gilles' alchemical experiments had led him into other fields of inquiry, including adventures in explicitly Satanic magic. He was charged with having attempted to invoke the Devil as a means to acquiring riches, and having—in the service of these rituals—abducted, tortured and murdered 140 children. Some alleged remains were produced, although no evidence survives of any substantial number of children having gone missing in the vicinity.

Gilles was arrested in 1440 and tried in Nantes. At first he refused to answer the charges, but after being threatened with excommunication he entered a plea of not guilty. He was convicted of heresy by an ecclesiastical court and of murder by a civil court, and it was not until his fate was sealed that he was persuaded (having now come under threat of torture) to confess. The vividly elaborate confession which he was persuaded to sign—thus ensuring that his inevitable death would be quick and reasonably dignified—was held up at the time as an extraordinary example of Christian repentance and the reclamation of Gilles' soul from the grip of Satan became a key example of the Church's power to redeem the world from the awful power of the devil. The powerful financial interest which his accusers—including the Duke of Brittany himself—had in his ruin attracted far less attention from contemporary and later observers.

Subsequent rumor swiftly increased the alleged mass and significance of the evidence against Gilles by several orders of magnitude; the lurid confession that he signed was particularly newsworthy. The conviction of Gilles de Rais thus helped to cement in many minds the belief that the active and unashamed worship of Satan was not merely a possibility but a reality in the late fifteenth century. How influential that idea might have remained in other circumstances, it is impossible to judge, but it provided a significant exemplar when Christendom entered into period of sustained crisis as soon as the sixteenth century began and widespread protests against the manifest corruption of the Roman Church gave birth to the Reformation.

III.

SATAN'S HARLOTS

Witch-Beliefs and the Early Church

Almost all cultures—even the rationalistic cultures of modern times—have some belief in magic, and a set of images of what people who practice magic are like. Many preliterate cultures have "official magicians" whose job-descriptions usually include divining the future by various means and treating illness. These official magicians are often believed to be engaged in a constant battle against anti-social practitioners of illicit magic: witches.

Ideas of what witches are like and what kinds of things they do vary from culture to culture, but certain stereotyped features crop up repeatedly. Many different belief-systems agree that that there is a species of witches whose members are active by night, have the power of flight, violate graves, use parts of dead bodies—especially those of babies—in their potions, practice cannibalism, and indulge in various sexual perversions. It is not unnatural that these ideas should be so commonplace, because witches of this general kind are, by definition, evil incarnate, and cultures mostly agree in their definitions and characterizations of evil. It is only to be expected that similar ideas of evil will produce similar notions of the most horrific imaginable activities; images of what these "nightmare witches" do are therefore harmonized across a broad spectrum of societies.

In most cases, these kinds of witch-images belong entirely to the realm of the imagination, as one might expect of something that is really just a handy summary of the idea of evil. The natural medium of allegations of night-riding, cannibalism and necromantic sorcery is storytelling, and witches are common characters in the oft-repeated tales that form the folkloristic core of many oral traditions. In societies that employ specialist diviners and "witch doctors" to identify witches as a matter of routine, however, images of the nightmarish kind usually co-exist with rather different sets of ideas about what witches do.

The notion of witchcraft that is involved in cases of actual accusation is usually much more mundane than the one contained in nightmarish tales. The "everyday witches" identified by diviners in various preliterate society as visitors of sickness and misfortune upon their fellows are usually charged with specific crimes, and forced to make limited and straightforward reparation. Such societies may indeed contain people who do indulge in magical rituals and divinatory practices that are "unofficial" or illegal, but practitioners of those kinds of "witchcraft" rarely, if ever, imagine that the nightmarish image of the witch applies to them; they usually represent their motives and methods as fundamentally benign, in spite of their actions being unlicensed.

Anthropologists studying preliterate societies have sometimes been confused by the fact that accusations of "everyday witchcraft" seem to take no account of the more nightmarish aspects of witchcraft beliefs, thinking that this is irrational. The tribesmen themselves, however, have no difficulty in compartmentalizing their beliefs, and in seeing the common sense of their own ways of doing things.

It is not the case that people must always travel to distant places and encounter cultures completely alien to their own in order to be confused in this way; it is sometimes difficult for educated, city-bred people to understand the customs and beliefs of rural areas only a few miles away. When people do travel abroad and encounter the strange tales and strange customs of other cultures, though, it is very easy indeed for them to become confused about the implications and the significance of different items of belief. Other people's superstitions always seem more bizarre and more ominous than our own, for which familiarity has bred an entirely appropriate contempt.

Post-Renaissance Europe was a time of great contrasts in education and ways of life; it was also a time when a great deal of traveling was done, not only by merchants and pilgrims but by inquisitive scholars. Although ways of life in remote rural areas were still Medieval, the way of life of educated men in towns had changed greatly. The changes in the intellectual climate brought about by the Renaissance cleared the way for the demolition of many old misunderstandings and the growth of modern science, but it also prepared the ground for new confusions. Witch-hunting in post-Renaissance Europe was, to some extent, the result of a series of such confusions regarding the significance of nightmarish witch-imagery and everyday "magical" practices.

The history of this confusion may seem to our rationalistic eyes to be rather silly, but we must remember that similar confusions still arise today, as an inevitable corollary of our habits of thought and our rationalistic outlook on the world. We still search for connections between "witchcraft" as it is occasionally manifest in actual behavior and the lurid witch-fantasies of the imagination. This search is still capable of leading observers to "discover" entirely imaginary sets of connections, just as the witchfinders of sixteenth-century Christendom were led to do.

It can presumably be taken for granted that witch-images like those to be found in other preliterate cultures existed in all the various regions of Christendom, where oral traditions continued in parallel with the narrow and highly specialized literate culture of the clergy. These oral traditions undoubtedly took aboard a great deal of officially-sanctioned Christian material—the legends of the saints as well as formalized doctrines—but many of the idiosyncratic customs and beliefs typical of particular areas, including ideas of nightmarish and everyday witchcraft, were presumably preserved in parallel. These ideas would have been largely disconnected from matters of religious faith, and from one another; it would be assuming far too much to try to find within them any kind of coherent system, or to assert that they constituted stubborn secret relics of organized pagan religion.

The attitude of the early Church to these elements of local oral tradition was fairly tolerant, because they were not seen as any threat to religious faith. Although attempts to practice magic were frowned upon, in accordance with Biblical instruction, belief in the efficacy of certain kinds of magic and divination was not opposed, unless it implied a failure of faith in orthodox dogmas. Rather than condemning the beliefs and practices of existing traditions outright, the Church's tendency was to "adopt" them and absorb them into its own festivals, as various customs associated with the pagan Yule were absorbed into Christmas.

Medieval Churchmen had no doubts about the theoretical possibility of most kinds of believed-in magic, but in the early days of the Church they tended to be dismissive of the idea that magic played a substantial role in everyday affairs. Augustine conceded that demons were ready enough and quite able to aid malicious humans in destroying crops or causing sickness, but he was unimpressed by accounts of magical metamorphosis, and credited them to illusion. Subsequent writers tended to be even more skeptical about the role played by magic in the real world, and were ever-ready to attribute anecdotes concerning magic to the delusions of those who claimed to have been involved.

It was generally believed in early Christendom that the images of the nightmare-witch that remained current in various regions were quite straightforwardly imaginary. This was affirmed by what was taken for canon law, although the authenticity of the actual canon involved is rather dubious. Its earliest known appearance is in a book of canons compiled by Regino, one-time abbot of Prum, as a guide-book to ecclesiastical discipline; the book dates from about 906 and the relevant canon is known as the *Canon Episcopi*. Because it follows a canon originating from the Council of Ancyra in the fourth century the *Canon Episcopi* has sometimes been attributed to the same source, but there is no real warrant for this assumption.

The *Canon Episcopi* exhorts bishops "to uproot thoroughly from their parishes the pernicious art of sorcery and malefice invented by the Devil" and goes on to say that "some wicked women perverted by the Devil, seduced by illusions and phantasms of demons, believe and profess themselves, in the hours of the night, to ride upon certain beasts with Diana, the goddess of the pagans, and an innumerable multitude of women, and in the silence of the dead of night to traverse great spaces of earth, and to obey her commands as of their mistress, and to be summoned to her service on certain nights". The canon is unequivocal in declaring all such beliefs to be false, based in delusion. Its writer is anxious that such delusions be condemned, because the women involved not only believe that they really do fly by night but also believe themselves to be doing good, and hence fail to recognize the Satanic source of their delusion.

The particular item of folklore referred to in this canon is not a nightmare-witch fantasy, but this was long held to be the authoritative statement applicable to *all* cases in which magical beliefs in oral tradition came into apparent conflict with articles of religious faith. Such folk-beliefs were held to be the result of the pollution of dreams by Satan, whose aim was to draw people away from the pure faith by creating confusion. Lay practitioners of healing and divination were thus held to be victims of Satanic delusion, but certainly not active servants of Satan.

This attitude went unchallenged until the thirteenth century, when the itinerant friars of the Dominican and Franciscan orders began to travel far and wide in search of heresy. Inevitably, they found marked differences between the folkloristic beliefs of their own countries and those of the countries which they visited. The unfamiliarity of these oral traditions must have made them seem more sinister to the inquisitors than they did to local priests and bishops—and the inquisitors were, of course, men avid for any evidence of dangerous unorthodoxy.

To some of the traveling friars, such elements of oral tradition seemed suspiciously like extensions of the heresies that they had been commissioned to detect and root out, and it is not difficult to understand how they might have begun to think of these alien beliefs as a species of heresy—and then to wonder what kind of conspiracy against orthodox belief they might contain. In this way, the groundwork was laid for the spread of the idea that local witchcraft beliefs might be evidence, not of a fairly harmless delusion, but of a widespread and horrific internal conspiracy against the Church.

The assimilation of fantasies of Devil-worship to the persecution of heretics was, as the last chapter pointed out, wholly natural. Heretics were, by definition, those who had yielded to the temptations of Satan, and thus might be thought of as worshipping him even if they thought of themselves as good and virtuous Christians. Pagans, after all, frequently thought of their gods as good even though Christians "knew" that all such idols were the Devil in disguise, and it seemed obvious that the ostensibly-Christian God worshipped by heretics was simply a disguise of a more cunning kind. Heretics, therefore, were credited as a matter of course with holding secret nocturnal gatherings where all kinds of obscene events took place. The relationship between what heretics were alleged to do by the vilificatory fantasies invoked in their persecution and what the nightmare-witches of folklore were supposed to do was understandably close.

The assimilation of witch-fantasies to the idea of heresy was basically a matter of setting aside the implication of the Canon Episcopi that the nocturnal gatherings commonly referred to in oral tradition did not actually happen. The idea that most of what was said to go on at these meetings was illusory could be retained, but the gathering itself had to be real. This was what eventually happened, but the process of assimilation was a gradual one, involving changes in the role that was attributed to the Devil at heretical assemblies and changes in ideas about the actual practices of witchcraft.

The Devil's Party, by Brian Stableford

Pacts with the Devil

The initial assumption of heresy-hunters tended to be that heretics had been deluded by the Devil without recognizing his nearness—that, by means of his masquerade as an angel of light, Satan had led them away from the true path by persuading them that they were following it. The unwillingness of many heretics to admit to this, however, put some strain on the interpretation, and, as the use of vilifying slanders escalated, the whole idea of the heretic's relationship with the Devil changed; instead of being the Devil's dupe the heretic became his willing instrument. This first became official during the career of Conrad of Marburg, when Conrad reacted to the angry criticism of local bishops by writing a series of letters to Pope Gregory IX, in which the supposed threat of the heretics he was searching out was gradually exaggerated by imaginative embroidery.

After Conrad's assassination in 1232 Gregory issued a bull in which he reproduced numerous allegations about the way in which people were initiated into heretical cults. Far from being deluded, these heretics were said to pay explicit homage to an animal—usually a giant toad—by kissing it on the mouth or anus, and then to pay similar homage to a man with black eyes or a black hat and a cold touch. A third gesture of obeisance might be required later, when the Devil re-appeared as a huge black cat. Later accounts tend to be more economical, referring to a single loathsome entity rather than a series, but the pattern remained the same. Thus were the gatherings of heretics represented as occasions when homage was consciously and calculatedly paid to Satan, and the way was opened up for the invention of more fanciful accounts of what happened on such occasions.

In thirteenth century accounts of such heretical "conventicles" it is usually assumed that the evil president requires no more of his subjects than that they should hold heretical beliefs and spread these beliefs among their neighbors. This was the extent of their part in the "agreement" which they had made with the Devil (it was, of course, quite enough to justify persecution, torture and burning). As time went by, however, more careful consideration was given to the matter of what was implied by what came to be called diabolical "pacts", and the question began to engage the interests of numerous scholars, whose examination of the logic of such pacts was crucial to the reinterpretation of heresy and witchcraft as species of explicit Satanism.

THE DEVIL'S PARTY, BY BRIAN STABLEFORD

The thirteenth century saw the beginning of the various intellectual movements that we associate with the Renaissance, including the revitalization of scientific inquiry. Paris and Bologna were the leading intellectual centers in Europe in the year 1200, but Oxford was just beginning to establish an international reputation and several other new universities had emerged, offering organized teaching and tests of attainment in all recognized areas of learning. Among these recognized fields of knowledge were alchemy and various kinds of divination. Not unnaturally, these were areas of study that attracted many students; the practical advantages that might be gained, if only the problems of these "sciences" could be solved and their methods mastered, seemed enormous.

Studies in the occult sciences were to some extent handicapped by the disapproval of the Church, but curious scholars persistently found ways of arguing the orthodoxy of their beliefs and the legitimacy of their enquiries. Most of the new universities were funded by the cities in which they stood—which meant that their support came from the mercantile community rather than directly from the Church—and this permitted more freedom of thought than might otherwise have been the case. It did not take long for rumors to grow up concerning the interest taken in such matters by leading scholars, and wild allegations were sometimes made concerning their knowledge of the magical arts. It was at this time that Roger Bacon first provided a prospectus for experimental scientific inquiry, and much scandal was spread regarding the nature of some of his experiments. Both Bacon and Albertus Magnus acquired considerable posthumous reputations as magicians, the latter being credited with several apocryphal works on magic.

It is difficult to determine whether anyone in this period was actually experimenting with demonic magic, but some scholars had certainly begun to wonder whether a parallel species of "angelic magic" might be practicable—and, if so, whether its mastery might be reckoned the highest ideal of devout Christian scholars. Inevitably, there was much scholarly interest in the theoretical aspects of these subjects, and the attempt to distance worthy studies in occult science from unworthy ones meant that a lot of attention had to be given to the theoretical basis of demonic magic, for the purpose of comparison and contrast.

The question of why demons should carry out the bidding of those magicians who were rumored to be able to command them was an understandably intriguing one. The chief hypothesis offered in speculative explanation of this enigma was that such magicians must have made a contract with the Devil, which gave them this power in return for the pledging to him of their souls. Augustine had earlier recognized a kind of pact in the possibility of intercourse between humans and demons, but that had been was an *implicit* pact—a covert element of the intercourse, of which the human was not aware. In the thirteenth century, however, scholars began writing about *explicit* pacts, which were formal contracts between men and demons. The possibility that would-be magicians might make this kind of explicit pact was recognized by Albertus Magnus, William of Paris and Thomas Aquinas—three of the leading scholars of the period.

Whether any thirteenth century would-be sorcerer actually attempted to make a pact with Satan or any lesser demon we cannot know. It appears, however that books eventually began to appear that purported to contain magical recipes of various kinds, including spells for conjuring demons and instructions for making pacts with them. Most Renaissance references to such books are second-hand—for instanced, William of Auvergne fulminated against a demon-summoning handbook he called *Liber Sacratus* in the thirteenth century, although no manuscript of that title has survived. It is possible that later manuscripts entitled *Liber Sacer* are copies of the text to which he referred, but it is also possible that such texts were produced in response to dark rumors of their existence rather than occasioning them.

The best-known of these "grimoires" was the *Clavicula Salomonis* [Key of Solomon], which is reputed to date back to the fourteenth century, although the extant manuscripts are much later. The *Grand Grimoire* allegedly dated from the thirteenth century, but is probably a much later fake. William of Auvergne's condemnation of demon-summoning is primarily an assault on the misappropriation of a particular symbol, the five-pointed star known as the pentagram. The pentagram had been adopted by neo-Platonists as a key symbol within the human microcosm, its five points echoing a variety of human attributes (not merely the number of senses and the number of digits on a hand but the body itself, displayed—as in an image that still remains archetypal—with its four limbs extended within the arc of a circle and the head forming the fifth point. Often called "the pentacle of Solomon", the symbol seems to have been used as a device for exorcising demons before acquiring a role in their summoning; the power of its symbolism was such that it was subsequently taken up by many "secret" organizations, including the Freemasons, and plays a significant role in literary fantasies, making an early exemplary appearance in *Gawaine and the Green Knight* (c1320).

Any evaluation of Satanic spells based on reprinted grimoires is bound to be hazardous, but the general impression they give is that the recipes are usually concerned with issues of safety, suggesting ways in which a magician might summon a demon and complete a pact without actually imperiling his immortal soul. The grimoirists seem to take the view that cheating the Devil of his due is an entirely virtuous, though difficult, thing to do—an attitude echoed and celebrated in countless literary representations of diabolical pacts.

This theoretical interest in the possibility of pacts between men and Satan, and in the design of rites for the purpose of doing so, was soon co-opted into the vilifying fantasies that were put about in connection with heretics. Ritual sorcery of the kind described in the grimoires was added to the list of what heretics were supposed to do as their part of the bargain with the Devil, and this brought the vilifying fantasies aimed at heretics even closer to images of "nightmare witchcraft".

Early Treatises on Satanic Witchcraft

The first significant treatise arguing that witchcraft was a species of heresy was included in the fifth volume of a work known as the *Formicarius*, which was written by Johannes Nider between 1435 and 1437, although it was not published until 1475 or thereabouts (the printing press having been invented in the interim). Nider's interest in witchcraft was purely theoretical, and his analysis of it forms part of a more general examination of the nature and efficacy of maleficent magic. His treatise presents an elementary classification of magical feats, illustrated by anecdotes, including such standard examples as raising storms, causing sickness and striking people dead with curses. Other aspects of everyday witchcraft are, however, included. There is a substantial chapter on amatory magic (love-potions were, along with medicines of various kinds, significant marketable products of everyday witchcraft).

The *Formicarius* also pays lascivious attention to the mythology of incubi and succubi: demons that have sexual intercourse with women and men as they sleep. There is a constant preoccupation with these species of demons in monastic writings, and their special importance in Christian demonology seems to be connected with the demand for celibacy among the clergy. Ordination does not stop the production of sperm in the testicles, and their periodic release in nocturnal emission is usually accompanied by erotic dreams. The likelihood that monks would interpret such incidents in terms of nocturnal visits by demons is obviously strong.

Nider's account of what witches actually do is confused because, on the one hand, he believes many of the anecdotes he quotes concerning magical misfortunes, while, on the other hand, he feels bound to accept the *Canon Episcopi*'s judgment on the illusory nature of night-flying. He quotes one particularly interesting anecdote in support of the *Canon Episcopi*, which was copied and re-copied by many other writers. This concerns a Dominican who was told by a woman of her night-flying experiences with Diana and who undertook to prove that these were illusory; when next she intended to go night-riding she called the friar, who brought several witnesses who were able to assert quite positively when she awoke that she had not left her bed.

It is important to note that if this incident ever actually happened (the likelihood is that it is no more than an illustrative fable) it was done as a demonstration, not as an experiment. The authority of the Church and the law lay, at that time and in Nider's eyes, behind the implication of the *Canon Episcopi*, and the friar of the story did what he did to simply show the merit of that authority, not because he doubted it. In many actual witch-trials the testimony of witnesses that their husbands, wives or children had been in bed when they or others claimed that they had been at conventicles—or, as they came to be called, Sabbats—was simply rejected.

This illustrates a vitally important difference between the Medieval way of thought and our own. We live in a rationalistic age and we place high value on experimental evidence and the testimony of witnesses; we have considerable faith in the evidence of our own senses. In the Middle Ages, by contrast, the real test of truth—and one which was given priority far beyond the evidence of the senses—was reference to authority. A scholar of the sixteenth century who wanted to argue that something was true still followed the style of Medieval scholarship to a great extent; he did not say "This is true because I have seen it with my own eyes" if he could possibly say "This is true because St. Paul clearly said so". The written word still had tremendous power of persuasion—far more so than the experience of ordinary people. It could hardly be otherwise in a culture whose fundamental world-view was based on sacred writings.

The period of history in which the great witch-panic happened was intermediate between the Medieval way of thought and the modern one. It was a period of transition, when the idea that the evidence of authority was paramount gradually and grudgingly gave way to the idea that the evidence of the senses ought to be given greater priority. For a long time, the balance of power between these mutually-incompatible assumptions was uncertain and confused. Nider's *Formicarius* provides a classic example of that uneasy co-existence and awkward confusion—as, indeed, do virtually all the books that were written about witches and witch-finding between the fifteenth and seventeenth centuries. The evidence of authority and the evidence of anecdote sit beside one another and mingle, and their interaction breeds all manner of speculations and strange conclusions.

Nider was a scholar, not an inquisitor, and his emphasis on the delusory aspect of many of the things supposed to be done by means of witchcraft should be seen in this light. It was the inquisitors—the Church's "field-workers"—who first became convinced of the reality of the witches' conventicles and of the actual results of their evil magic. They were the people in daily confrontation, not only with the beliefs that came to be associated with the new witch-image, but also with the real misfortunes that were habitually attributed to imaginary witchcraft. The inquisitors were the front-line troops in the Church's war against heresy, who were actually *using* vilificatory fantasies in their work, and were thus bound to take them wholly seriously. For this reason, early treatises written by inquisitors are different in emphasis from those written by scholars.

Jean Vineti, an inquisitor active in the Carcassonne, states in his *Tractatus contra daemonum invocatores* (written c1450) that the witchcraft he has encountered is a new heresy, not the one covered by the *Canon Episcopi*, and that demons are capable of much more than mere delusion in the matter of transporting people through the air by night. The historian who first assembled many of the key documents relating to the Inquisition and its persecution of witches, H. C. Lea, quotes from another tract written at about the same time by an inquisitor in the Savoy, which gives a detailed account of witch-meetings, accepting their reality without question, although this never reached print. In both these works, the confessions of witches later burned are cited as proof that the meetings took place. Other treatises followed to supplement these, most of them arguing that the *Canon Episcopi* did not refer to the heresy of witchcraft at all, but to something quite different. Their arguments had some force, but the point was not an easy one to win.

It appears from the materials painstakingly assembled by Lea that those on the sidelines of the dispute were gradually swayed to the side of the inquisitors. Evidence to this effect is provided by *Lamiarum sive Striarum opusculum*, written by Girolamo Visconti in 1460 or thereabouts. Visconti belonged to the famous noble family and was Professor of Logic in the University of Milan in the 1440s. His tract carefully presents the arguments for and against the reality of the witches' conventicles, and finally comes down in favor, ultimately circumventing the *Canon Episcopi* by saying that what is an illusion in one instance may be a reality in another, provided—and this he claims to have demonstrated by his arguments—that it is within the bounds of possibility.

These works and others opened up an area of intense interest for scholars and an intriguing problem for theologians. The debate created its own momentum, and the printing-press was now available to carry it forward, providing the inquisitors with new authorities, which they could use as instruments of persecution. All that was needed to complete the process was a book that would provide a supposedly-definitive summary of the debate and its conclusions: a work that would serve both as a textbook for scholars and as a handbook for inquisitors; an eminent and definitive authority on the whole subject of Satanist witchcraft. It was in order to fulfill this function that the *Malleus Maleficarum* was written.

The Hammer of the Witches

The authors of the *Malleus Maleficarum* were Jacob Sprenger and Heinrich Kramer (also known as Institoris). Both were Dominicans, and both had been active as inquisitors, although Sprenger was primarily a scholar. Kramer, when serving as an inquisitor in the Tyrol, had met the usual local opposition to his activities, and in 1484 he sought a special bull from Innocent VIII to silence it.

The bull in question refers to "many persons of both sexes" who had "abandoned themselves to Devils, incubi and succubi" and who "by their incantations, spells, conjurations, and other accursed charms and crafts, enormities and horrid offences", had cursed unborn children, crops and animals, and had afflicted humans and animals with various diseases and impotence. It further alleges that "at the instigation of the Enemy of Mankind they do not shrink from committing and perpetrating the foulest abominations and filthiest excesses to the deadly peril of their own souls, whereby they outrage the Divine Majesty and are a cause of scandal and danger to very many." It goes on to confirm that Kramer and Sprenger have been commissioned to deal with such individuals and that they should in no way be hindered in their task.

What this bull actually amounts to is a confirmation of the authority of the two Inquisitors, which might be used to quell local opposition to their activities; in this respect it is little different from hundreds of other bulls issued by various popes during the previous two centuries. In doing this, however, the bull also offered confirmation that the particular heresy Sprenger and Kramer were searching out did actually exist and was a species of Satanism. This seems to have been the first official recognition of the legitimacy of bringing witch-beliefs under the heading of heresy (and thus conceding reality to many aspects of witch-beliefs previously held authoritatively to be illusory). Sprenger and Kramer set out to use this official recognition to begin a crusade against witches.

The *Malleus Maleficarum* was submitted to the Faculty of Theology at the University of Cologne, who were asked to certify its orthodoxy. Sprenger was Prior to the Dominicans of Cologne and thus in a position of some influence, but the Faculty refused to approve the book. Sprenger and Kramer persuaded those members of the Faculty who did support them to compose a notarial act implying that the Faculty as a whole *had* approved it, and this was appended to all editions of the book except those printed in Cologne itself. Innocent's bull was printed at the beginning of the book as if it were a papal certificate of approval. Although the book's veneer of dogmatic respectability was largely fraudulent, it went through a dozen editions between 1486 and 1520, when the first epidemic of witch-hunting (which it did much to create and sustain) petered out; when the epidemic was renewed in the 1570s it was quickly revived, and went through a further sixteen editions before 1670.

The *Malleus* is divided into three parts. The first is an examination of the supposed facts of the matter—an assertion of the reality of witchcraft, followed by the sifting of authorities for supporting statements and a commentary on the implications of the "facts"; its main arguments are directed against skeptics who believe that there are no such things as witches, and the intensity of the rhetoric suggests that Sprenger and Kramer expected to find many such among their readers. The second is an examination of the "theory" of demonic magic and of the methods supposedly used by witches in its administration, followed by a list of remedies by which witchcraft might be opposed and its effects cancelled (folk remedies are condemned as further witchcraft). The third is concerned with the conduct of witch-trials—not only with formal procedures but with all the strategies that can be used to extract confessions, including suggestions regarding the organizing of threats and deceptions; there are also comprehensive instructions with regard to sentencing. As a whole, therefore, the book comprises a complete guide to witch-hunting, telling the would-be witchfinder what he must do, and why, and how to justify what he does to himself and to others. The great utility and unfortunate effect of the *Malleus* arose from this practical value, not in its claim to be a considerable work of scholarship.

It may seem incredible to modern observers that the Christian witchfinders could go on and on extracting confessions and burning people, apparently without ever suffering crises of conscience or moments of doubt—but we know only too well the kind of personality that insists on proceeding *by the book*, surrendering all personal initiative to the dictates of some external authority, its rules and its precedents. Our legal system still operates in this fashion, and the habit-forming propensity of bureaucratic procedures is notorious; it could hardly have been otherwise in an era where the principal test of truth was reference to authority. Once an apparently-authoritative document like the *Malleus* was produced, and made generally available, there is little need to wonder that it was used—and used, it seems, almost unthinkingly.

The arguments by which Sprenger and Kramer try to confound and defeat skepticism are weak even in the context of thought of the day. Appeals to authority are constantly supported by anecdotal evidence because the relevance of the authorities cited is manifestly dubious. Many of the arguments are circular—misfortunes are recorded, interpreted in terms of witchcraft, and these wholly speculative interpretations are then held to prove the existence of witchcraft.

Skeptical arguments to the effect that witches do not need Satan in order to perform maleficent magic (and thus are not heretics)—or, conversely, that Satan does not need witches to attain his ends—are not so much countered as sidestepped; Sprenger and Kramer admit that there are species of magic that do not need Satan's aid, and that Satan can affect men directly, but simply say that these kinds of events are not what concern them. To counter the argument that witches are mere instruments, and therefore ought not to be punished, they simply state that witches retain their free will within their compacts with Satan. Through all the arguments runs a steadfast insistence that witchcraft exists "by the permission of God"—that God, for reasons unknown, permits Satan to seduce men and women into the pact and then to give them magic powers to afflict the innocent.

Apart from its utility as a witchfinder's handbook and its influence as a treatise "proving" the existence of witches, and their status as Satanist heretics, there is a third aspect of the *Malleus* that proved vitally important to the history of Satanic abuse: its contribution to an increasing body of "case histories", which was copied by other writers, each reproduction adding further apparent authority to every individual tale. These anecdotes are scattered throughout the text, but fall mainly in part two. Many are simply beliefs from folklore, quoted as illustrations of the supposed power of witches, and it is surprising, taking census, how very few of them even claim to be real events. Some are no more than bawdy jokes or little horror stories, such as the oft-quoted tale of the man who loses his penis and approaches the local witch to demand its restoration (she tells him to climb a tree and pick one from her collection, assembled in a nest, but when he reaches for the biggest one admonishes him because it belongs to a priest). A few pages later, quoted in evidence in support of the metamorphic powers of witches, we find another frequently-repeated tale concerning a man attacked by animals who beats them off with a stick, injuring them, only to find similar injuries on the bodies of three women, who charge him with assault (but he is acquitted after he tells his story).

Some of these tales had been previously written down, and many were perpetrated in oral tradition throughout Europe, but the *Malleus* collected them together and renewed their effect with the gloss of "truth". "Urban legends" of a kindred sort still circulate freely today in Europe and America, represented by their narrators as things that happened to "a friend of a friend"; they still rely for their effect on the pretence and insistence that they are true. The aesthetic fascination of the *Malleus* and other well-known books by post-Renaissance witchfinders that are still occasionally reprinted is largely dependent on these anecdotes. Why such tales have the power to fascinate us is not entirely clear, but they certainly do, and the prolific use of them by witch-hunters undoubtedly made some contribution to the willingness of readers at least to entertain the notions that were advanced as "explanations" for them. (In today's world, too, considerable success can be achieved by books that claim to have found melodramatic explanations for arbitrarily-assembled collections of petty mysteries.)

One curious aspect of the witch-lore collected in the *Malleus* is a total lack of interest in the events said to take place at the witches'

Satanist Sabbats. Many other witchfinders were much preoccupied by the matter of the Sabbat, and some—notably Pierre de Lancre—showed an obsessive curiosity about what went on there. The reasons why it does not figure large in the *Malleus* are probably twofold. On the one hand, de-emphasizing the nocturnal gatherings made it much easier for the authors to sidestep the *Canon Episcopi* by making it seem irrelevant to the image of the witch that they were building. On the other hand, Sprenger and Kramer were primarily concerned with blaming witches for all manner of routine catastrophes; their immediate interests were the ability of witches to inconvenience their neighbors, and the way to go about prosecuting them for such crimes, with appropriate legal procedures and sentences. The more nightmarish aspects of the image of the witch are treated rather evasively in the treatise; there are the customary allegations of infanticide and cannibalism, but these are not the focal points of concern. Far more attention is paid to the matter of witchcraft as a prolific cause of commonplace misfortunes; the real work that the book did was to establish that acts of everyday witchcraft, such as were very widely believed in—and presumably practiced—throughout the rural areas of Western Europe were, in fact heretical and explicitly Satanic.

It was largely to the *Malleus Maleficarum* that the post-Renaissance witchfinders owed the idea that most witches were female. The Inquisition made no distinctions of sexual grounds when they selected victims for persecution, but the blame for heresy was more frequently put on men than women, simply because men were assumed to be the progenitors of ideas and their wives mere followers. There was nothing in the image of the witch drawn up by Nider and other scholars to suggest that witches were more likely to be female than male—and many male witches were, of course, accused and brought to trial—but Jacob Sprenger, who was presumably the writer of the theoretical parts of the *Malleus*, seems to have harbored a particularly bitter streak of misogyny, which he made every effort to communicate to other inquisitors.

The point has already been made that the restrictions of celibacy imposed upon monks must occasionally have been uncomfortable. Dominicans were forbidden sexual activity, but this did not make them immune to sexual arousal, and the temptation to account for their troublesome sexual feelings in terms of the supernatural assaults of Satan must have been strong. It cannot have been very difficult for men of Sprenger's stripe to associate the supposed Satanic nature of those assaults with the actual female persons "responsible" for particular instances of arousal.

This kind of thinking is presumably what lies behind the extraordinarily confused and vituperative answer to the subsidiary enquiry of Question VI of the *Malleus Maleficarum*: "Why it is that women are chiefly addicted to Evil Superstitions". Sprenger alleges there that women "are feebler both in mind and body" than men and are "more carnal". He argues that Eve was a defective being, by virtue of being formed from a bent rib, and that this innate imperfection is reflected in the deceitfulness of all women. He suggests that women are naturally spiteful and given to hate, and he quotes from Seneca an observation to the effect that Hell hath no fury like a woman scorned. He concludes his extraordinary diatribe with the observation that "a woman is beautiful to look upon, contaminating to the touch and deadly to keep" and thanks God for having made the males of the human species so much less lustful that they are far less likely to be seduced by Satan; he implies strongly that Christ only suffered and died for men, not for women.

Other witchfinders were by no means as extreme in this emphasis as Sprenger, but the prevalence of females accused and convicted of witchcraft throughout the period of persecution testifies to the commonness of such opinions. Sexual feelings and sexual behavior have, of course, always been an aspect of experience much charged with real and imaginary anxieties, and even men who have not taken vows of celibacy may often feel that women have an altogether unreasonable power to "bewitch" them. The politics of persecution always involve attempts to make scapegoats responsible for the failings of persecutors, and it is not entirely surprising to find itinerant friars projecting their own neuroses upon their victims. The understandability of the tendency, however, does make it any less despicable.

The Documentation of the Great Witch-Hunt

The documents relating to the witch-hunts of the sixteenth and seventeenth centuries fall into three main categories: official records of accusations and trials preserved within court records; accounts of trials given from memory by judges and inquisitors in treatises or autobiographies; and pamphlets issued after the trials to acquaint the public at large with the events.

The official records are reliable insofar as they offer us a reasonably objective account of what kinds of person were most likely to be charged, what the charges amounted to, and the usual outcomes of the trials. They are not very detailed, and the implications of the record of confessions is sometimes misleading (many inquisitors used a prepared list of questions which the accused had to answer affirmatively, and this helps to account for the repetitiveness of the things confessed) but they do contain some hard data. The preservation of such documents to the present day has been rather haphazard, but in many places official documents have been zealously hoarded; H. C. Erik Midelfort was able to survey a considerable number of such records in compiling his study of *Witch Hunting in Southwestern Germany 1562-1684*.

The accounts left by the inquisitors themselves are, of course, far less trustworthy. They are the testimony of witnesses who interpreted everything that happened according to a strict set of preconceptions, and the way in which those preconceptions filtered and distorted the actual events makes them unsafe as sources of information. Much of the material is given anecdotally, to exemplify points made in discussion, and in adapting evidence for such exemplary purposes a certain amount of license was undoubtedly taken. These disadvantages would be extreme if we were only concerned with extracting hard data—the "bare facts" of the matter—but if these documents are treated purely as a record of what people *thought* they are more valuable than the official trial records.

The most famous witch-trials are the most famous because they were the ones that attracted the keenest attention of the public at the time, encouraging people to write about them in pamphlets and books. Such accounts are, by and large, sensationalist accounts written—like today's tabloid newspapers—more to entertain than to inform; the priority of the writers in most cases was to exploit to the full their scandalous, morbid and horrific elements. Such pamphlets were the yellow journalism of their day, and they undoubtedly functioned as a kind of pornography; their deft combination of sadism and the supernatural follows a formula that still works well today. It is not surprising that these accounts continue to fascinate people, because they were formulated with exactly that motive: they are cocktails to feed the avid thirst that people have for exotic melodrama spiced with sex and violence.

What most people "know" about witchcraft and Satanism is almost entirely derived from documents of this third kind, whose lurid stories have been copied and re-copied by generations of journalists and "popular historians". The historian who desires to mine undistorted facts from such accounts has an impossible task; no method will allow it to be done. Future historians endeavoring to discover the "facts" behind the stories in today's entertainment-orientated tabloid newspapers will have similar difficulty. Even where court records and the testimony of inquisitors are also available, it is still difficult to weed out the journalistic inventions and embellishments from particular cases, because the inventions and embellishments are designed to make the more powerful impression on the imagination. Even as guides to what people thought, rather than what they did, these documents are highly unreliable, although they do constitute an intriguing record of what people *wanted* to think, at least temporarily, for the purpose of experiencing a thrill. To the extent that they are a useful historical resource, they need to be treated very carefully, as works of the imagination rather than as reportage.

The implication of these observations is that those items of the witch-craze that are most likely to be familiar to modern people, by courtesy of everyday reading and everyday conversation, are the least trustworthy. If we are to understand what happened in the course of the great witch-hunt, we must beware of what we think we already know, and must also beware of plausibility itself. When we find exciting stories and interesting cases, and theories that appeal to our aesthetic sensibilities, then we must be very careful indeed, for we are almost certainly being misled by the glamour of journalistic artistry. The "best" stories about the witch-craze have been retold repeatedly, and what was added to them in the telling was always more significant than the contribution of actual events.

The witch-panic was a product of the human imagination, and so are the accounts of it that have been handed down to us through the last five hundred years. In trying to comprehend it, we have to take into account the imagination of ordinary people who were called upon to produce elaborate and detailed confessions of things that never happened, often under torture and always under duress. We also have to take into account the imagination of inquisitors and commentators, many of whom believed the temporal world to be under a tremendous supernatural threat. Then again, we have to take into account the imagination of onlookers who found in accounts of these trials all the kinds of stimulation that we still derive from horror stories, pornography, popular magazines and tabloid newspapers. All these imaginative contributions were important in determining the continuing evolution of the idea of Devil-worship and the practices of Satanic abuse.

THE DEVIL'S PARTY, BY BRIAN STABLEFORD

The First Phase of the Witch-Panic

There is no reliable evidence of any witch-trials occurring before the end of the fourteenth century, although the sorcery trials of the Knights Templar and Lady Alice Kyteler provided important exemplars of persecution by means of Satanic abuse. Two supposed instances from the early 1300s that are sometimes quoted by modern historians, one involving mass trials in Toulouse, and the other involving a witch-hunt in Italy, are shown by Norman Cohn in *Europe's Inner Demons* to be mistaken, the former being a nineteenth century invention of a prolific writer of popular histories and the latter the work of a sixteenth century forger. H. C. Lea's *Materials* include mention of one fourteenth century trial involving the charge of making an image to disclose the whereabouts of buried treasure, and a number of cases brought before secular courts where individuals were charged with making poisons, love-potions and wax figurines for use in magic, but all these cases were treated as straightforward affairs of trivial criminality.

The first occasion we know about when strategies developed by inquisitors for use against heretics were employed in a trial involving charges of "everyday" witchcraft occurred shortly after the beginning of the fifteenth century, in the Alps. The escalation of such isolated incidents into large-scale panics was fairly rapid; in the Swiss canton of Valais and the neighboring French province of Dauphiné there was an extensive witch-hunt during the late 1420s, which resulted in about two hundred people being burned. The spread of the panic was aided there, as in later panics, by the fact that accused witches were required not only to confess but to name other witches, thus allowing charges to multiply exponentially.

The confessions made by the witches follow a stereotyped pattern that was to vary only slightly through the various phases of the hunt. One Pierre Vallin confessed in 1438 that he had given himself body and soul to the Devil sixty-three years before, that he paid the Devil a yearly tribute and that he had given his six month old daughter to the Devil to be killed. He admitted to raining tempests at the Devil's command by beating the water of a brook (a traditional method), and to riding on a stick to Sabbats, where he had intercourse with the Devil in the form of a twenty-year-old girl and participated in cannibalistic feasting. The majority of those accused and implicated in this particular affair were male but the lists of those actually burned suggest that the conviction rate for females was far higher than that for males.

Persecution remained endemic to the region after this first wave of panic, but some time passed before the scare expanded out of the Alps. The locale is significant; many writers have noted that the geography of witch-scares is rather idiosyncratic, and that mountain areas were particularly prone to outbreaks. This presumably has something to do with the fact that fantasies of night-flying tend to be prevalent in such areas, but there are also sociological factors to be taken into account, and in particular the relationship between the Church and its inquisitorial representatives and the local people. Special attention to this matter was paid by Hugh Trevor-Roper in his long essay on *The European Witch-Craze of the 16th and 17th Centuries*, where he suggests that feudalism had never really established its dominion in mountain areas, and that Christianity itself had made relatively little impact on independent-minded local cultures. The Church had sent its inquisitors into the mountain regions in search of Waldensians, but it seems that what many of them found there was an alien-ness of belief that cut much deeper than sectarian asceticism, and which therefore seemed to some friars even more sinister.

Witch-hunting spread from the Alps to the Pyrenees, where there appears to have been a considerable panic during the 1430s. It was in the Alps, however, that the first wave of the witch-hunt made its greatest impact. Nider's essay on witches in the *Formicarius* seems to have been inspired largely by the activities of a Swiss magistrate, Peter of Berne. Although it was as a result of experiences in Germany that Sprenger and Kramer wrote the *Malleus Maleficarum* those experiences were not of witch-panics *per se* but of the difficulties in importing the witch-mythology into a territory where skepticism reigned; there were no mass trials in Germany during the first wave of the hunt. Despite the notorious precedent established by the sensational trial of Gilles de Rais, attempts to start mass trials for sorcery in lowland France were mostly quashed. In 1459-60 inquisitors tried to initiate a witch-hunt at Arras in Northern France, but after they had tortured a considerable number of people and burned five their activities were halted by the Parlement de Paris, which exonerated the accused, declaring that the inquisitors had acted in error and had employed "inhuman methods".

The *Malleus Maleficarum* was published in 1486, while this situation was still normal. It is difficult to estimate its influence on the number and distribution of trials, and if we consider the number of people actually burned in the ensuing years it could be argued that it had less effect than its authors presumably hoped. Mass trials between 1486 and 1500 were mostly confined to areas where witch-hunting was already entrenched; although there was an increase in accusations in areas the panic had not previously touched it is possible that this gradual infection would have followed much the same pattern even without the *Malleus*.

The first phase of the witch-panic petered out in the 1530s. As far as we can tell from official records, the number of people executed in this phase was probably somewhere in four figures; it is unlikely to have been as high as ten thousand, and the best estimate may be about half that. This number is, of course, very tiny compared to other mortality factors effective in the regions affected: death by disease, deaths resulting from common crime, and deaths occasioned by simple poverty. By 1540 the persecution of witches had virtually ceased, and for twenty years there were hardly any witch-trials at all. Explaining this decline and the subsequent explosive rebirth of witch-persecution is one of the most difficult challenges facing the historian of the period.

The Lull Before the Storm

There are two major hypotheses that attempt to explain the substantial pause in the history of the great European witch-hunt. The first, put forward by Robert Mandrou, takes the view that the inquisitors only turned to burning witches in the first place because of a scarcity of manifest heretics, and that the lull was associated with the Church's urgent concern with the rapid spread of new Protestant heresies during the sixteenth century.

In Mandrou's view, it was only when the attempt to prevent the Reformation had manifestly failed that both Catholics and Protestants turned away from the purposive business of persecuting one another to the scapegoating of witches. Mandrou supports this thesis by quoting specific examples of regional persecution where prosecution of witches began again in the late sixteenth century at exactly the time when prosecution of heretics was abandoned. A variant of this hypothesis was offered by Hugh Trevor-Roper, who saw the second phase of witch-persecution as a means of expressing the tensions between Catholics and Protestants, whereby the anger of both parties could be redirected against a common enemy. The resurrection of witch-persecution was, in this view, a by-product of the wars of religion that raged between 1560 and 1590.

The second hypothesis, advanced by E. W. Monter, claims that the geographical distribution of the witch-panics that began the second phase of the hunt simply does not fit the explanations suggested by Mandrou and Trevor-Roper. In Monter's view, both the Protestant Reformation and the subsequent Catholic "Counter-Reformation" led by the Jesuits are best understood as different aspects of a spirit of religious revival rather than as a social conflict, and the persecution of heretics ought be seen as an index of religious zeal rather than straightforward enmity. He argues that because witchcraft was the very worst sort of anti-Christian heresy—supposedly being evidence of the existence of an organized sect of active Satanists—the persecution of witches became a useful way of displaying the magnitude of one's religious zeal.

Monter's hypothesis, like its rival, is primarily intended to explain the revival of witch-persecution, and tacitly regards the decline of the original bout of witch-hunting as a more-or-less natural process, although the decline may well be more problematic than the revival. In any case, Monter's hypothesis is easily combined with that of Mandrou and Trevor-Roper if one is prepared to regard the upsurge of religious zeal on the part of Catholics and Protestants as a product of the challenge that each version of the faith presented to the other. The Protestant movement offered harsh criticisms of the Catholic faith, to which the Catholics then had to produce their own answers. There might, however, have been more to the decline of witch-hunting in the early sixteenth century than the mere passing of a fad; it could be viewed as a deflection of attention, which happened because many members of the Church began to see their problems in a new perspective.

The prosperity that had come to Europe by the late eleventh century had allowed the Church to build a powerful organization, which dominated Medieval Europe, but the same growth in prosperity eventually began to redistribute power, by creating economic power where none had been before. The Church's authority was primarily moral authority; it had armies only by virtue of the loyalty of fighting men and their secular leaders, and money only by virtue of the generosity of its followers. After 1100, the loyalty of political leaders had been slowly eroded, because the possible gains to be made in this world began to engage the attention and endeavors of powerful people, at the expense of the hypothetical gains of salvation.

The authority of the Church was first resented, and then challenged; the career of Philippe le Bel of France provides an outstanding example of the re-ordering of priorities on the part of secular leaders. Independence of spirit spread like an infection; the printing press invented in the fifteenth century—which facilitated the mass-production of ideas, and made the sacred writings of Christianity available on a wide scale for direct contemplation by ordinary men—posed a powerful threat to the Roman Church's role as custodian and interpreter of wisdom. As the mass-production of books opened up the way for the spread of literacy beyond the monasteries and the universities, the extent to which people could and did think for themselves increased rapidly; in this fashion, the Renaissance became the mother of the Reformation.

The upsurge of religious zeal to which Monter refers was, in part, the expression of a new confidence in the human individual, and the individual's ability to make his own way even in a corrupt world. The notion that society had gone wrong, and that the Church had lost its way, was offset by the idea that the relationship between individual men and God could be remade, and that the situation could be corrected. Martin Luther's vision of the world seems terrible and pessimistic to modern readers of his tirades—we find such statements in his writings as: "The world and all that belongs to it must have the Devil as its master"; "We are servants in a hostelry where Satan is the householder, the world his wife, and our affections his children"; "The whole world is possessed with Satan"; and "The world is the Devil and the Devil is the world"—but in his supposed personal encounters with Satan, Luther claimed to have emerged triumphant, and his triumph was embodied in his idea of a new and more personal relationship between man and God.

Protestantism was more than simply a new heresy. Earlier heretics had forsaken the established Church in favor of other mediators who claimed a better understanding of the word of God. The Protestants, however, opposed the whole notion of mediation, wanting to give men direct access to the word of God (as represented by the Bible). It was not by any means a rebellion against scriptural authority, but rather against the hierarchical "bureaucracy" that had arisen between men and the only true authority. In their acceptance of, and adherence to, the authority of the Bible the Protestants were rather more determined than the Catholics.

The chronology of the Reformation fits the gap in the pattern of witch-hunting very closely; the witch-scare waned as the movement for Reform grew. The movement gained its vital substance with the work of Erasmus, who outlined his new theology—discarding the layers of commentary imposed upon scripture by the Church—in a "Handbook for the Christian Warrior" published in 1503. He published a new Latin translation of the Bible in 1516 and was an active propagandist for the wider circulation of the Holy Word and its translation into the vernacular languages of Europe. In 1520 a Papal Bull drove Luther into public defiance of the Church; he was excommunicated in 1521 and refused to recant at the Diet of Wurms held in that year.

The "Protest" itself, from which the movement took its name, was delivered by a few minor princes at the Diet of Speyer in 1529, and by 1531 the Protestant princes of Germany were linked in the Schmalkaldic League. The reform of Zurich by Ulrich Zwingli in the 1520s was notionally independent of the Lutheran movement, but John Calvin—who made his key contribution to the Swiss Reformation in the 1540s—was heavily influenced by both reformist doctrines. The Church of England was divorced from Rome by Henry VIII in 1534, although Reform and Protestantism made relatively slow and problematic progress until stability was established during the long reign of Elizabeth I, which began in 1558. By 1560 Switzerland, Germany, Austria, Denmark and Scandinavia were all predominantly Protestant—but that was where the movement reached its limits, for the time being; by 1600, only a small further expansion had taken place, the only major additions being Scotland and Holland.

Erasmus never formally declared himself a Protestant, continuing to press for reform of the Catholic Church from within. His cause was subsequently taken up by Ignatius Loyola, who founded the Society of Jesus in 1540. The Jesuits soon became one of the major forces in the Catholic world, coupling their own kind of reform with zealous opposition to the Protestant movements. The Catholic "reformation" was formally effected by decrees issued by the Council of Trent, which opened in 1545 and closed in 1563; by 1570 the Roman Church had redefined itself as a religious and political entity.

It was undoubtedly this self-conscious and self-critical redefining of means and ends by the Church's scholars and missionaries that deflected attention away from the "problem" of witchcraft. It is significant, too, that this was not merely a time of soul-searching doubt but also a period of unexpected new opportunity, because of the opening up of the new world. Cortés conquered Mexico in 1519 and Pizarro conquered Peru in 1531; adventures of these kinds provided further new scope for the zeal of the Church's servants, and helped to make the kinds of misfortunes allegedly caused by witches seem woefully trivial.

The Devil's Party, by Brian Stableford

Unfortunately, the fervor of self-consciousness and self-criticism did not last. By 1570 a new equilibrium had been established, with Europe divided and the Americas divided up between various groups of European colonists, and each party was more or less sure of its own position. It was then that ideologies hardened and a tortuous tension developed between two unyielding positions. This tension bred extremism in doctrine and action, stimulating zealous defenses of each faith and fierce expressions of the defensive temperament. It was an age when martyrdom came back into vogue, and it was an age when Catholics and Protestants alike began searching for witches to burn.

The Second Phase of the Witch-Panic

The second phase of the great witch-hunt lasted only a little longer than the first, but it was far bloodier. It was not confined to mountain areas, but spread much further through rural regions of Europe. The business of cataloguing witch-trials from the 1560s to the end of the seventeenth century is an exhausting one, and the descriptions which we have of the more celebrated trials are often horrifying, but again we must be careful not to overestimate the number of people who were actually involved.

There are more than ten times as many known cases of execution of witches in the second phase of the hunt than in the first phase, but this is likely to be a greater proportion of the actual total because the records we have are better (though far from complete). On this basis, we may conclude that the total number of deaths was in the tens of thousands, although it was probably not more than fifty thousand. This is still a small figure compared to the overall mortality rate, and even by comparison with the number of people who died after being convicted of ordinary criminal offences—but it remains an appalling total in connection with an imaginary crime and a judicial procedure of such cruelty and irresistibility.

The revival of the witch-hunt in such nations as France and various regions of Germany was simply a resumption on an exaggerated scale of what had happened in the first phase of the hunt, though many more areas were affected. There were more trials in these regions, and hence more epidemics of incrimination. Other nations, however, differed considerably in the extent to which they allowed the panic to spread. In Spain there had been mass trials of witches by secular courts in Navarre in 1526, but, after an investigation by the Suprema of the Spanish Inquisition, the trials had been stopped. The Spanish Inquisition was no less suspicious of witchcraft accusations during the second phase of the hunt, and stifled virtually all the witch-panics that threatened the country, in spite of a new wave of panic that afflicted Navarre in 1610.

The British Isles had been unaffected by the first phase of the witch-hunt, but witch-mythology was imported during the second phase, although it had noticeably different impacts in England and Scotland. Henry VIII, whose reign extended into the "interregnum" between the phases of the witch-hunt, had enacted a law prohibiting the practice of medicine by people who were not accredited members of the medical profession, in order to protected the privileges of the Royal College of Physicians, and the act justified its protectionist stance with the allegation that traditional practices of folk medicine were a form of sorcery. The law was not used as a device of persecution, however, and was repealed after Henry's death in 1547 because the Royal College of Physicians had taken such advantage of its "closed shop" that only those who could pay got any medical attention at all. When Elizabeth came to the throne, however, a new act in a similar vein was issued against "conjurations, enchantments and witchcrafts" in 1563. This established hanging as the ultimate penalty for causing death by witchcraft, but did not prescribe death simply for being a witch and did not license the torture of suspects or the use of inquisitorial procedure in trials.

Elizabeth's reign was constantly troubled by the uneasy relationship between Protestants and Catholics, but the government of the kingdom remained securely in Protestant hands. In Scotland, by contrast, the battle for control was still going on in the latter half of the sixteenth century. The Scottish Catholics had begun a campaign of extermination against the Protestants in 1539, but in 1542, following the death of James V, Protestant lords seized power and enthroned the Earl of Arran. The victory was short-lived because Arran switched sides, but the pendulum swung back again as John Knox emerged as an outspoken reformer and there was a popular uprising against the Catholics. The French intervened to put down the revolt, and Knox spent two years in the galleys, but by 1560 the French had been expelled, the Scottish parliament had repudiated the authority of the Pope, and Knox had drafted his Confession of Faith. The settlement between the Protestants and the Catholics remained uneasy, and Parliament would not give any legal backing to the Book of Discipline intended to establish the system of Presbyterian Church government—with the result that, from 1560 onwards, there was a continuing struggle to establish the system, with or without the legal force to make it compulsory; it was this struggle that became the context of Scottish witch-hunting.

In Scotland, unlike England, torture was legitimate and convicted witches were burned. Accused witches were permitted legal representation, but most of them were too poor to afford counsel. A confession had to be extracted in order to ensure conviction, but the use of torture facilitated such extractions. In all, approximately four thousand witches were burned in Scotland, the great majority between 1590 and 1700. There were a few further executions after 1700, but the act under which the prosecutions were conducted was repealed in 1736. In England, records show only a few hundred hangings, and. even when some correction is made for the incompleteness of the records, the best estimates made by such careful historians as C. L'Estrange Ewen are less than a thousand.

Witch-hunting reached Wales at a late date, and operated on a very small scale. Although the first translation of parts of the Bible into Welsh was made in 1567, Reform did not become effective in Wales until 1650, and it was after this date that witch-trials first appeared in the records of the Welsh courts, although the accused seem to have been acquitted in almost every instance prior to the advent of John Wesley's Methodist revival in the early eighteenth century. This was some time after persecution in Europe had ended, and Wesley was never able to ignite any real fervor for witch-hunting. Ireland, although it had its troubles during the period, was hardly affected by the witch-craze at all.

North America imported witchcraft beliefs from Europe, but there too they remained virtually ineffective for many years. When the mythology finally did give birth to a mass trial—at Salem in 1692—it caused such a sensation that no repetition was possible. Although the Salem affair became *the* archetypal witch-trial, so far as Anglo-American society is concerned—and will be discussed as such in due course—it did so because it was such a bizarre exception to the normal state of affairs in the colonies.

The Conduct of Witch-Trials

The procedure of witch-trials was already stereotyped when the second phase of the witch-hunt began. The standard pattern was virtually invariable in continental Europe. Suspects were seized, cast into prison, and then formally charged by the magistrate. The accused was invited to confess, and if he or she refused, the process of persuasion began. This was organized in several graded stages.

The first stage was simply imprisonment and verbal pressure. Imprisonment itself could be a frightful ordeal—prisons were damp, filthy, pest-ridden places where prisoners were not adequately fed and had no protection against cold. Those in charge of the questioning could say, in all honesty, that the only way the prisoner could avoid worse torture would be to issue a full confession. Other psychological pressures could also be brought to bear; it was possible for the inquisitors to play upon any guilt—specific or vague—felt by the prisoner, and to exploit all emotions connected with religious faith and sentiment. They often offered mercy as a reward for a full and open confession and a display of repentance, and sometimes meant it, although the *Malleus* and other handbooks stressed that inquisitors were perfectly entitled to lie to the suspect in this matter.

If no confession was forthcoming under this first stage of pressure the suspect was deemed "impenitent" and subjected to "preparatory" torture. This involved stripping the accused person naked, shaving the body to remove all hair, and binding with rope, often to a ladder. Suspects were often stretched on the ladder by hauling on the ropes that bound them, after the manner of the rack. Once bound, they were often whipped. This kind of pressure was quite adequate to secure a confession in many cases, but, as formal torture had not yet begun, such confessions were usually said to have been given "freely". Some confessions really do seem to have been given freely, but the elasticity of the term means that the official records give a dramatically distorted picture of their frequency. It was not until suspects passed on to the third stage of interrogation that they were officially acknowledged to have been tortured

The most usual method of formal torture employed in France, Germany and Switzerland was the strappado. The hands of the victim were tied together behind the back and attached to a system of pulleys which allowed the body to be lifted clear of the ground. The system could be used either to juggle the victim up and down or to drop him or her from a height, arresting the fall just before the ground interrupted it. This process twisted the arms so as to cause great pain, and ultimately dislocated the shoulders. A variant producing constant rather than periodic pain involved suspending the victim and then tying heavy weights to the feet.

There were many variations of this standard pattern, and fashions in torture tended to be local. In Scotland the standard tortures involved the crushing of limbs with vices or by wedges inserted into clamps. These methods—especially the thumbscrew, which had the advantage of being cheap and easily portable—were also used in

Europe. Pincers were sometimes used to tear the flesh, and branding was not uncommon. Particularly well-equipped prisons often had more complex apparatus specially constructed, and individual torturers were sometimes wont to design highly imaginative engines of torture whose mere contemplation was terrifying: spiked chains, iron suits that could be heated externally by fires and so on. Such elaborate devices probably did not add significantly to the efficacy of torture, but the ingenuity of their design offers a curious insight into the aesthetic sensibilities of the sadistic imagination. (The Marquis de Sade was a prolific, but purely hypothetical, designer of imaginary engines of torture.)

Some of the most bizarre torture devices devised in this period have been carefully preserved as museum pieces, and some of those lost (or never actually built) have been carefully "reconstructed"; all such exhibits remain very popular. They are extravagantly deployed in oral tradition and popular fiction for the purpose of inspiring horror, and that has always been their true purpose; the simple business of inflicting pain can be accomplished much more easily and cheaply. With or without their aid, however, the success of torturers in extracting confessions is not at all surprising.

The Confessions of Accused Witches

It seems obvious to modern observers that the kinds of pressure used by the inquisitors could extort a confession of absolutely anything from almost anyone. When we study the appalling catalogue of ordeals we can only marvel at the fact that a few people actually endured the whole process and remained obdurate. We must remember, however, that the inquisitors saw things differently, and so did the victims. If we wish to understand how and why it was that some people confessed "freely", while others refused to confess even under the most terrible of tortures, we must try to look at the whole process not from our relatively detached and rational viewpoint but from the viewpoint of those concerned—both inquisitors and suspects.

A detailed examination of the records of witch-persecution in Lorraine was carried out by the French historian Étienne Delcambre, who made a strenuous effort to analyze the attitudes of the people involved and to understand the psychology of the confessions which resulted from the processes of enquiry.

Delcambre is willing to accept the total sincerity of the judges, who saw themselves engaged in a battle with the Devil for the souls of human beings. The one victory that mattered to them was the salvation of the souls of the accused, and the method which they used to achieve that end was, in their eyes, wholly justified by the fact that it was authoritatively held and experimentally proven to be the only one that was effective in cases of witchcraft. The inquisitors were always prepared to plead with their victims to allow God's grace to redeem them and allow them to confess their sins, and Delcambre accepts that neither they, nor many of their victims, suspected that there might be an element of hypocrisy in this endeavor. He concludes that many accused witches not only accepted the sincerity of their tormentors but were prepared to be moved by it; indeed, he notes that a kind of *rapport* seems sometimes to have grown up between inquisitor and accused, perhaps not unlike the kind of *rapport* that is sometimes established nowadays between hijackers and their hostages.

Delcambre is convinced that many of the accused who confessed—whether before or after torture—really came to believe in their own guilt. In many cases confessions *were* given simply to avoid further pain (and were often retracted later) but this was by no means always the case. Confessions first extracted under torture had later to be repeated and affirmed "freely", and many of these eventual "free" confessions appear to Delcambre to have been sincere. Many people apparently found in their inability to withstand torture "proof" of their guilt, which they took more seriously than their knowledge of their innocence. This may seem irrational, by our standards, but it becomes understandable when we recall that these people did not live by our standards. Many of the accused looked upon torture as a kind of trial by ordeal—a test of their faith. They trusted in God to give them the strength to demonstrate their innocence. When that strength failed they often responded, not by losing faith in God, but by losing faith in themselves. When they failed to withstand torture, they began to doubt their own innocence, their own worthiness in the sight of God. They began to consider themselves guilty, if not of witchcraft then of *something*: something that justified what was being done to them, and their eventual acceptance of it.

The image that people have of their own selves is to a very large extent developed and maintained by the image that other people have of them. We are, to a large extent, what other people know us to be, and we can be changed when other people change their attitude to us. People who were called witches could indeed be made to think of themselves as witches, especially with the kind of emphasis that was lent to the charge by the nature and procedures of seventeenth century witch trials. We may assume that the people accused of witchcraft were all guilty of *some* sin, and that none had a completely clear conscience. Everyone charged with deserting the cause of God in favor of Satan could easily find thoughts and deeds by which they had failed the prescription for the ideal moral life. It was not difficult, once the wall of faith was tested and breached, for it to be carried away altogether. Once guilt has been accepted, what matters is the degree to which it is felt—and the pressures of the inquisitors were calculated, not only to break down the will to resist, but also to magnify any sensation of guilt and failure.

According to Delcambre's analysis, many accused witches, under torture, found themselves capable of confessing in all honesty to sins of the mind and heart. Confession really can be "good for the soul", in that it permits relief, and the relief it permits can be proportional to the enormity of the sins confessed rather than to those actually committed. It is not uncommon in today's world for people burdened with a sense of guilt to confess to crimes that they have not committed, and police interrogators inevitably become expert at eliciting such confessions. In the Post-Renaissance era, when so much more emphasis was placed on sin and confession, this tendency must have been even more common—and the natural form for such confessions to take was provided by the context of witchcraft. It is far less difficult than we might suppose for people to come to believe—or be induced to believe—that they have deserted God and made a pact with Satan; the path from metaphorical to literal desertion, from the admission of an implicit pact to the confession of an explicit one, could not have been a difficult one to travel under the pressure of skilful interrogation.

This kind of process surely accounts for many confessions of diabolism that were issued freely, or which were freely reiterated after being extracted under torture. One notable British case is that of the Scotsman Thomas Weir, who had an outstanding reputation as a soldier, parliamentarian and evangelical leader, but who suddenly and spontaneously confessed in 1670 (at the age of seventy) to an astonishing array of sins, including incest, sodomy, bestiality and witchcraft. His sister joined him in the orgy of self-abuse and they were both burned, although there was not a shred of evidence that any of the alleged crimes actually had been committed.

Delcambre notes that about one in ten of those submitted to torture persisted in their denials and ultimately escaped the stake. In stating that many of the confessions appear to have been sincere he makes conscientious reference to hallucinations, amnesia, epilepsy and other psychiatric conditions, but the core of his argument is what happened was far less abnormal than we might initially suppose, and that quite ordinary people—who were not in any sense "mad"—were persuaded to accept the judgment of their inquisitors. Such people were certainly deluded, but they were not mentally ill; they yielded to pressure and came to believe things about themselves that were not true, but we all believe things about ourselves that are not true, and many of these beliefs are imposed upon us by the beliefs of others, communicated to us in various direct and indirect ways.

The most curious thing to emerge from Delcambre's study was not the number of confessions that were more-or-less freely given but the number of partial confessions. Many people admitted some of the charges but not others. There is no logic to this as a strategy of evasion, in that any admission of any degree of guilt was enough to guarantee execution, while partial obduracy was likely to prolong the torture. Delcambre noted that a considerable number of people were prepared to admit to bewitching humans, while insistently denying that they had ever casting spells on animals, even though the former offence was far more serious. The only conceivable explanation for this sort of discrimination, as Delcambre observes, is that people really were persuaded that their resentful feelings had acquired actual magical force, and were therefore prepared to admit to injuring people by magic, while still taking offence at the idea that they might ever have wished harm on innocent animals.

It is hardly surprising that people accused of witchcraft by their neighbors should find themselves guilty of harboring malice toward those same neighbors, while remaining perfectly certain that they had never had evil thoughts regarding a pig or a cow. Further evidence of this sort is provided by Delcambre's observation that some of the accused persons who subsequently retracted confessions given under torture only retracted parts of the confessions, while affirming others. This, too, attests to a genuine concern with the accurate assessment of personal guilt-feelings.

The witch-trials Delcambre studied often involved denunciations as well as confessions, and the pattern of denunciations is even more puzzling to superficial examination than the pattern of confessions. Delcambre notes that, in other places, people from whom confessions were wrung occasionally attempted a kind of revenge by naming their jailers and inquisitors as fellow witches they had seen at the Sabbat. How common this was we cannot tell, because such accusations were rarely written down, but it appeals to us as a singularly appropriate stratagem. However, Delcambre notes that there is no note anywhere in the Lorraine records (which are unusually full) of anything like this ever having happened. Even if it is simply a matter of non-recording, though, there remains for explanation the pattern of the denunciations that *were* made. This aspect of the trials obviously horrified Delcambre more than any other, his observations of the behavior of some accused persons being offered in a frankly condemnatory manner.

Delcambre observes that, once accused persons became convinced of their own guilt, they frequently became very enthusiastic in denouncing others. Although their torturers would normally have been content with one or two names, several individuals offered lists of other people they claimed to have seen at Sabbats that extended into double figures. Delcambre cites instances of newly-accused witches being confronted by the friends and relatives that had accused them, tearfully begging them to tell the truth, but receiving only reproaches and further accusations by way of reply. He notes that although denunciations of brothers, sisters, uncles, aunts, brothers or sisters-in-law were relatively rare, instances of spousal accusation, mothers-in-law accusing daughters-in-law, and children accusing their parents of taking them to the Sabbat, were far more numerous, as were instances of parents admitting to corrupting their children. These patterns provide an obvious reflection of the different extents to which people are likely to feel guilty about their treatment of close relatives.

Delcambre reserves his greatest amazement and horror for his reportage of the evidence given by some children below the age of puberty, for its extraordinary enthusiasm and the extent of its embellishment; this phenomenon played a key role in many of the most notorious witch-trials, which were often fuelled by the local assumption that small children were quite incapable of making up the kind of accusations that they were prepared to level at their parents and other adults known to them—an assumption that rings very hollow indeed when all the evidence is amassed and considered. The passions generated by family tensions can often be very powerful, all the more because they are not permitted expression in the normal course of affairs, due to the obligations and responsibilities of the relationships involved. It is particularly easy for adults to underestimate the extent to which children resent the powerlessness associated with their low status and small size—a point of considerable relevance to the key role played in very many witch-trials by the confessions and denunciations of children.

Delcambre's analysis helps us to see that witch-trials were not simply cruel events in which innocent people were made to confess to imaginary crimes. Many modern commentators have been misled by their own knowledge of the impossibility of the charges to a bitter condemnation of the supposedly-psychopathic viciousness of the inquisitors. The point has already been made, though, that the purpose of a "show trial" is not so much to prove something as to obtain affirmation of a belief. The victim, ideally, has not only to capitulate but to participate. Most inquisitors presumably believed in what they were doing, and reaffirmed their own belief by persuading their victims to share it. Many post-Renaissance witch-trials were not so much straightforward exercises of brutality as careful "brainwashing" procedures, and in this respect they often seem to have been spectacularly successful. The witch-hunters did not simply create the image of the Satanist witch; they also convinced a significant number of their victims that they really were Satanist witches.

The Decline of Witch-Hunting

The second phase of the witch-hunt reached its peak in different areas at different times. Midelfort's figures for south-western Germany show a peak around 1630, with the last trials involving more than ten accused persons in the 1660s. Alan Macfarlane's figures for the Essex assizes in England show a peak in the period 1580-99, with a steady decline thereafter interrupted by a minor peak in 1645. In France, the main peaks were in the 1580s, when Nicholas Rémy was active in Lorraine, and in 1609, when Pierre de Lancre embarked upon his crusade in the Labourd. In all three of these countries, witch-hunting had virtually ended by the year 1680. Although America's witch-scare began later than that, in 1692, persecution was ended for good by the published recantation of the Salem jurors only four years afterwards.

The question of why the witch-craze died away in this period may seem to be almost rhetorical. The answer that seems immediately obvious is that it was the eventual victory of reason over superstition and skepticism over credulity, but this is not so much an explanation as a restatement of the observation. The question of how and why skepticism triumphed over credulity, and reason over superstition, is actually rather complicated and not at all straightforward. Because the victory is now taken for granted, it seems perfectly obvious that the skeptics were right and that rationality had to win the day, and most modern commentators consider that it only took so long because of an obduracy on the part of the credulous that they find as exasperating as many inquisitors must have found the obduracy of supposed witches—but the war between skepticism and belief was not the simple battle between sense and nonsense that it may seem to us. It was, in fact, a battle between two whole ways of thought, each with its own internal integrity.

If we want to understand why witch-hunting died out when it did it is not enough simply to observe that too many people had ceased to believe in it by the end of the seventeenth century. In fact, belief of a theoretical kind persisted long after, and is far from extinct even today. What really happened was that people, by and large, stopped *acting* on those particular beliefs. The slow spread of doubt as to whether the beliefs were warranted was undoubtedly important in securing that result, but it may not have been as important as the erosion of the psychological pressures that created the compulsion to act. As E. W. Monter, Robert Mandrou and Hugh Trevor-Roper all argued, the witch-hunt was in large measure an expression of religious zeal, and that zeal was guided in its expression by the tensions within Christendom resulting from the Reformation. By 1680, the tension in question had by no means died away, but its character had changed, and it no longer called for expression in the same fashion.

The Reformation not only divided the Church but served to make necessary the separation of secular power from religious influence. Rulers themselves might be Catholic or Protestants, but their subjects were likely to include adherents to both causes. As the seventeenth century extended, the interests of secular leaders became more and more disposed to the problems of maintaining order and promoting trade rather than to the matter of homogeneity of belief and the persecution of heretics. By 1648, the year that saw the end of the Thirty Years War, there was still a great deal of bitterness and hatred between Catholics and Protestants, but the notion that anything significant could be done about it died away as secular influences persuaded rulers that their primary interest lay in suppressing conflict rather than encouraging it.

Fervent faith is still perfectly viable as a way of thinking and a way of coping with the world in today's world. It still results in various kinds of violent persecution, but for the most part, abuse—however violent its rhetoric might be—is only rarely translated into action, and when such actions do occur they are normally considered to be horrible aberrations by the vast majority of onlookers and commentators. The Christian witch-craze did not die because fervent faith and its associated fears and resentments disappeared, allowing rationality to put a full stop to the whole business. The process was much more complicated than that, and the interaction between dependence on authority and dependence on the testimony of the senses in the intellectual debates of the period is more subtle than the common distinction between reason and credulity would have us believe. We must bear this in mind while attempting a more detailed analysis of the sixteenth- and seventeenth-century writings on Satanist witchcraft, and in trying to interpret the related writings of our own day.

IV.

THE WAR OF SKEPTICISM AND BELIEF

The Problems of Skepticism

From the very beginning, Christian witch-hunters faced opposition from skeptics who would not accept that accused witches were really members of an organization of Satanists. The tenor of the skepticism varied from place to place and from time to time, but in its most common form it did not hold that witchcraft was an imaginary crime, or that making pacts with Satan was impossible. The orthodox Christian of the sixteenth or seventeenth century had to concede the theoretical possibility of humans working maleficent magic with the aid of the devil. Because of this, the skeptic was always open to attack through his own essential doubt. It was, in many instances, the very reasonableness of skeptics that made them vulnerable to conversion to belief in witchcraft, because believers had two powerful arguments on their side.

One of these arguments was the appeal to authority, which—the *Canon Episcopi* notwithstanding—could easily be made to sanction belief in witches; the other was the appeal to the experiences of witchfinders and the confessions of convicted witches. Both these arguments became seemingly stronger with the passage of time. Authorities piled up as more and more writers produced treatises on witchcraft, and new translations of the Bible into vernacular languages often added considerably to the authoritative pronouncements to be found therein. The register of confessions also grew, along with the weight of a new oral tradition of witch-anecdotes, which was continually augmented.

It was partly because of this steadily increasing power of these arguments that the kinds of opposition that succeeded in containing the first phase of the hunt were less effective in inhibiting the second phase. The opposition case had actually lost ground as the case for belief had literally gained substance. The skeptics could never have won the argument had it continued to be conducted in the same arena. As long as the accepted "rules" for distinguishing a good argument from a bad one remained the same, the believers were winning; they would still be winning today if we still gave arguments from authority priority over arguments based on experience, using the former to determine the interpretation of the latter rather than using the latter to test and undermine the former.

It was a particular mixture of the two modes of argument—in which a specific interpretation of authority controlled the interpretation of experiential evidence—that proved so deadly in promoting witch-fantasies to the level of social action. It was the change of allegiance to a different mixture—in which experiential evidence gained far more control over the interpretation of authority—that demoted them back to fantasies again. The story told by the major documents of the great witch-hunt is not so much that of a slow but steady growth in non-belief in witchcraft, but that of a gradual shifting of the argumentative battleground, in such a way as to redefine the implications of certain arguments from authority and to deny them the privilege of justifying certain kinds of social action.

Strix (1523) by Gianfrancesco Pico della Mirandola offers an excellent example of the argument between skepticism and belief as it was conducted during the first phase of the witch-hunt. It is cast in the form of a dialogue, in which three men put their case for believing or doubting in the account of herself given to them by the witch Strix, at the end of which—being scrupulously reasonable men—they reach agreement.

Pico has Strix define her activities in terms of the conventional stereotype. She attends Sabbats (which she calls "the game"), where she indulges in feasting and making love, flying there on a linen-mallet after anointing herself with ointment. Her magical activities include storm-raising and killing babies by sucking their blood. Whenever she attends mass she makes covert obscene gestures at the elevation of the host, to emphasize her renunciation of Christ. Her account is ridiculed by Apistius, who thinks that it is a tissue of lies, but he is opposed—and ultimately converted—by Phronimus and Dicaste, whose grounds of attack are markedly and significantly different.

Dicaste simply quotes the scriptures, and bases his whole argument on the word of the Bible. His faith is simple and straightforward. Phronimus is much more sophisticated; his recourse, too, is to the authority of ancient writings, but he is thoroughly eclectic, as an educated man would be. He uses Apistius' own considerable learning and respect for classical philosophy against him, recalling images of the witch in Greek literature and comparing them to aspects of Strix's confession, and reminding Apistius that the gods of Greece and Rome were really the minions of the Devil. Phronimus is the dominant figure in the debate; it is his arguments that convince the educated Apistius, although he also serves to confirm, by means of the best and most scholarly arguments of the day, that Dicaste's simple and straightforward faith in the Bible is wholly justified. Phronimus demonstrates, according to Pico, that all the knowledge of the ancient world does not serve to put aside one word of Christian dogma, even though it has led the unwary Apistius into doubt.

This is a clear reflection of the intellectual climate of the day. The Renaissance had allowed the intelligentsia to acquaint themselves with the literature and the philosophy of the ancient world, but this interest had to be justified, relative to the Christian faith, by the careful assertion that all the new learning supported and supplemented the dogmas of the Church, and could not come into conflict with them.

The author of *Strix* was the nephew of the neo-Platonist scholar, Giovanni Pico della Mirandola, a follower and one-time associate of Marsilio Ficino, the leading figure in the Renaissance revival of neo-Platonism. Ficino had been given a copy of the *Corpus Hermeticum*—one of the key documents promulgating the idea of the Hermetic Tradition—by Cosimo de Medici, who had acquired it in 1460. Ficino's version of the *Corpus*, published together with his commentary and extrapolations of its claims, was widely circulated thereafter; its admirers included Rodrigo Borgia, who became Pope Alexander VI, and Giordano Bruno, one of the most prominent advocates of the heliocentric theory of cosmology. Giovanni Pico's own attempts to reconcile Christian theology with the Hebrew Kabbalah resulted in his condemnation for unorthodoxy by Pope Innocent VIII, and he was briefly imprisoned before coming under the protection of Cosimo de Medici's grandson, Lorenzo, nicknamed Il Magnifico. Under the influence of Lorenzo's arch-enemy, the ardent reformer Girolamo Savonarola—who briefly took political control of Florence after Lorenzo's death—Giovanni moved back towards orthodoxy: an example his nephew was enthusiastic to follow.

Gianfrancesco Pico was a skeptic of sorts himself, but he was not the same kind of skeptic as Apistius. He was prepared to doubt everything except the divine revelation of the scriptures, including the evidence of the senses. His treatise *On Imagination* (1501) dwells extensively on the delusions of the senses that may be caused by malicious demons, and regards the evidence of the senses as essentially weak, not in the same league as the evidence of the Holy Word. A skeptic adopting this position would have been very hard pressed indeed to resist the arguments of a Phronimus.

The first important scholarly attack on the activities of witch-hunters was launched by the Lutheran physician Johann Weyer, who served for most of his adult life as physician to William III, Duke of Cleves. His most important book, *De Praestigiis Daemonum* [On the Wiles of Demons] was first published in 1563, and was revised several times for new editions. It became the subject of fierce controversy. Modern commentators devoted to what Herbert Butterfield dubbed "the Whig interpretation of history", which sees history as a series of battles between heroic progressives and evil reactionaries, tend to view Weyer as a hero who stood up for common sense in an era of credulity, but this is something of a misrepresentation.

Weyer was skeptical about the acts attributed to witches only because he was convinced that the blame really lay with cunning demons that made witches appear to be responsible for their own supernatural maleficia. His treatise contains not only a defense of those accused as witches but also a vitriolic attack on other supposed magicians who allegedly *did* solicit the aid of demons, while pretending to be virtuous themselves. Weyer believed wholeheartedly in the reality of maleficent magic and in punishing those guilty of it, but he saw witches as the dupes of demons, not as arch-criminals. As a fervent Protestant, he classed the rituals of the Catholic Church as evil magical practices, and he considered Catholic priests to be Satanist idolaters. The essential passion of his work is an unusually extreme expression of Reformist zeal.

The first part of Weyer's treatise is a history of the Devil, which stresses Satan's unceasing activity and dreadful cunning, and the awesome ingenuity of his triumph in seducing the entire Catholic Church to worship him in exactly the same manner as the pagans of the ancient world. The second part considers the work of magicians. All magic, Weyer says, consists of illusions wrought by demons; Christ's miracles were real and accomplished without demonic aid, but no one else has this power. He goes out of his way, *en passant*, to declare that his old teacher, Cornelius Agrippa von Nettesheim—whose name, like that of Albertus Magnus, had been co-opted for use in scurrilous anecdotes concerning black magic and had been attached to an apocryphal book of black magic—was entirely innocent of any involvement with magic. The third part describes the way in which the new image of the witch was concocted and attacks the *Malleus Maleficarum*. Weyer rejects entirely the notion of the diabolical pact. He attempts to account for confessions made by witches by reference to the medical theories of the day, attributing them to fantasies initiated by "melancholia".

The fourth part of Weyer's treatise is devoted to the matter of demonic possession, which was often discussed in connection with witchcraft. Numerous people were accused of bringing about the demonic possession of innocent people, but Weyer's contention is that all cases of possession are the fault of the demons involved, and that people accused of instigating them are quite blameless. In the fifth part, which deals with the methods used to counter maleficent magic, Weyer condemns exorcism as the use of diabolical magic to fight diabolical magic. The sixth part deals with appropriate punishments for the various crimes discussed; it prescribes deterrent fines for those who attempt to conjure demons, exile and confiscation of property for Catholic exorcists, exile for diviners who claim to detect witches, and death for poisoners. The greater part of this section is, however, devoted to railing at the inquisitors and judges who try and execute so-called witches.

In the context of his own era, Weyer's arguments were rather weak. His medical contentions lacked recognized authority, and his attempt to distinguish "real" sorcerers from accused witches was logically incompetent. He conceded that all the things that witches were said to do could be done, but contended that they were all done by other entities, while accused witches were necessarily guiltless; this could hardly be reckoned a convincing argument. Catholics were bound to find his opinions intolerable, and his association with Agrippa von Nettesheim aroused suspicion in itself. Agrippa's *De Occulta Philosophia* (written 1510; published 1533) was an assertive repopularization of neo-Platonist ideas, with all the problems associated with them, making much of the notion of a quasi-Gnostic secret wisdom. Oddly enough, Agrippa did not publish the book until three years after he had apparently recanted the views expressed therein; like other writers who followed Marsilio Ficino's lead in trying to establish the virtuousness and potential orthodoxy of some kinds of non-demonic magic—most famously Theophrastus Bombastus von Hohenheim, alias Paracelsus—Agrippa ran into severe political and practical difficulties, but his recantation seems to have been perfectly sincere and it is unclear why he published a work that had already been superseded. Nevertheless, it was *De Occulta Philosophia* that made Agrippa's posthumous reputation; an apocryphal work of black magic that claimed to be a supplementary volume soon made an appearance.

Weyer's defense of his old teacher was somewhat disingenuous, in that Agrippa certainly had been interested in demonic magic, if only as a theoretical corollary to his interest in a kind of purified "spiritual magic" for which Ficino had labored long and hard to provide an apology. In any case, Weyer's attempt to direct attention away from witches and towards scholarly would-be magicians was doomed to failure, partly by its own inadequacies and partly because scholarly magicians enjoyed far higher social status and influence.

The Backlash of Belief

Weyer's views were attacked by many Catholic writers, and were not widely supported even among Protestants. Their most significant effect was to enrage a famous magistrate and expert in jurisprudence, Jean Bodin, to the point where he sat down to produce a book that became a key element in the believer's repertoire of authorities: *De la démonomanie des sorciers* [On the Demonic Madness of Witches] (1580).

Bodin's refutation of Weyer is scathing, criticizing both the logic of his arguments and the authority of his medical evidence. The tone of the main text is careful and dryly academic, but the author added a furiously angry appendix occasioned by the appearance of a new essay by Weyer, which had been appended to a new edition of *De Praestigiis Daemonum*.

Bodin begins his study of witchcraft with a witch-trial at which he happened to be present, and which was primarily responsible for his fascination. This appears to have been a fairly typical witch-trial: a woman named Jeanne Harvillier was accused of killing a man by witchcraft and, after initially denying the charge, confessed under torture. What particularly fascinated Bodin was a legal nicety raised in the course of proceedings: the matter of whether convicted witches should be hanged as murderers or burned as heretics. Around this delicate point, in the manner of so many committed intellectuals, Bodin gathered a comprehensive assessment of the whole legal, philosophical and theological context that rendered the question meaningful and—in his view—forced the argument to its logical conclusion. It is not surprising that Bodin, a jurist of great reputation, should focus his attention on the legal aspects of witch-trials; nor is it surprising to find that his philosophical and theological ideas are arranged about the central concept of the law of God. Because of this orientation, his book had much the same practical utility as the *Malleus*, as well as being vastly superior in the quality of its scholarship and its prose.

Of all the writers who devoted themselves to the cause of the witch-hunt Bodin was the most prestigious and probably the most intelligent, and yet he was the most credulous of all. He appears to have been a man whose entire consciousness was dominated by the authority of the written word. The *Démonomanie* was his fourth book; his first dealt with the methodology of law and history, his second was an analysis of an economic crisis that subjected France to runaway inflation in the late sixteenth century and his third extended the same analysis into a discourse on political theory. The *Démonomanie* must be seen, in the context of these earlier works, as a product of a lifelong theoretical interest in the legal, economic and political relationships that existed between human beings as defined and arbitrated by reference to the relationship between human beings and God.

Bodin accepts without question in the *Démonomanie* what such writers as Sprenger and Kramer had "discovered" concerning witches, just as he accepts without question the confession wrung from Jeanne Harvillier. His main concern is with the method by which such individuals should be found out, tried and punished. He does not attempt to make any distinctions between different varieties of magic, but he does make a careful distinction between those who knowingly invoke demons and those who do so unawares—a natural point of insistence for a lawyer.

The first part of Bodin's treatise concerns the unwitting employment of diabolical agencies, while the second goes on to construct a taxonomy of magical practices according to whether they involve no invocation of spirits (and are therefore spurious), implicit pacts or explicit pacts; he assesses the degree of culpability in each case. It is followed by chapters on the Sabbat, night-flying, lycanthropy and copulation with incubi or succubi. Bodin's main aim here is to systematize his data, bringing material culled from many sources into perfect order. Data deriving from cases reported to him personally are used primarily as token confirmation of data derived from written sources. In the third part of the treatise, though, he makes rather more use of his personal experience of witch-trials, and the legal procedures connected therewith, in a discussion of the legitimate counter-measures to be taken against witchcraft. These he believes to be quite effective; unlike most active witch-hunters, Bodin was so confident of the success of the hunt that he believed witchcraft to be in terminal decline already.

The final part of the *Démonomanie*, dealing with punishment, expresses Bodin's belief that the witch is the most miserable of creatures, subject to unspeakable humiliation as a result of being bound to the Devil. He states that burning alive should not be seen as an addition to a witch's suffering but as a release from it, and that torture is part of the same process of merciful release, so that witches should not be pitied on account of the treatment they receive. He therefore supports all the deceits suggested by Sprenger and Kramer for use by inquisitors, including feigned kindness, false promises, and even the construction of false accounts of evidence given. With his habitual neatness, Bodin establishes that the witch offends against God on nine separate points, and is guilty of a further six offences against his or her fellow men.

Although Weyer is cited in the main body of the book Bodin does not single him out for special attention, but the appendix occasioned by Weyer's repetition of his views is a virulent attack upon the man as well as his ideas. Bodin contends that Weyer must be a magician himself because at one time he had published—in order to expose the evils of the scholarly magicians—part of a textbook of black magic: a version of the most famous of the Renaissance grimoires, the *Clavicula Salomonis*. (His ire was not without justification, as Weyer's version of that text was far more widely circulated than any other.) He concludes his whole argument with a scornful suggestion that Weyer, as a physician should stick to judging the color and consistency of urine, and to leave infringements of divine and human laws to judges.

By the standards of assessment applicable in his own era, Bodin's argument was a much stronger one than that advanced by Weyer. Indeed, it was very difficult for any of Bodin's contemporaries, however skeptical they might be, to find adequate grounds for assaulting his case. Even so, Bodin did not remain unchallenged; just as Weyer had provoked him to put pen to paper, so he in his turn provoked the production of a skeptical account much more assertive and convincing than Weyer's.

A New Kind of Skepticism

Reginald Scot's *The Discoverie of Witchcraft* (1584) is a remarkable book, from which Elizabethan poets and playwrights took considerable inspiration. Although Scot's purpose was to subject witch-beliefs and witch-hunting to scathing ridicule, the net effect of his efforts was actually to win them a secure place in the canon of English literature, most conspicuously in William Shakespeare's *Macbeth*.

Scot was an unlikely participant in the debate, his principal acknowledged employment being that of surveyor of flood defenses at Romney Marsh, but when he wrote the *Discoverie* he was a close associate of Thomas Digges, one of the leading mathematicians and military engineers of the day; he assisted Digges and his own cousin, Sir Thomas Scott, in the design and construction of the defenses of Dover Harbor. He was a devout Protestant who had read his Bible assiduously, and his rejection of many of the authorities with which he contended made much of their Catholicism, but he also launched a rigorous attack on the Protestant translations that had introduced references to witchcraft into the Bible, and he reserved particular ridicule for the common determination to attribute misfortune to forces of evil rather than accepting them as the vicissitudes of life.

"The fables of Witchcraft," Scot began, "have taken so fast hold and deep root in the heart of man, that few or none can nowadays with patience endure the hand and correction of God. For if any adversity, grief, sickness, loss of children, corn, cattle or liberty happen unto them; by and by they exclaim upon witches. As though there were no God in Israel that ordereth all things according to his will; punishing both just and unjust with griefs, plagues, and afflictions in manner and form as he thinketh good: but that certain old women here on earth, called witches, must needs be the contrivers of all men's calamities and as though they themselves were innocents, and had deserved no such punishments. Insomuch as they stick not to ride and go to such, as either are injuriously termed witches, or else are willing to be so accounted, seeking at their hands comfort and remedy in time of their tribulation, contrary to God's will and commandment in that behalf, who bids us resort to him in all our necessities.

"Such faithless people are also persuaded, that neither hail nor snow, thunder nor lightning, rain nor tempestuous winds come from the heavens at the commandment of God: but are raised by the cunning and power of witches and conjurors; insomuch as a clap of thunder, or a gale of wind is no sooner heard, but either they run to ring bells, or cry out to burn witches; or else burn consecrated things hoping by the smoke thereof, to drive the Devil out of the air...

"But if all the Devils in hell were dead, and all the witches in England burnt or hanged; I warrant you we should not fail to have rain, hail and tempests, as we now have: according to the will of God, and according to the constitution of the elements, and the course of the planets, wherein God hath set a perfect and perpetual order."

Having concluded that common misfortunes need no explanation in terns of witchcraft, Scot reconstructs the image of the witch in an equally strikingly fashion. He does not deny that there are people who think themselves witches—he characterizes them as "women which be commonly old, bleary-eyed, pale, foul, and full of wrinkles; poor, sullen superstitious, and papists; or such as know no religion: in whose drowsy minds the Devil hath gotten a fine seat; so as, what mischief, mischance, calamity or slaughter is brought to pass, they are easily persuaded the same is done by themselves; imprinting in their minds an earnest and constant imagination hereof"—but he is utterly scornful of their delusions, and the parallel delusions of anyone stupid enough to believe that people of this sort can wreak any kind of havoc.

"These miserable wretches are so odious unto all their neighbors," Scot goes on, "and so feared, as few dare offend them, or deny them anything they ask: whereby they taken upon them; yea, and sometimes think, that they can do such things as are beyond the ability of human nature. These go from house to house, and from door to door for a pot full of milk, yeast, drink, pottage, or some such relief; without the which they could hardly live: neither obtaining for their service and pains, nor by their art, nor yet at the Devil's hands (with whom they are said to make a perfect and visible bargain) either beauty, money, promotion, wealth, worship, pleasure, honor, knowledge, learning or any other benefit whatsoever.

"It falleth out many times, that neither their necessities, not their expectation is answered or served, in those places where they beg or borrow; but rather their lewdness is by their neighbors reproved. And further, in tract of time the witch waxeth odious and tedious to her neighbors; and they again are despised and despited of her: so as sometimes she curseth one, and sometimes another; and that from the master of the house, his wife, children, cattle etc. to the little pig that lieth in the stye. Thus in process of time they have all displeased her, and she hath wished evil luck unto them all; perhaps with curses and imprecations made in form. Doubtless (at length) some of her neighbors die, or fall sick; or some of their children are visited with diseases that vex them strangely: as apoplexies, epilepsies, convulsions, hot fevers, worms etc. Which by ignorant parents are conceived to be the vengeance of witches. Yea, and their opinions and conceits are confirmed and maintained by unskillful physicians... Witchcraft and enchantment is the cloak of ignorance....

"The witch on the other side expecting her neighbors' mischances, and seeing things sometimes come to pass according to her wishes, curses and incantations (for Bodin himself confesseth that not above two in a hundred of their witchings or wishings take effect) being called before a Justice, by due examination of the circumstances is driven to see her imprecations and desires, and her neighbors harms and losses to concur, and as it were to take effect: and so confesseth that she (as a goddess) hath brought such things to pass. Wherein, not only she, but the accuser, and also the Justice, are foully deceived and abused; as being through her confession and other circumstances persuaded (to the injury of God's glory) that she hath done, or can do that which is proper only to God himself."

Another kind of witches, Scot adds, are simple tricksters; later chapters of his study offer a survey of the methods used by conjurors and illusionists, which was separately reprinted as a pioneering guide to stage magic, in which form it was continually reprinted and augmented over several centuries. Scot was such a remarkably clear-sighted man by the standards of his age that many modern reader may have difficulty in understanding how it was that he did not have a more telling effect on the ongoing debate, but it is necessary to understand how alien his whole way of thought was to that of the great majority of his contemporaries.

Scot refers continually to Bodin's rules for the conduct of witch-trials, attacking the idea that such a process could ever be an efficient way of determining the truth and arguing that torture and the fear of death would extract confessions from anyone. He constantly refers to "witchmongers" rather than "witch-hunters" or "witch-finders" (the latter being the more common expression in England). He devotes sections of his book to scornful analyses of the preposterousness of accounts of sexual intercourse between men and demons, lycanthropy and so on. He ridicules the constant appropriation by witchmongers of literary works as "authorities" on witchcraft. He provides an extensive catalogue of contemporary magical beliefs, charms and spells, amulets and magical medicines, and ridicules them all—though not to the extent of preventing these chapters being used as a reference-work by playwrights in search of incantations. His principal recourse throughout is an appeal to the logic of common sense, but wherever he can test the claims made on behalf of the magical formulas he reports that he has done so and that they have failed. He also quotes experiments carried out by others to detect trickery.

This massive job of debunking reaches its climax when Scot outdoes Weyer by reproducing, almost *in toto,* a version of the *Key of Solomon* (not the same one that Weyer had excerpted), including instructions for conjuring demons, consulting the spirits of the dead, enclosing spirits in crystal stones, etc. Like Weyer, Scot can see no difference between such conjurations and the rites of the Catholic Church, noting in one chapter gloss "That it is a shame for papists to believe other conjurors' doings, their own being of so little force". In the final section of the book, "A Discourse upon Devils and Spirits"—which was omitted from most later editions—he summed up his case and drew his own ultra-skeptical conclusions regarding the purely metaphorical significance of almost all the spiritual beings referred to in the Bible.

Scot's skepticism goes far beyond that of Weyer. Not only does he say that all apparent magic is due to illusion, but due to illusions perpetrated by ordinary men using mundane means. He sees no role in human affairs for demons, nor for Satan himself. In his view, the Age of Miracles is long past, leaving no contemporary residue at all. Scot stopped short of denying that spiritual beings exist at all, being delicate in his anxiety to avoid the charge of Sadducism (the denial of the reality of spiritual beings and of the immortality of the soul) but his critics were virtually unanimous in considering him guilty of this heresy, and many of his modern champions agree with the charge. Thomas Digges probably agreed with him, in spite of having long been the ward and protégé of John Dee—whose notorious attempts to communicate with spirits by means of Edward Kelley's skrying stone were just getting under way as the *Discoverie* was published—but he had few other sympathizers.

It is never easy to persuade people that their superstitions are false. Even today there is little popularity to be gained by "debunking" other people's ideas, however irrational they may be. Wrong ideas often thrive on their aesthetic appeal, and attempts to point out their wrongness inevitably seem dry, pedantic and colorless. No Catholic, of course, was ever going to take note of Scot's arguments, but very few Protestants were willing to give him a hearing either, because they too relied very heavily on the mythology of the Devil, and found more than adequate support for that reliance in their own reading of the Bible. For the vast majority, conceding—or even contemplating—the possibility that the references to spiritual beings in the Bible might be metaphorical was out of the question. Scot had little effect simply because he was so completely right. He asked his readers not merely to give up their belief in witchcraft but to give it up because virtually all the beliefs they held relating to misfortune and the problem of evil were manifestly absurd. This turned out to be asking far too much.

Scot's reply to Bodin did little or nothing to turn the tide against Bodin's view of things because Scot's arguments never really *met* Bodin's: they were waiting on a different battleground, owing allegiance to very different criteria determining what was and what was not "knowledge" and "reasoning". They had to wait a long time for the battle to move on to that battleground, so that their effect might tell at last. In the meantime, James I—the King of England who succeeded Elizabeth I, during whose reign the *Discoverie* was published—ordered that all existing copies of the book should be seized and burned by the public hangman.

The Royal Expert

It is not surprising that James VI of Scotland and I of England took strong exception to Scot's book. He had played a major role in one of the most famous journalistic accounts of a British witch-trial before ascending to the English throne, and once there he had a considerable influence on English witch-hunting. He helped to popularize the continental image of the witch in England by writing his own fierce rebuttal of Scot's *Discoverie* but what he did not do—and this is a matter of very considerable significance—was to encourage, or even allow, English witch-finders to operate unhindered.

James spent much of his time on the continent in his youth, while Scotland as beset by political turmoil, and became familiar with the standardized witch-mythology of Europe, but there is no evidence that he took any active interest in witchcraft before 1590, when his attention was claimed and gripped by a trial in North Berwick. Mainly because of his involvement, that affair was very widely popularized by a sensational pamphlet called *Newes from Scotland* (1591), which became one of the biggest best-sellers of its day.

According to the pamphlet, the affair began when a deputy bailiff of Trenent, David Seaton, became suspicious of his maidservant Geillis Duncan, who was in the habit of leaving the house "every other night". She had acquired a reputation for treating the sick, and Seaton was suspicious of the fact that this might be done "by some extraordinary and unlawful means". He and some of his friends took it into their heads to search her body for a "Devil's mark"—they found a blemish on her throat—and to torture her. Her fingers were crushed by a device known as the pilliwinks and ropes were twisted about her head to squeeze her skull; this procedure was entirely illegal, but when she eventually confessed to being a witch she was thrown into to prison, where she was persuaded to implicate others, including a schoolmaster named John Cunningham, allegedly also known as Dr. Fian.

James, hearing that one of the accused was supposed to have murdered the Earl of Angus by witchcraft, decided to interview some of the accused himself, and had some of them brought to Holyrood House. After initial denials, they were persuaded to confess, and a woman named Agnes Thompson produced a bizarre story about the accused having met together on the previous All Hallows Eve, putting to sea in sieves and meeting at the Kirk of North Berwick to dance to the music of a "Jew's trump". Satan had attended this Sabbat and, after receiving the customary homage, had taken the trouble to rail against King James in person. She claimed that she had collected venom from a black toad in order to procure the king's death but had been unable to acquire an item of his clothing in order to complete the spell. Thus frustrated, the witches had tied various parts of a dead man to a cat and cast it into the sea while the king was in Denmark for his marriage, in order to raise a storm to sink a ship carrying gifts for his queen. The same spell was said to be responsible for winds that separated James' ship from those accompanying it when he returned from Denmark with the queen; only his faith, it was alleged, had saved him.

James initially reacted to all this by declaring it a pack of lies, but the pamphlet states that he was convinced of its truth when another of the accused witches "declared unto him the very words which passed between the King's Majesty and his Queen at Oslo in Norway the first night of their marriage, with their answer each to other". This journalistic masterstroke has joined the long list of marvelous anecdotes associated with witch-lore, being offered even today as evidence to shake the incredulous. It might be worth noting, however, that the pamphlet refers to the personal acquaintance of Agnes Thompson with John Kerr, an "attendant in His Majesty's chamber". Whatever the source of the item of gossip in question might have been, the king seems to have become convinced of the threat of witchcraft to the temporal world and its appointed protectors.

THE DEVIL'S PARTY, BY BRIAN STABLEFORD

The trial of the Berwick witches continued with the torturing of Cunningham/Fian; the pamphlet avidly relates that he had his legs crushed by wedges hammered into an iron boot, forcing him to make a confession of minor acts of sorcery that he subsequently retracted. In order to encourage him to repent of his retraction, needles were thrust underneath his fingernails, which were then torn off, and his legs were crushed in the boot so "that the blood and marrow spouted forth in great abundance"; even so, he stood by his retraction and was burned as an impenitent.

James appeared personally at several other witch-trials in the 1590s, and the eventual result of his preoccupation with witchcraft was a short book called *Daemonologie*, published in 1597. The volume represented a tiny fraction of his voluminous literary output, which mostly consisted of erudite treatises on theology and politics, and the relationship between the two, but it was his most widely-read publication by far. It takes the form of a dialogue, akin to Pico's *Strix*, in which the doubting Philomathes is delivered from confusion by the clever Epistemon, who establishes by argument and careful citing of authorities the reality of witchcraft and the various aspects of witch-mythology. Scot and Weyer are named in the introduction for specific disapproval, and Bodin is prominent among the many sources cited and in the suggestions offered for further reading.

Daemonologie is not original in a scholarly sense; the main thrust of its argument is simply that the scriptural references to witchcraft in the Bible must be taken seriously. It is hardly surprising, in that context, that the version of the English Bible that James authorized as a standard text in 1611 did not stint on such references. The text is, however, more cautious than most continental texts, admitting that witches are deluded by the Devil and that, in consequence, individual confessions must sometimes be doubted in their detailed claims. This may seem like a very tiny breach in the wall of faith, but it was a highly significant one, as can be seen from James' subsequent involvement with English witch-hunting. Arguably, this tiny loophole in the king's witch-theory did more to inhibit English witch-hunting than the entire weight of Scot's scathing skeptical arguments.

In 1603 James became king of England and went to London. His arrival did not precipitate a burst of witch-persecution in England; Alan Macfarlane's figures for the Essex assizes show a steady continuing decline after the end of the sixteenth century. James did involve himself in a number of English trials involving alleged witchcraft—there were several in 1605 and at least two others, in 1616 and 1620—but they were concerned with charlatan "prophets" and fake demoniacs; in each case, he was readily convinced that trickery was responsible. In all the cases that he investigated he appears to have been skeptical of the actual claims made, in spite of his firm commitment to the theoretical possibility of witchcraft.

On the face of it, this skepticism seems out of keeping with the views of *Daemonologie*, but this is not so. Because he was prepared to doubt the contents of individual confessions, James was able to approach each individual case on its own merits. Unlike most witchfinders, when he took an interest in particular cases he was relatively open-minded about the content of a confession, and was always disposed to wonder whether it might be a delusion—and, if so, whether it was one induced by the Devil or not. Because of this willingness to take individual cases on their own merits, rather than applying stereotyped preconceptions, he did not find it difficult to detect trickery in supposed marvels, and spite in accusations. Thus, without for a moment surrendering his belief in the reality of witchcraft, he was able to conclude in every case he scrutinized that the accused persons were guilty of nothing more than deception, or were in fact innocent victims of circumstance.

We, as rationalists, might expect that a man who found so many individual cases of supposed witchcraft to be spurious would begin to doubt the general case, but James was no empiricist, and he held his general beliefs because of the sound authority that lay behind them. That he was then prepared to doubt individual instances of supposed witchcraft in the real world reveals a double standard of belief, but it was a double standard that was easy to maintain and intellectually comfortable. In the eyes of modern commentators, who consider the European witch-craze to have been horrific and almost incomprehensible, James remains something of a villain by comparison with Scot, the heroic champion of rationality. In actual fact, though, it was James' brand of skepticism—which approached individual cases on their merits while not putting forward any serious or dogmatic challenge to theoretical beliefs about the nature of witchcraft—which was more in tune with the intellectual context of the day and gained such ground during the seventeenth century that it was eventually able to stifle the witch-craze.

Despite the prestige and the popularity of King James's *Daemonologie*, witch-hunting in England remained at such a low level that most English horror stories of this sort are wildly exaggerated—none more so than the myths surrounding the career of Matthew

Hopkins, the initiator of a mass trial in Essex in 1645. Hopkins was made by rumor and anecdote into such an ogre that even Montague Summers, the twentieth century's most ardent apologist for the witchfinders of Europe, had not a kind word to say about him, describing him as "the foulest of foul parasites, an obscene bird of prey of the tribe of Judas and Cain". Alan Macfarlane, however, argues that Hopkins was only one of a group responsible for the prosecution of the supposed witches, that he was probably sincere, and that there is no evidence to back up the claim of subsequent popular mythology that he traveled from village to village discovering witches for a fee. Whether Macfarlane or rumor is correct in this matter, the dearth of evidence makes it difficult to be certain—but if the lack of documentary evidence can be taken at face value, then Hopkins' elevation by rumor to the status of "Witchfinder General" provides a notable example of table-turning. Having indulged himself in slanderous persecution, Hopkins then became the victim of sly vilification by those who disapproved of what he had done.

The trial in which Hopkins was involved was unusual for several reasons. Firstly, there was an uncommon emphasis on familiars or "imps" allegedly kept by the witches; the main charges alleged no more than that the women accused entertained evil spirits. Secondly, the methods used to extract confessions—including denying them sleep—were uncommon, as were the techniques of divination used to "prove" that the accused were witches, which included pricking their flesh in order to detect dead spots that did not bleed and were supposedly insensitive to pain, and which were then deemed to be "witch-marks". Pricking was common in Scotland but had not been widely used in Southern England. Another form of divination used in this case was "swimming the witch"—a test based on an old superstition to the effect that witches floated while honest people sank if they were thrown into ponds or rivers with their thumbs tied to their toes (this was rationalized by the notion that because witches had renounced their baptism the water would not accept them). Because of the high profile of the case these exceptional elements have become standard elements of conventional British witch-lore.

Hopkins was singled out for attack in 1646 by a clergyman named John Gaule in a pamphlet called *Select Cases of Conscience*. Gaule held Hopkins responsible for the pressures put upon the suspects and condemned his methods strongly. Hopkins replied in his own pamphlet, *The Discovery of Witches* (1647), which is not the work of a scholar, and reveals a considerable lack of intellectual sophistication on the part of its author. King James' *Daemonologie* is the only authority Hopkins cites, and his reliance upon "common knowledge"—i.e. local folklore—for his understanding of witchcraft presumably explains the unusual features of the trial and the charges. Hopkins denies that he kept his victims awake in order to torture them, claiming that he only sought to assure that the witches remained active enough to summon their imps, and commenting that "peradventure their own stubborn wills did not let them sleep". In reply to the charge that the accused were walked about until their feet were blistered in order to keep them awake he claims that the suspects had to be kept standing because when they lay down their imps appeared and frightened those watching. With reference to swimming, he claims that the suspects wished to be so tested in order to demonstrate their innocence. In seeking justification for his actions Hopkins is content to quote a list of "imps" seen by ten witnesses (he does not say where), including one that looked "like" a white kitten, another "like" a black rabbit, and a third "like" a polecat; the others were more bizarre, one being like a legless spaniel, another like a "long-legged greyhound with a head like an ox".

The most interesting feature of the Hopkins affair is the readiness with which it attracted criticism and the alacrity with which Hopkins' own name was blackened. The mass trial took place in the early years of the Civil War, when the political situation could hardly have been more uneasy, and the brief crusade might be seen as a reflection of the anxious zeal of the Puritans, who were on the threshold of political dominance. As in the celebrated trial of the Lancashire witches in 1612, many of the accused were actually executed, but there was a swift aftermath of bitter recrimination, which cast severe doubt on the justice of the action taken. There may seem to be a certain rough justice in the retaliatory vilification of Hopkins by Gaule and others, but there is also an undoubted irony in the fact that its main effect was to make the man so famous that his name is still remembered and reviled today; had no one taken the trouble to slander him, he would probably have been utterly forgotten.

The outcry against English witch-trials was largely successful. The notorious Lancashire witches who were tried and hanged in 1612 were singularly unfortunate; a second mass trial in Lancashire, in 1634, was abruptly aborted when news reached London and Charles I promptly signed a reprieve for all concerned; parliament wanted no repetition of the earlier scandal. All in all, skepticism of the kind embraced by King James seems to have become widespread in England in the early seventeenth century. Many individual witches were hanged, mostly in rural areas, but panics were very rarely able to escalate according to the continental pattern.

Memoirs of Witch-Hunting Men

The suspicions of skeptics motivated a considerable number of witch-hunters to publish memoirs in justification of their careers, and these works are a major source of information about particular trials and the attitudes of the inquisitors. They tend to be stereotyped, in that the basic features of the witch-image are set out again and again, and painstakingly established by reference to the same standard authorities, each point being further supplemented by instances drawn from personal experience. Nicholas Rémy's *Demonolatria* [Demon-Worship] (1595) is a notable type-specimen.

Rémy was a Privy Councilor in Lorraine, where he boasted of having destroyed nine hundred witches in fifteen years. He found time to write his book when he was driven to take refuge in the country from an epidemic of the plague. His ostensible purpose in writing it, spelled out in the dedication to Prince Charles of Lorraine, was to combat "atheism" by revealing the hideous menace of diabolism. In order to confound skeptics he brings forth the classic argument that there cannot be smoke without fire. Rémy's conviction of the prevalence of skepticism is interesting, especially as he operated in an area where belief was as deep-rooted as anywhere. It is also worth noting that the skeptics he takes most seriously are not those who, like Reginald Scot, "have set their course by the light of reason"—who are deemed unworthy of consideration—but the followers of Weyer, who accept the fact that witches are guilty of heresy but argue that this is not their fault.

The most idiosyncratic feature of Rémy's accounts of the activities of witches is his continual insistence that witches can take no possible pleasure from any of them. Copulation with the Devil is said to be "cold, joyless, vain and barren", and even their dancing is unusually fatiguing and "little short of madness". He observes that "just as their banquets are attended by hunger and bulimy, their copulations by pain and disgust, their largesse by poverty and want and all their benefits by loss and damage to the recipient of them; so also those dancings and caperings, which are ordinarily a pleasure, never fail to cause weariness and fatigue and the greatest distress." In this insistence Rémy seems to be elaborating Bodin's opinion that witches are already so miserable that nothing the inquisitors might do to them can make things worse.

THE DEVIL'S PARTY, BY BRIAN STABLEFORD

A noticeable unease attends Rémy's consideration of the matter of storm-raising, which he clearly finds incredible, although he will not deny its possibility. Similar doubts seem to attend his accounts of many of the other wonders supposedly worked by witches, and he leans much more to the use of imagination as an explanation for the fantastic aspects of the mythology of the Sabbat than do his predecessors. Such doubt is evident when he first insists that freak births are natural and not to be regarded as the progeny of demons, and then states that of course copulation with demons *might* cause such deformations indirectly, because the impression made upon the imagination of a mother by the sight of a demon might be transmitted to the fetus so as to transform it by means of a natural process.

Rémy's evident intellectual discomfort regarding some of the aspects of witch-mythology never shook his basic faith, but it testifies to an occasional willingness to try to work things out for himself, resolving anomalies by the power of his own reason. He regards himself as an expert—and hence an authority in his own right—by virtue of his long experience, and he tends to quote from that experience with great pride and delight. This adds considerably to the appeal of his work as a collection of horror stories, and the continuing popularity of the work (it was frequently reprinted in the seventeenth century) owed much more to its power as sensational journalism than to its informative value or its utility as a handbook for inquisitors. Most of the works that followed in the wake of the *Demonolatria* showed a continuing tendency to become mere anthologies of horror stories.

Henri Boguet's *Discours des sorciers* [Discourse on Witches] (1602) grew out of the trial of a particular group of witches in 1598, most of them incriminated by Françoise Secretain, who had been charged with responsibility for the demonic possession of a child. Boguet, a Burgundian magistrate, goes through the various points of the confession eventually extracted from Secretain and diverges therefrom to a discussion of the various elements of contemporary witch-mythology. The book is short and relatively straightforward; Boguet is far more readable than Bodin and much better organized than Rémy. The book's popularity cannot have been due to its competence as a work of scholarship or its rhetorical force, but it does conclude with a guide for magistrates, laid out as a series of brief Articles, which comprised the simplest set of instructions for witch-hunters that was then available.

The *Discours* is not as sensational as Rémy's book, although it is not short of intimate detail, but it testifies to the same intellectual discomforts. For instance, Boguet "confirms" the myth that witches are unable to shed tears by initially stating that none of the witches he examined were ever able to shed tears in my presence, but immediately concedes that he had actually seen them *appear* to weep, hastily insisting that if the tears were not actually fake they must have been conjured up with the greatest difficulty. Boguet also "demonstrates" that Satan can give witches foreknowledge of what will happen to them by observing that several convicted witches were able to predict that they would die painfully in the flames, while Françoise Secretain was heard to say several times that she would *not* be burned before she committed suicide in her cell. As with Rémy, Boguet obviously finds difficulty in believing in some aspects of witch-lore, but stoutly refuses to give way to doubt.

One of the most interesting books belonging to the *genre* of Rémy's *Demonolatria* and Boguet's *Discours* is Francesco Maria Guazzo's *Compendium Maleficarum* [Compendium of Evil Magic] (1608). Guazzo was a friar, who was obviously very interested in witch-trials but who does not seem to have worked as an inquisitor. In compiling his *Compendium* he functions only as an anthologist, never referring to any personal involvement with the prosecution of witchcraft. The book takes a series of issues one by one, in each case presenting an introductory argument deriving from authoritative sources, followed by a series of examples taken from the already-massive stock of anecdotes.

The *Compendium*'s arguments from authority contain nothing new and are usually rather cursory; it is obvious that the real purpose of the book is its assembly of anecdotes, many of which are presented more melodramatically than in their previous versions. It is much more a literary work than a justification of persecution or a text to confound skeptics, and it is significant that the text begins with an essay on the power of the imagination. Guazzo is always ready to fall back on the logic of illusion when he finds some particular marvel hard to believe. "Any man." he observes, "who maintained that all the effects of magic were true, or who believed that they were all illusions, would be rather a radish than a man. Most often the Devil, being the father of lies, deceives us and blinds our eyes or mocks our other senses with vain illusory images."

Guazzo goes on to argue that, whenever the effects achieved by demonic magic are authentic, then they are accomplished through "natural" means. He is very conscious not only of the difference between the natural and the supernatural, but also of the difference between the natural and the artificial. Artificial magic, he contends, is wrought by human trickery, and is either "mathematical" or "presti-digital". He regards demons as being little more than extremely accomplished conjurors. This is a very different assessment of demonic power from that found in Bodin, and is suspiciously similar to the central arguments of Weyer and Scot. In Italy (Guazzo was from Milan), as in Spain, there was not a great deal of witch-persecution, and this may well have been partly due to the prevalence of this logic of illusion and trickery. As with James I of England, this kind of thinking permitted skepticism to intrude into the consideration of individual cases without posing a significant threat the underlying theoretical belief. Guazzo is not significantly different in his interests and concerns from Rémy and Boguet; he is simply much more confident of the common sense of his doubts—and rather than put them behind him, he exploits the logic of illusion to indulge them.

In contemplating the psychology of Rémy, Boguet or Guazzo, the modern reader is likely to find much that is disturbing: a blood-curdling insensitivity to the suffering of the supposed witches, and an unhealthy interest in the substance of the vilifying fantasies used against them. In all likelihood, though, these men were not sadists, nor were they in any sense "mentally ill". It is only the most extreme documents in this *genre* that offer significant cause to doubt the sanity of their authors. There is, however, one such book that had a very considerable influence: *Le Tableau de l'inconstance des mauvais anges et démons* [A Depiction of the Inconstancy of Fallen Angels and Demons] by Pierre de Lancre, first published in 1610 and further augmented in 1613.

In 1607 de Lancre had published a very long book called *Tableau de l'inconstance et instabilité des choses* [A Depiction of the Inconstancy and Instability of Things], which was an extensive meditation upon the impermanence of worldly things and the vanity of worldly desires, which drew the conclusion that people ought to concentrate their efforts on the cultivation of the spirit. His crusade against the witches of Labourd in 1609 and his book on witchcraft must be seen in the context of this more general philosophy. Witchcraft, to de Lancre, was the evidence *par excellence* of the vileness of lusting after worldly advantage. It was the ultimate evil, and he considered that the world was completely in its grip. De Lancre saw witchcraft everywhere, and was utterly convinced that the entire population of the country in which he conducted his persecutions was given over to Satan-worship. He had such confidence in his own powers of witch-finding that he believed he could detect witches simply by looking them in the eye. In 1622 he published a polemic against those who were lax in prosecuting witchcraft and in 1627 he published a further treatise on countermeasures effective against witches, including an alphabetically-arranged guide to witch-finding.

De Lancre's *Tableau* is framed as urgent propaganda attempting to make people aware of a danger that surrounded them, but which they stubbornly refused to see. It is the most personal of all the witch-hunting manuals, with very copious illustrations drawn from experience, although it quotes the customary battery of authorities to establish the basic scholarly credentials of the ideas expressed therein. De Lancre's methods of judgment seem to have been extreme even for a witch-hunter; he assumed that all suspects were guilty, and used torture to extract confessions of an unusually elaborate and detailed nature. His star witnesses and denouncers were eventually persuaded to be carried away to Sabbats almost every night, in order that they might feed his hunger for information about what went on there. These witnesses, who were almost all between ten and nineteen years of age, found it greatly to their advantage to feed de Lancre's appetite for the lurid; they functioned almost in the manner of Scheherazade, delaying their own destruction by appealing to his curiosity, stringing out an endless chain of denunciations and ever-more-horrific tales of obscene revelry.

De Lancre appears to have been more adventurous in the manufacture of evidence than any other witchfinder in history, and his assiduity presented a considerable challenge to the imagination of his informants, some of whom rose to the occasion with great enthusiasm. The number of those seen at a typical Sabbat climbed from a mere handful to thousands during the course of his investigation, and the obscene activities in which they indulged in grew much more various as time went by. The accounts of the Sabbat extracted by de Lancre far surpassed in their detail anything previously written down, despite the fact that very many of those accused and burned were Basques, and could only communicate with him via an interpreter. Later editions of the *Tableau* featured a highly-elaborate and oft-reprinted frontispiece designed by the Polish engraver Jan Ziarnko, which offers a pictorial summary of these accounts.

De Lancre's obsession with "inconstancy" helps him to explain the predominance of female witches over male, and his book also contains an elaborate explanation for the inconstant temperament of the Basques in terms of social, geographical and climatic factors. Inconstancy is not a difficult thing to find when one sets one's mind to it, and, when all inconstancy becomes proof of demonic activity and susceptibility to witchcraft, it is not surprising that de Lancre could identify witches just by looking at them. He knew, for instance, that most of the local priests had to be witches—and when he turned for confirmation to his child witnesses they promptly reported having seen them all at the Sabbats.

At one point de Lancre refers to the "marvelous pleasure" of one of his witnesses in telling what she has seen at the Sabbat. It might, perhaps, be unjust to accuse him of taking a similar pleasure in the tales of abomination that he sought so eagerly, but the excitement of his recounting of them is unmistakable. De Lancre's fascination with the minutiae of Satanic rites is extensively reflected in the spurious mythology of "black masses", which was to be elaborately developed in literary fantasies and lifestyle fantasies. The modern interest in such things is a prurient one, and the mythology of the black mass is essentially a species of horror-pornography. It is hard to set aside the suspicion that de Lancre's own interest was essentially prurient, and that many of his readers must have found a similar excitement in reading what he wrote. It is significant that de Lancre argues very fervently against the opinion that the Sabbat, or any other element of witch-mythology, might be illusory. For him, it all had to be real.

The panic that de Lancre fed and exploited spread across the border into the Spanish Pyrenees, and resulted in several witch-trials there, including one in Zugarramundi in 1610, as a result of which seven witches were burned in an auto-da-fé, five others were burned in effigy (having already died), and eighteen were more reconciled to the Church after confessing, repenting and asking for mercy. One of the three inquisitors who supervised the trial, however, was not content with the evidence. After reporting back to the Suprema of the Spanish Inquisition, which had stifled witch-panics during the first phase of the hunt, this inquisitor—Alonso de Salazar y Frías—was commissioned to make further investigations of accusations of witchcraft.

Salazar examined over a thousand children who, like Pierre de Lancre's informants, told stories of particular maleficia or recounted tales of the Sabbat. Unlike de Lancre, he asked for evidence to back up the claims, and found none. He compared accounts and found them very various as to events. Few referred to actual places, and when he investigated those places that were named he found no traces of any gatherings of any kind. He was able to disprove many of the claims simply enough, pointing out that several young girls who claimed to have had intercourse with the Devil were still virgins, and demonstrating that several witnesses were asleep when they claimed to have flown to the Sabbat. His conclusion, having weighed up everything "with the proper objectivity and rectitude" was that none of the events referred to by his informants had actually occurred.

Salazar was forced to defend this opinion against criticism from other inquisitors, but the Suprema accepted the report and embodied its conclusions in a memorandum of 1614, which kept Spain almost entirely free from the witch-craze thereafter. The members of the Suprema were evidently prepared to accept Salazar's arguments, which were based entirely on experience and experiment—but they would not license publication of the report. Despite its effect on the policy of the Spanish Suprema, it was not allowed to become a weapon in the war between skepticism and belief. The reason for this was, of course, that the orthodoxy of the view Salazar expressed, and the way he supported his conclusion, were highly dubious. The Suprema did not want to endorse them, or even to condone them, because its members could not and would not renounce the authoritatively-supported beliefs that were challenged by the report. What they *were* prepared to do was accept that the particular cases that Salazar had investigated were not cases of witchcraft, and that, in all likelihood, any other particular accusations of witchcraft would be unfounded. The attitude of the Spanish Inquisition to witchcraft was, therefore. essentially similar to that of James I of England, invoking a double standard of belief that allowed its members to accept the theory of witchcraft but to reject its application to events in the real world.

The Spread of Skepticism

Another man who came to the same conclusions as Salazar, and who seems to have been desperately torn by an ensuing conflict of conscience and emotion, was a German Jesuit named Friedrich von Spee, who officiated as a confessor in Wurzburg during a witch-hunt in the 1620s. He found that the confessions offered openly by the accused after torture and the confessions they made to him in the privacy of the confessional often differed completely. Many people confessed to their inquisitors to save themselves further torture, but they continued to make their true voices heard in the privacy of the confessional, knowing that the communications were privileged. Von Spee comforted the accused, and came to believe that every last one was innocent, but he dared not speak out, because to do so would have exposed him to instant accusation and almost certain conviction. In 1631, however, he wrote a tract entitled *Cautio Criminalis*, in which he made his views public.

Cautio Criminalis does not deny the reality of witches, but is couched as a desperate appeal for legal procedures more in accordance with the principles of justice. Von Spee is bitter in his condemnation of those who sanctioned witch-hunts: theologians and prelates allegedly devoted to the enjoyment of speculation, who knew nothing of the squalor of prisons and the reality of torture; judges who found such trials lucrative by virtue of the confiscation of the accused persons' property; and wicked individuals who found accusation of witchcraft a convenient way to pay off their grudges. In von Spee's view, the Wurtzburg witch-hunt was such a grotesque miscarriage of justice that he it could only be explained by the conclusion that it must have been initiated and motivated by the malevolence of real witches, who were among the accusers rather than the accused.

A second attack on the methods of the witchfinders and the iniquities of torture, very similar to von Spee's, was Johann Mayfarth's *Christliche Erinnerung* (1635). Both these works seem to have had some influence in engendering doubt about the practice, if not the theory, of witch-hunting. It was, of course, much safer to doubt the legal system than religious authorities, because such doubts were not in themselves heretical. This kind of skepticism was more easily able to take root than non-belief in witchcraft, and fell on fertile ground in some places because of long-standing conflicts between itinerant friars and local bishops. The experience of von Spee suggests that thousands of other confessors must have heard similar insistences from convicted witches, and said nothing in public at all, but we can only speculate as to the effect it had on opinions regarding the utility of the existing legal system as an instrument of justice. By the end of the seventeenth century, court systems throughout Europe had begun a process of gradual reform, the vestiges of the Inquisitorial system being set aside in favor of more balanced adversarial systems, in which arguments for the prosecution were matched against arguments for the defense. The replacement was gradual, but the manifest injustice of witch-trials must have helped to impress a great many people with a sense of its necessity.

The voices of men like Salazar y Frías and von Spee were mostly stifled, constrained by the preconceptions of dogma, but there was also a more general intellectual movement towards broad-ranging skepticism that gained support throughout the 1600s. By the middle of the seventeenth century, a growing population of freethinkers deliberately engaged in casting off the shackles of arguments from authority, in favor of a new philosophy of knowledge based in the evidence of the senses. These were the founders of modern scientific thought; their pioneering ranks included Galileo, Francis Bacon, Christian Huygens, René Descartes, Thomas Hobbes, and Nicolas Malebranche.

All of these men struck pious poses, but, beneath the diplomatic masks their philosophies wore, they advanced the cause of subversive doubt, carefully undermining the edifice of accumulated authority, which was made to seem more ramshackle by every new discovery in empirical enquiry. Unlike Scot fifty years before, they were sufficiently influential to command a hearing, and their impact on the climate of European thought was very considerable. Their works helped to convince large numbers of their contemporaries that there was far more to the quest for knowledge than a mere "renaissance" and augmentation of the ideas of long-dead sages, and that much of what the ancients believed had simply to be rejected. They already had one crucial victory to their credit, in the firm establishment of the heliocentric theory of the solar system—in frank defiance of both Plato and Aristotle—by Galileo and John Kepler, whose telescopes enabled them to confirm and further elaborate sixteenth-century astronomical observations carried out by Tycho Brahe, John Dee, and Thomas Digges.

Francis Bacon, who popularized the notion that human wisdom was confounded by a whole series of "idols" of false belief, accepted the reality of witchcraft, but was set solidly in that English tradition of thought which doubted individual cases and individual confessions. "And therefore," he wrote, "as divers wise judges have prescribed and cautioned, men may not too rashly believe the confessions of witches, nor yet the evidence against them. For the witches themselves are imaginative and believe oft-times they do that which they do not: and people are credulous in that point and ready to impute accidents and natural operations to witchcraft. It is worth the observing, that both in ancient and late times, as in the Thessalian witches and the meetings of witches that have been recorded by so many late confessions, the great works which they tell, of carrying in the air, transforming themselves into other bodies, etc., are still reported to be wrought, not by incantations or ceremonies, but by ointments and anointing themselves all over. This may justly move a man to think that these fables are the effects of imagination: for it is certain that ointments do all, if they be laid on anything thick, by stopping of the pores shut in the vapors and send them to the head extremely."

This particular theory—that the contents of the confessions of witches were heavily influenced by hallucinogenic experiences brought on by drugs—was often reiterated, and became increasingly fashionable as the modern psychotropic pharmacopeia increased; twentieth century images of Satanist rites almost invariably refer to the use of psychotropic drugs. There is some evidence to support Bacon's theory, in that herbs used in the seventeenth century for their supposed curative powers or for their efficacy as poisons included deadly nightshade, whose belladonna alkaloids can indeed have hallucinogenic effects. As to whether sensations generated by hallucinogens contributed anything to the mythology of the Sabbat we can only speculate, although many officially-sanctioned magicians in preliterate cultures do make calculated use of psychotropic drugs, but the presence of the argument in Bacon's speculations is important as an example of a new way of looking at the whole issue of witchcraft, and of a determination to search for alternative, "natural" explanations of evidence that could not yet be forthrightly denied.

The same emphasis on the Sabbat-experience as an artificial hallucination is found in Malebranche, who similarly does not doubt that witches *could* exist, or that demons do sometimes influence human affairs, but similarly goes in search of other possible causes for reported instances of witchcraft. Malebranche was one of the first authors to take a keen interest in the psychology of belief in Satan and his human minions, and the psychology of the story-telling that promulgated such beliefs. He commented on the psychological plausibility of the idea of invisible malignant powers determined to do us harm, the strange pleasure derivable from recounting stories about witches, both in frightening others and in frightening oneself, and the psychological stubbornness of superstition. In making those points, he also called attention to the anger and resentment routinely felt by believers against people who wanted to "demystify" their convictions, comparing them to hypochondriacs who are desperate to follow medical advice but do not actually want to be cured.

Malebranche was a monk, who had devoted himself to the study of the Bible and the Church Fathers before discovering the philosophy of Descartes, with its insistence on the power of the intellect and the necessity of doubting everything that could not be asserted with absolute confidence. Descartes himself said little about witchcraft (though he believed that it was all an illusion) but when Malebranche applied his perspectives ruthlessly to the problem he provided a new voice within the Church. The book in which he addressed the topic, *Recherche de la vérité* [Seeking the Truth] appeared in 1674, and French witch-hunting came to a final halt shortly thereafter.

Such changes in philosophical outlook among the intelligentsia of Europe made the continuation of the witch-hunt impossible. The implementation of the new logic was hardly immediate, because accusers and witch-hunters still went very much their own way, according to their own beliefs, but central authorities became increasingly determined to take control of such cases, partly as a way of emphasizing their hegemony; this was the period in which the processes of consolidation began that created modern nation-states.

The new emphasis on the evidence of experience at the expense of arguments from authority did not, however, cut the ground from under the feet of the witch-hunters; they continued to argue that the evidence of their own experience was entirely adequate to justify their belief and their conduct. An example of the new way of thinking applied in support of witch-mythology and witch-hunting can found in the most important British work promoting witch-beliefs to appear after King James's *Daemonologie*, Joseph Glanvill's *Saducismus Triumphatus* [Sadducism Defeated] (1681).

Saducismus Triumphatus was published a year after Glanvill's death and was augmented several times in subsequent editions. It is a collection of anecdotal material similar to Guazzo's, all secondhand save for one story told to Glanvill by an epileptic. Its subtitle is "Full and Plain Evidence Concerning Witches and Apparitions", and that is its ambition; its method is strikingly different from books with the same aim published a hundred years earlier. It relies hardly at all on arguments from authority but throws the entire weight of its argument on its catalogue of "experiences". The first part of the text is claimed to contain "philosophical considerations" which defend the possibility of witchcraft and ghostly apparitions, but it is immediately clear that these are not the same kinds of philosophical considerations that commended themselves to Bodin. We find Glanvill arguing defensively against Sadducism, not by trumpeting Biblical authority as final, but by means of the conspicuously weak argument that demons and other "apparitions" might comprise a class of animate beings elusive to our senses, much as the creatures recently revealed by microscopes had previously passed unobserved.

Glanvill is clearly conscious of fighting on a new battleground, and he attempts to deploy new argumentative weapons to the advantage of his credulity—but on this kind of battleground, disputing with this kind of ordnance, there could be no possible justification for the *methods* of witch-hunters. Whether or not Glanvill's arguments could persuade his readers that there might, after all, be such things as witches, they could do nothing to support the instrumentality of the Inquisition. Once witchfinders were called upon to produce proof of the guilt of individual witches, according to the criteria of truth demanded by empiricists, they were confounded—and the demand for this kind of proof slowly spread. It had to be imposed from above and from without in rural areas where belief in witchcraft was still widespread and unchallenged, but it was nevertheless firmly imposed.

The Last Large-Scale Witch-Trials

Most of the anecdotal "evidence" quoted by Glanvill in *Saducismus Triumphatus* is trivial, consisting of mere repetition of familiar stories. Appended to the book, however, is a moderately detailed account of one of the most famous of the late seventeenth-century witch-panics: the Swedish "Blokula scare" of 1669-70. This case is also described in detail in a skeptical work by the Dutchman Balthasar Bekker, *De Betoverde Weereld* [The World Bewitched], published in 1691.

The Blokula affair began in the Swedish village of Mora in 1669, when a fifteen-year-old boy reported that a girl of eighteen had stolen children for the Devil. When the girl denied it, the boy went on to accuse others, all of whom denied it save for one seventy-year-old woman. After pleas from the villagers, the king of Sweden reluctantly set up a commission to look into the affair, with the declared purpose of redeeming the supposed witches by prayer. The news spread rapidly, and when the commissioners began to conduct their prayer-services three thousand people traveled to hear the sermons.

Many other children now began to offer accounts of having been seduced by witches and taken to Sabbats against their will, and some seventy people were accused. Twenty-three of them eventually confessed—freely, according to the documents of the case. All seventy were eventually burned, and with them fifteen of the child-accusers, who were deemed equally culpable. Thirty-six other children adjudged less culpable were made to run the gauntlet and to submit to caning on their backs once a week for a year, but those under nine years old were only caned once every three weeks.

The speed with which this panic was communicated once the crowds gathered at the prayer-meetings was remarkable, but not so remarkable as the nightmarish descriptions of the Sabbats offered by the children, who claimed that these had been held at a house called the Blokula (no such location was ever identified.) The sheer bizarrerie and apparent spontaneity of these accounts seem to have been the major factors involved in convincing the inquirers that something monstrous must be happening; the similarities between this affair and late-twentieth-century scares related to Satanic ritual child molestation are very striking. A "composite confession" was put together by the commissioners and was offered to all the children to sign, which contained such details as accounts of riding through the air to the Sabbat on a spit stuck into the anus of a goat; signing Satan's book in blood; giving birth to sons and daughters after copulation with Satan—which, when coupled in their turn, gave birth to toads and snakes—and familiar spirits called "carriers", which foraged for food to be brought to the Blokula. The report of these marvels concluded with the note:

"The Lords Commissioners were indeed very earnest, and took great pains to persuade [the children] to show some of their tricks, but to no purpose; for they did all unanimously confess, that since they had confessed all, they found that all their witchcraft was gone, and that the Devil at this time appeared to them very terrible, with claws on his hands and feet, and with horns on his head, and a long tail behind, and showed to them a pit burning, with a hand put out; but the Devil did throw the person down again with an iron-fork; and suggested to the witches, that if they continued in their confession, he would deal with them in the same manner."

The friend of Glanvill who appended an account of this scare to *Saducismus Triumphatus*, Henry More, offers it as solid proof of the abilities of spirits, but Bekker interprets it very differently. Unlike Glanvill's friend, Bekker takes the story to its conclusion, observing that the panic spread from Mora into Finland and other districts of Sweden, but was stopped as it approached Stockholm by the voice of a doctor, Urban Hjarne, who preached against the panic and claimed that the confessions were all due to morbid imagination, simple malice and the impulse to attract attention. Until this dissenting voice was heard the panic had spread unchecked, but as soon as it was challenged and opposed it seems to have evaporated as quickly as it emerged.

THE DEVIL'S PARTY, BY BRIAN STABLEFORD

Bekker agrees with Hjarne that the whole affair was a clear case of collective delusion, and constructs his own more general skeptical case to the effect that, although spirits exist, they cannot interfere with human affairs. He claims that witch-mythology infected Christianity from paganism, being adopted by the Catholic Church for the purposes of terrorism and profit. Like Scot before him, Bekker attacks the elevation of Satan to the status of anti-God, and professes himself a true monotheist. His opinions were, however, held to be outrageous by his fellow Calvinists, and he was dismissed from his ministry.

The Blokula affair was the last major panic in Europe, and the pattern that it followed, of rapid expansion followed by equally rapid dissolution, was also the pattern followed by the last and most famous scare of all, whose progress was much better chronicled: the case of the witches of Salem, Massachusetts.

The social situation in New England in the years immediately prior to the Salem witch-scare was very uneasy. The previous twenty years had seen several attempts by English kings to interfere with the religious solidarity of the Puritan communities by commanding the establishment of an Anglican Church. The Charter that established the rights and principles of the colonial government was revoked by James II in 1686, but when William III of Orange came to the throne, a man named Increase Mather went to England to ask for its reinstatement. Mather returned in 1692 with a replacement charter, but it embodied various religious reforms calculated to disturb the Puritans—significantly, the widening of the electorate to include property-owners of other Protestant denominations.

The new charter effectively removed the Puritans' erstwhile monopoly on political power. There was also a more subtle crisis of religious feeling; the Puritan ethic itself seemed to be under threat. It was not that the Puritans of the colony had not received just reward for their diligence and asceticism, but that everyone else seemed to be prospering too, suggesting that success was dependent upon human endeavor rather than the favor of God. These political and religious factors, while in no way explaining the particular accusations of witchcraft that were made, are important to an understanding of the actions and opinions of one of the leading figures in promoting the scare: Increase Mather's son, Cotton Mather.

The genesis of the Salem scare, as with so many European scares, was a series of accusations made by a group of children. The children had been subject to strange convulsions and screaming fits, which were eventually diagnosed by the town physician as bewitchment. Thus encouraged, they identified their tormentors. One was Tituba, a colored servant in the house of the minister Samuel Parris, who had apparently taken some delight in telling the children lurid tales of the supernatural that she had learned in Barbados. The second was Sarah Good, an old beggar-woman with a nasty disposition. The third was Sarah Osbourne, a woman of high social standing whose reputation had been tainted by living in sin with a man for some months before marrying him, and who did not attend Church. In a Puritan community, these three were ready-made targets for abuse.

The three women were examined publicly, and the examinations were made extremely melodramatic by the antics of the children, who rolled on the ground in apparent agony, screaming that they were being tormented by the witches' spirits, which they could clearly see, although they were invisible to everyone else. These performances received unexpected support when Tituba enthusiastically confessed the charges laid against her, declaring that she and the other two accused were by no means the only witches in Salem. The combination of melodrama and mystery promoted the affair into a panic. Appeals were made to the children to identify the other witches. One of them, Mary Warren, attempted to back out when accusations began to name ordinary and respected members of the community, but the others blamed her reluctance on capitulation with the Devil, and she was quickly persuaded to return to the conspiracy. Weeks passed while the children held the center of the stage, producing new names at regular intervals. The county jail was soon full, and a long list of trials scheduled. The panic spread from Salem to Andover, and then beyond.

The policy adopted by the magistrates was markedly different from that employed in Europe; the only witches who were hanged were those who remained adamant and refused to confess. Those who did confess were allowed to live, although they were imprisoned and their property was confiscated. Faced with this dilemma, several of the accused thought it wiser to confess. The one man who "escaped" the dilemma was Giles Corey, who refused to plead at all, knowing that if he pleaded not guilty he would be hanged, and that if he pleaded guilty his property would be forfeit. He was placed under a wooden board on which heavy stones were piled in the attempt to force him to plead; he persisted in his refusal and was crushed to death.

As the panic spread, the accusations became indiscriminate. The wife of the governor of the colony was named, and so was Samuel

THE DEVIL'S PARTY, BY BRIAN STABLEFORD

Willard, the president of Harvard College and pastor of the First Church of Boston. This proved too much, and magistrates began contradicting their informants. Once such contradictions began, the value of the "spectral evidence" by which the girls identified the spirits of their tormentors was considerably undermined. Its validity had always been a matter of dispute, and in generating its wildest accusations it betrayed its incompetence. Governor Phips instituted a new court to try those cases actually scheduled and ordered the rest to be dismissed. The magistrates in the special court did admit spectral evidence, although with some reluctance, but still found forty-nine out of the fifty-two accused innocent; the governor reprieved the other three. Nineteen people, however, had already been hanged and two had died in prison.

Cotton Mather's involvement with the affair began when Governor Phips and his council requested the advice of the Boston clergy with respect to the trials already conducted. Mather had earlier written a book entitled *Memorable Providences Relating to Witchcraft and Possessions* (1689) to demonstrate the power of the Devil and the reality of witchcraft, and he was thus a recognized "expert". He immediately lent his support to the prosecution in Salem, and was convinced of the truth of the accusations in spite of his doubts about the use of spectral evidence. Phips appointed him to prepare an official report on the whole affair once it was over, and this he did, compiling a book entitled *Wonders of the Invisible World* (1693). It seems to have been written rather hurriedly, and the elaborate extension of the prefatory material suggests that there was some delay in his actually getting hold of the court records, but it sold very well. The work is redolent with melodrama, and this is especially evident in the essay "Enchantments Encountered", which forms part of the prefatory material:

"The New Englanders are a people of God settled in those, which were once the Devil's territories; and it may easily be supposed that the Devil was exceedingly disturbed when he perceived such a people here accomplishing the promise of old made unto our Blessed Jesus. *That He should have the utmost parts of the earth for his possession....* I believe, that never were more Satanical devices used for the unsettling of any people under the sun, than what have been employed for the extirpation of the vine which God has here planted, casting out the heathen, and preparing a room before it, and causing it to take deep root...the Devil is now making one more attempt upon us; an attempt more difficult, more surprising, more snarled with unintelligible circumstances than any we have hitherto encountered; an attempt so critical, that if we get well through, we shall soon enjoy halcyon days with all the vultures of hell trodden under our feet. He has wanted his incarnate legions to persecute us, as the people in other hemispheres have been persecuted...a malefactor, accused of witchcraft as well as murder, and executed in this place more than forty years ago, did then give notice of an horrible *plot* against the country by *witchcraft*, and a foundation of *witchcraft* then laid, which if it were not seasonably discovered, would probably blow up, and pull down all the churches in the country. And we have now with horror seen the discovery of such a witchcraft! An army of Devils is horribly broke in upon the place which is the center, and after a sort, the first-born of our English settlements: and the houses of the good people there are filled with the doleful shrieks of their children and servants, tormented by invisible hands, with tortures altogether preternatural."

In Cotton Mather's view, the entire Salem affair was a kind of test to which the New England colony and its threatened Puritan ethic were subjected. This notion arises out of the sense of threat felt by the Puritan ministry, and Mather seems to have seen the trials more as a means to fight against that threat than as an issue in their own right. He seems to have had no difficulty in reconciling his conscience to the fact that people were actually hanged in order that this demonstration should be made, on the basis of evidence of no real value; he simply convinced himself that the accused really were guilty.

The Salem panic was not only stifled but turned back upon itself. Many of those involved subsequently admitted publicly that they had made a dreadful mistake, having been carried away by panic—demonstrating by this admission that there could be smoke without fire after all. On the 15th of January 1697 there was a day of fasting in the colony to show repentance for the injustice of the trials. A confession of error was signed in 1696 by the jurors who had brought in the convictions in Salem, which included the following paragraph:

"We do therefore hereby signify to all in general, and to the surviving sufferers in especial, our deep sense of, and sorrow for our errors, in acting on such evidence to the condemnation of any person. And we do hereby declare that we justly fear that we were sadly deluded and mistaken, for which we are much disquieted and distressed in our minds; and do humbly beg forgiveness, first of God for Christ's sake for this error, and pray that God would not impute the guilt of it to ourselves nor others. And we also pray that we may be considered candidly and aright by the living sufferers as being then under the power of a strong and general delusion, utterly unacquainted with, and not experienced in matters of that nature."

The movement of repentance that provoked the production of this document, casting about for a villain to blame instead of the witches, settled upon Cotton Mather—who, despite his reputation and standing in the community, was then vilified much as Matthew Hopkins had been in England. In *More Wonders of the Invisible World* (1700), Robert Calef mounted a vitriolic attack on Mather, presenting some data that had been left out in Mather's hasty attempt to justify the trials. He insinuated that Cotton Mather and his father had obtained a perverted sexual satisfaction from interrogating hysterical young girls, printing (without permission) Mather's own account of his attempt to "save" a girl supposedly possessed by the Devil. An outraged Mather denied the innuendo, but in so doing only drew attention to it, while Calef smugly denied that he had intended to imply any such thing.

Whether Mather deserved such treatment is a matter of opinion, but there is no need to doubt his essential sincerity. He was a representative of a world-view that was in decline, and a way of thinking that was not only opposed but derided by a new way, which seemed to him unholy and dangerous. He was not himself a zealous witchfinder, but he was the kind of man who permitted witch-finding to flourish and praised its fruits. He did so because he was the victim of a strong sense of threat, and there is a sense in which there really was an urgent threat to his ideology and way of life, although it did not come from witches. Mather's whole way of understanding the world was being subverted by the corrosive skepticism of modern philosophy; he had no way available to him to think of that subversion save as the activity of the Devil, and no way to think of its human agents save as a Devil-led conspiracy. He was wrong, but he was not—as Calef implied—sadistic or mad.

Anyone can be wrong, and it is, unfortunately, much easier to fall into the kind of error that was made by the witch-hunters and their supporters than most of us would like to think. That is why some people in today's world are still prone to such errors, especially if they are religious believers inclined towards Puritanism. People who hold views of that kind can hardly help but think that everything they hold dear is nowadays under threat, and might perhaps be forgiven for the desperation that sometimes drives them to extraordinary lengths in the search for explanations.

V.
LITERARY FANTASIES

Early Literary Treatments of Witchcraft and Black Magic

We have a moderately clear idea today of the difference between "fiction" and "non-fiction", but the line separating them remains rather blurred. A rich folklore of anecdotes, often represented as events that happened to "a friend of a friend" continues to thrive. Such stories rely for their effect on an insistence that they are "true" and they often reach print eventually, sometimes in newspaper reportage. These anecdotes are often rich in horrific material, and sometimes explicitly supernatural, especially ghost stories; the circulation of such tales helps to sustain popular belief in the supernatural (or, in modern parlance, the "paranormal").

The importance of tales of this kind in sustaining witch-beliefs during the period of the great witch-hunt was probably considerable, and such tales did not die away when witch-hunting ended. Indeed, many episodes of the witch-hunt were added to the standard repertoire of startling tales handed down with considerable relish from generation to generation. Nor is this process new; many of the textual "authorities" of Greek and Roman origin cited by the better-educated authors of treatises on witchcraft, from Pico della Mirandola onwards, are works of fiction, and others are the kind of reportage in which the boundary between fact and fantasy is calculatedly blurred.

Whenever a newly-literate culture sets out to commit its history to paper for the first time it can only begin by recording the "mythic past" of oral culture, which is bound to consist of an intricately interwoven net of fact and fantasy. The mythic past, which is a product of memory and legend, is subject to constant reworking, in which actual events are blended into a background of quasi-religious beliefs and items of folklore. In oral tradition, everything is mixed up together, and the attempt to recover accounts of what "really happened" during the careers of those kings and heroes of legend whose exploits are still recalled is doomed to failure.

The early generations of a newly-literate culture frequently write down what oral tradition tells them of their own prehistory, but their representation of it as "history" usually includes a tacit recognition that there is much in it that is fanciful and much that is metaphorical; future generations, however, are inevitably confronted with the written word, shorn of its original context of understanding, and the exact significance of written records becomes more difficult to determine as time passes. The Jewish compilers of the Old Testament attempted to reserve writing for the preservation of a set of sacred texts, which were to be taken entirely seriously, if not entirely literally, but the Greeks were much more promiscuous in their use of the new intellectual tool. Classical writing is much more various in its nature, and it is much more difficult to figure out what different writers might really have believed, or how seriously they took their beliefs.

The religious mythology of Greece and Rome, unlike that of the Jews and Christians was never systematized. It remained diffuse and changeable—changeable sometimes even as a result of conscious whim. The Graeco-Roman attitude to religion was very different from that of the Hebrews, although its owners took religion just as seriously, in their own fashion. Their beliefs were not rigid, and particular aspects of belief could wax and wane while the ideas contained within them remained alive. This is why, in the course of a few centuries of astonishing progress, the Greeks were able to invent philosophy, political analysis and geometry as well as giving new form and new evolutionary scope to epic and lyric poetry, drama, and prose fiction. The Romans, who inherited the gifts of Greek literacy, were unable to replicate, or even to preserve, this capacity for innovation; Christendom only recovered it after an interval of a thousand years, and it took a further five hundred to surpass it.

Greek literature apparently featured magic very extensively, both in official and illicit contexts, as did the Roman literature that succeeded it. It features many characters describable in retrospect as witches, some of whom were, allegedly, persons who had actually existed, while others are frank and unashamed fictional inventions. These images are of some significance to the history of witch-belief because of the influence they had on the Renaissance writers of treatises of witchcraft, but they are also of considerable interest in their own right, as illustrations of the transformations that mythical and folkloristic ideas undergo when they move out of oral tradition and on to the written page.

The Graeco-Roman world was remarkably heterogeneous as to patterns of belief and degrees of commitment to particular beliefs. The Romans, in particular, were almost obsessed with omens and divination; diviners of various kinds were supported by the state. The Sibylline Books, full of enigmatic comments on the future (which could usually be interpreted retrospectively to fit actual events) were preserved in the temple of Jupiter on the Capitol until they were lost in a fire in 83 BC. Such was their reputation that Jewish and Christian writers were later to use forged oracular hexameters as an aid to the conversion of the Roman Empire. The actual use of magic in the Graeco-Roman world was probably widespread, and this applies both to public magic used to secure legitimate social ends and to private magic used for personal ends (some of them presumably illicit). Sorcery was prohibited by law and prosecutions were successfully brought under those laws, but these beliefs were never universal and unquestioned in the sense that the beliefs of a preliterate tribe are universal and unquestioned. There was room in the Graeco-Roman world for many different shades of belief, from total credulity to outright skepticism.

The Greeks were the first people to bring logic to bear on questions of magic, religion and the way of the world. By the same token, they were also the first people to adopt the ideas associated with magic and witchcraft into the fictions of the drama and poetry, producing literary images that have become almost archetypal. It should not need to be emphasized that literary images cannot be taken as straightforward representations of beliefs—they mostly serve metaphorical and allegorical functions—but it must also be remembered that Greek drama still retained some of the functions of the religious rites from which it descended, and that its representations were considered to be in some sense "true". Plato was suspicious of the arts and suggested (perhaps with his tongue somewhat in his cheek) that poets would have to be banished from an ideal Republic, but Aristotle considered them socially valuable and held that the representations of art were universal statements, giving a better account of the nature of things than mere everyday experiences.

The most famous sorceresses in Greek literature are Circe, who turned Odysseus' crew into animals, and Medea, the wife of Jason.

THE DEVIL'S PARTY, BY BRIAN STABLEFORD

The antiquity of the images is considerable: the *Odyssey* dates from the ninth or eighth century BC, while the fifth-century *Medea* of Euripides undoubtedly borrows from earlier sources; both characters crop up frequently in later works. The divinities with which these and similar characters are associated, and from whom their power allegedly derives, are also female; they are the group of Graeco-Roman goddesses associated with the moon, including Hecate and Diana.

These literary images are very different from the image of the witch that the Christian witchfinders eventually consolidated. Both characters are sexually attractive and deploy their power in that connection, and there is a measure of tragedy about their eventual fates. Circe is eventually outwitted and humbled by Odysseus, and falls in love with him only to lose him after a year. Other works inform their readers that she had been disappointed in love on two previous occasions: she turned Picus into a woodpecker for preferring the nymph Canens, and when the youth Glaucus asked her for a love-potion to influence Scylla she tried to seduce him, failed, and took vengeance by giving him a potion that turned Scylla into a monster. Medea is the instrument by which Jason completes the superhuman tasks set for him by Hera, but her infatuation with Jason causes her to arrange the murder of her brother. When Jason eventually finds sanctuary in Corinth, Medea is unwelcome and he divorces her, but she murders his new wife-to-be.

Circe and Medea are by no means straightforward embodiments of evil. Both women are guilty of evil deeds, but they are driven to commit their crimes by passion and disappointment. They are victims rather than monsters, because their crimes are understandable, if not forgivable. These are certainly not the kinds of images that might be used in persecutory vilification; the original authors of these stories appear to have been primarily concerned with the painstaking exploration and hypothetical explanation of the sources of human malice and its tragic consequences.

Greek and Roman literature contain numerous items of witch-lore that would have seemed ominous to Christian witch-hunters. A poem by Theocritus from the third century BC tells the story of Simeta, who resorts to magic in order to win back a lover who has left her; with the aid of elaborate ritual and incantation she calls upon the help of Hecate and Selene. In Lucan's *Pharsalia* the witch Erichtho undertakes illicit divination using various repulsive ingredients taken from corpses. Horace's Canidia—another witch attempting to recover a former lover—joins with others to cast a spell, which involves such ingredients as a wild fig grown from a tomb, toad's blood and the feathers of a screech-owl. Ovid portrays a drunken and spiteful hag-witch named Dipsas, who has considerable knowledge of herbs and potions and great skill in conjuring spirits.

There is a great deal here that crops up again in the mythology of the post-Renaissance witchfinders: not merely the notion that most witches are women, often motivated by lust and jealousy, but notions of the kinds of spells they might work and the materials they might use. These literary fantasies, in fact, feature the first tentative fusion of ideas relating to "everyday witchcraft" and the image of the "nightmare witch". In these various literary works the fusion is clearly made for melodramatic effect, but the melodrama was mixed with comedy, emphasizing that its artificiality was well understood.

In the second century AD, Apuleius, borrowing extensively from an earlier story by the Greek satirist Lucian, produced the work known in translation as *The Golden Ass*, a flamboyant satire featuring the witch Pamphile, who can "call down the sky, hang earth in heaven, freeze fountains, melt mountains, raise the spirits of the dead, send gods to hell, put out the stars, and give light to Tartarus itself". She changes an innkeeper into a frog and a lawyer into a ram. This is a figure of fear made ludicrous by exaggeration, her powers inflated into parodic grotesquerie. The joke was undoubtedly shared by many, though there were some who did not share it; the author's apparent familiarity with powerful sorcery was cited and when he married a wealthy widow and was charged with employing magic to the end of seduction. He made a record of his defense, *Apologia sine Oratio de Magia*, which does not deny the real possibility of magic, but points out various implausibilities in the case made against him, making the telling point that, if he really were a powerful magician, how could his accusers possibly prevail against him?

The Graeco-Roman witch images are more sharply focused than any others belonging to the ancient world. This is because Circe and Medea—and even Canidia and Dipsas—are properly characterized; in being inserted into coherent narratives they become surrogate human individuals, possessed of personal histories and coherent sets of motives. In being so equipped, they inevitably become far more human than products of nightmare—and yet much of their fascination *as items of fiction* is intimately bound up with the elements of nightmare fantasy that they retain and embody.

The myths of Greece and Rome were not the only ones known to the scholars of Christendom, although the preservation of Roman lore in Latin—the language of the Church—allowed it to retain a gloss of respectability that other myths did not have. The native mythologies of the northern nations of Christendom also contained images of magic and its practitioners, which continued to thrive at the level of folklore and eventually became an important source of literary imagery. The radical disjunction of the oral traditions familiar to the itinerant friars of the Inquisition and the ones that they found in some of the areas they visited is easily illustrated by a superficial comparison of the mythology of Greece and Rome with the mythology of the Teutonic peoples.

The gods of Graeco-Roman mythology seem to lead lives of ease and pleasure, continually in search of diversion. Much of their interference with human affairs is conducted in a spirit of play. The gods of the Teutons, by contrast, have a much harder time, living constantly in the shadow of their own apocalyptic doom, the Götterdämmerung. The Graeco-Roman preoccupation with oracles implies a certain confidence in the future that is not evident in the Teutonic scheme, whose pessimistic anticipation is a terrible battle heralded by a bitter and unnatural winter. Teutonic mythology is dominated by magic; the gods and giants use it constantly, and are desperately dependent upon it. This idea of magic, with an illusion of systematization introduced into it by its association with runic writing, is perhaps closer to the idea of "natural law" than any other notion of magic in ancient Europe. Even Odin had to learn his magic from a magician, and such wise men—or, in English parlance, "cunning men"—seem to have been far more important in the ancient culture of the northern pagans than their counterparts in the Mediterranean countries.

From northern mythology—little of which was written down before Snorri Sturlasson compiled the Prose Edda in Iceland in the thirteenth century, but which was still perpetuated as oral tradition in mainland Europe for centuries thereafter—we obtain witch-images rather different from those enshrined in Graeco-Roman thought. Here the witch is always the hagwife or hedge-rider, old and ugly, essentially and inherently evil. She is usually busy mixing potions, according to disgusting recipes, in her cooking-pot or cauldron (magic cauldrons play key roles in Celtic mythology and Norse legend). In the post-Renaissance era, when vernacular languages were much more widely used in writing, the influence of these images on the ideas of witch-finders and writers of fiction became considerable.

THE DEVIL'S PARTY, BY BRIAN STABLEFORD

Our aesthetic appreciation of modern literary works in which various kinds of witches figure is in no way dependent upon our belief in the real possibility of their endeavors and achievements, and neither was the appreciation of the original audience. There is, however, an imaginative thread connecting that appreciation to the ever-present anxieties that generate belief in witchcraft. Literary representations of witches tug at that thread and stir up those anxieties, in ways we do not fully understand. A history of Satanic abuse which attempted to stick rigidly to images of Satanism and witchcraft deployed in the real world, ignoring those that never pretended to be anything more than fiction, would be incomplete; it would run the risk of becoming incompetent by virtue of neglecting an important source of insight into the fascination that even dedicated skeptics have for the idea of Satanic harlotry.

The Early Literary History of Satan and the Diabolical Pact

In the scriptures of the New Testament and the official doctrine of the Church, the role of Satan is clearly marked out: he is the ultimate embodiment of the idea of evil and of everything despicable. This is the way in which he is deployed in Medieval legend and Medieval art; he is extravagantly featured as a tempter, whose best efforts cannot prevail against the holiness of saints, and as the president of a horrid Hell that awaits sinners. He is usually portrayed as a repulsive creature, a chimerical compound of the human and the bestial. In more confident artistic representations, however, including pageants and miracle plays, his role could be ignominious, or even comical, rather than menacing.

Many of the great painters of the Renaissance were fond of apocalyptic imagery, and certain Satanic exploits—notably the phantasmagoric temptation of St. Anthony—offered unparalleled scope to the artistic imagination. While the great witch-hunt was beginning, Hieronymus Bosch was pushing back the limits of diabolical grotesquerie in his bizarre representations of Hell and the Garden of Delight. Other painters who used the emergent technology of oil painting to cultivate a new realism of representation, however, found that bringing Satan into sharper focus sometimes made him seem more human. In literature, too, he increasingly became a more ambiguous figure, even in the works of devout men. To some extent this ambiguity arose from the literary use of Satan as a purely metaphorical character, but even in those works where his literal existence was accepted he sometimes acquired a charismatic attractiveness befitting a skilful tempter.

Many early literary representations of Satan followed the example of Medieval artists who gave him a bestial face, horns and a tail; some writers, though, derived inspiration from the idea that, before his rebellion, Satan had been an angel, and presumably very handsome, or from the fact that his supposed shape-shifting abilities allowed him to present himself in any form at all. He was thus able to appear in some literary fantasies as a very beguiling figure: handsome (if only deceptively) and inordinately clever.

The archetypal image of Satan in English literature is that created by Milton in *Paradise Lost* (1667-74), written in response to Joost van den Vondel's reinterpretation of the War in Heaven as an anti-Puritan allegory, *Lucifer* (1654). This image provided a notable example of the effects of characterization and image-crystallization. Milton tried hard to make his Satan as repulsive and nasty-minded as possible, but the simple step of making the devil into a *person*, with recognizable feelings and coherent motives—not to mention a bold adventure to undertake—Milton opened up so much scope for reader identification that William Blake was moved to declare in 1793 that Milton had been "of the devil's party without knowing it".

The explicit purpose of *Paradise Lost* was "to justify the ways of God to man" by making his divine plan visible and comprehensible, but in characterizing Satan so memorably Milton also made *him* visible and comprehensible, and potentially sympathetic. How could it be otherwise, given that Satan's motives and seductions are, by definition, exactly those we find tempting, in spite of all the moral restrictions demanding that we deny them expression? When Satan becomes a literary character he is inevitably attractive, because evil *is* attractive—if it were not, repudiation of it would not have been such a vexing problem that our ancestors were led to invent the Devil in the first place.

The literary history of Satan is very largely one of increasing sympathy for the devil. As the Church's power waned in the aftermath of the Reformation. resentments against its attempted tyranny over the ideas of men were expressed in countless ways, including works of fiction that wondered, overtly or covertly, whether Lucifer had been entirely wrong to rebel against the dictatorship of his creator. Such ideas could be expressed in literature long before they could be stated openly, because the fictitious status of literary works cushioned writers against the charge that they were actually espousing Satanism. Sympathetic literary images of Satan were able to provide a kind of safety-valve for anti-clerical resentments, especially in France, whose literature produced a whole series of anti-clerical satires and romances in which Satan and his minions play an increasingly ambivalent role.

Once the great witch-hunt was over, and real fear of Satan's activities quieted by Enlightenment, the way was effectively clear for calculated literary flirtation with ideas that would earlier have seemed dangerously blasphemous. The way is not *entirely* clear even today, as is demonstrated by the *fatwa* issued against Salman Rushdie by the Ayatollah Khomeini on the grounds of the allegedly blasphemous contents of *The Satanic Verses* (1988), but modern Christian religious leaders rarely acquire the kind of authority that Khomeini had in Iran's Islamic republic.

In Alain-René Le Sage's *Le Diable boiteux* (1707; tr. as *Asmodeus; or, The Devil on Two Sticks*) the amiable demon Asmodeus assists the hero to penetrate the hypocrisies and follies of his countrymen. In Jacques Cazotte's *Le Diable amoureux* (1772; tr. as *The Devil in Love*) a demon disguised as a beautiful woman becomes very fond of the hero and loses her motivation to do him harm. Such stories as these paved the way for the eventual acceptance of Satan as a potential hero of the Romantic Movements that swept through Europe in the late eighteenth and early nineteenth centuries.

Percy Shelley, the leading spokesman for the English Romantics, followed up Blake's judgment of Milton with a more elaborate commentary in his calculatedly combative essay presenting "A Defense of Poetry" (written 1820). "Milton's poem," Shelley writes, "contains within itself a philosophical refutation of that system, of which, by a strange and natural antithesis, it has been a chief popular support. Nothing can exceed the energy and magnificence of the character of Satan as expressed in *Paradise Lost*. It is a mistake to suppose that he could ever have been intended for the popular personification of evil.... Milton's Devil as a moral being is as far superior to his God as one who perseveres in some purpose, which he has conceived to be excellent, in spite of adversity and torture, is to one who in the cold security of undoubted triumph inflicts the most horrible revenge upon his enemy...with the alleged design of exasperating him to new torments."

Shelley's *Prometheus Unbound* (1820) followed up this new ideology more radically than Blake's own quasi-Manichean fantasies, which had fused the roles of anti-god and redeemer into one. Charles Baudelaire abandoned diplomatic packaging in "Les litanies de Satan", included in *Les Fleurs du mal* (1857), although the first version of Gustave Flaubert's *Les Tentations de Saint-Antoine* (written 1848-49) had earlier been shelved in favor of a more diplomatic version published in 1874.

The most explicit and elaborate development of this kind of Romantic Satanism was eventually to be found in a series of works by the French Nobel prize-winning writer Anatole France. *Le Puits de Sainte Clare* (1895; tr. as *The Well of St. Clare*) is a collection of anti-Clerical satires, including "Lucifer", in which a darkly handsome Satan visits a Renaissance artist to complain about his representation in contemporary art, and "Le Tragédie humaine" (tr. as *The Human Tragedy*, in which a saintly Medieval monk, who preaches poverty and humility after the fashion of Jesus, is condemned by proud and wealthy Churchmen as a dangerous heretic and is saved from execution by Satan, whom he reluctantly recognizes as a friend and ally.

In France's *La Révolte des anges* (1914; tr. as *The Revolt of the Angels*) a guardian angel who takes to reading philosophy realizes that Jehovah is not what He represents Himself to be, and becomes enthusiastic to lead a new revolution—but when he eventually tracks down Satan and invites him to take charge of the fallen angels' army Satan declines, on the grounds that he has no wish to become a tyrant in Jehovah's image, and that the battle for the hearts and minds of men will be better won by passive resistance to the despotism of faith. Later writers who attempted to reconstruct Satan's version of the events allegedly misrepresented by Christian tradition included Jonathan Daniels, in *Clash of Angels* (1930), William Gerhardie and Brian Lunn, in *The Memoirs of Satan* (1932) and David H. Keller in *The Devil and the Doctor* (1940).

Reconstructed images of Satan could by this time be found even in works by devout writers. In Marie Corelli's best-selling *The Sorrows of Satan* (1895) a handsome and aristocratic Satan still has hope for his eventual salvation, if only men will cease to respond to his reluctant temptations. Other modern fantasies take pity on Satan, imagining him as an unfortunate creature whose battle to win men's souls is hopelessly out of date; Murray Constantine's The Devil, Poor Devil! (1934) is a sharply satirical example. Alongside these works, of course, conventional horror stories continued to appear in some profusion, so the literary history of Satan must be regarded as a bifurcation of evolutionary strands rather than as a single line of descent.

The glamour of the Romantic Satan inevitably rubbed off on at least some of those who made pacts with him. The notion of the diabolical pact itself had been a central motif of literary images of Satan ever since its emergence from the mists of oral tradition, mainly because of the story-value of the battles of wits involved in attempts to escape the consequences of such pacts. The best-known traditional version of the escaped pact is the story of Theophilus, a sixth-century bishop's seneschal, which was first written down in the tenth century. Theophilus was said to have made a bargain with the devil by which he granted the devil his soul and renounced Christ and the Virgin Mary in return for seven years of riotous living; when the seven years expired, however, he repented and prayed to the Virgin for pardon, which she duly gave.

The morality of the story of Theophilus is highly dubious. It seems to have originated in connection with the cult of the Virgin Mary—a popular Christian sideline that was finally given authoritative backing by Pius IX in the nineteenth century—in order to emphasize that the virgin is particularly merciful to the most extravagant of sinners, and therefore a particularly useful addressee of prayer. In post-Renaissance literature, however, a rather different myth became the foundation-stone of the majority of literary dramatizations of the pact with the devil: the story of Faust.

The legendary Faust was named after a scholar based at the University of Heidelberg in the early sixteenth century. After the actual person's death, the rumor spread that he had traded his soul to the Devil in exchange for "earthly knowledge"; his career thus became a parable in which science was represented as essentially satanic, by virtue of its concentration on the empirical at the expense of the spiritual. The printed version of the legend appeared in 1587, in a pamphlet signed by Johann Spies, usually known as the *Faustbuch*; it was translated into English as *Faustus: the History of the Damnable Life and Deserved Death of Dr. John Faustus* (1592) by "P.R., Gent" and the story was immediately appropriated by Christopher Marlowe in *The Tragical History of Dr. Faustus* (written c.1592; published 1604). The original pamphlet was rapidly followed by a sequel known as the *Wagnerbuch* (1593; tr. 1594 as *The Second Report of Dr. John Faustus; containing his appearances and the deeds of Wagner*), which added further attestation to the story and tracked the adventures of Faust's servant.

The most famous literary transfiguration of Faust's story after Marlowe's—and the most influential of all—was J. W. Goethe's *Faust* (1808-32), which shows a great deal more sympathy for the protagonist and whose two parts are often claimed to symbolize Goethe's conversion to the ideal and methods of Romanticism.

THE DEVIL'S PARTY, BY BRIAN STABLEFORD

Philip James Bailey's verse drama *Festus* (1839) similarly blended Christian ideas with Hegelian idealism, and included an educative cosmic tour—a motif also co-opted into Flaubert's quasi-Faustian *Tentation de Saint Antoine*—as a summary of his part in the bargain and prelude to his triumphant redemption. Many twentieth-century versions of the story further exploited its allegorical potential, including Thomas Mann's *Doctor Faustus* (1947; tr. 1948), Jorge de Sena's *O fisico prodigioso* (1977; tr. as *The Wondrous Physician*), Robert Nye's *Faust* (1980) and Michael Swanwick's *Jack Faust* (1997). The most earnest twentieth-century redeployment of the Faust myth was, however, Oswald Spengler's *Der Untergang des Abendlandes* (1918-22; tr. as *The Decline of the West*), which characterized the modern culture whose life-cycle was allegedly coming to an end as one possessed of a quintessentially "Faustian Soul".

As with the revision of the image of Satan, this literary process was a bifurcation rather than a metamorphosis. The melodramatic potential of diabolical pacts was carefully preserved and exploited in such Gothic romances as *The Monk* (1796) by Matthew Gregory Lewis and *Melmoth the Wanderer* (1820) by Charles Maturin, and in such folklore-based tales as Jeremias Gotthelf's *Die schwartze Spinne* (1842; tr. as *The Black Spider*) and Alexandre Dumas' *Le Meneur de loups* (1857; tr. as *The Wolf-Leader*). *Melmoth* was a particularly influential work; Honoré de Balzac wrote a crude imitation of it in the pseudonymous *Le Centenaire ou les deux Behringelds* (1832; tr. as *The Centenarian*), but used the notion of the diabolical pact far more seriously in his philosophical novel *La Peau de chagrin* (1831; tr. as *The Magic Skin*) and in a spirit of satirical travesty in "Melmoth reconcilié (1845; tr. as "Melmoth Reconciled"), in which the asking-price for souls has fallen dramatically in contemporary France.

Gothic fantasies of sinister diabolical pacts are far outnumbered by comedies in which the project of cheating the Devil becomes an ingenious game; notable examples include James Dalton's *The Gentlemen in Black* (1831), Eden Phillpotts' *A Deal with the Devil* (1895), Stephen Vincent Benét's "The Devil and Daniel Webster" (1937) and the twenty stories collected—alongside a translation of the *Faustbuch*—in Basil Davenport's showcase anthology of *Deals with the Devil* (1958). Such stories constitute, in sum, an extraordinary celebration of enterprise and imagination. Sometimes the ultimate victory is to the one side and sometimes to the other, but, whether the Devil or his human adversary wins, the victory is always a triumph of ingenuity; morality is a secondary issue.

THE DEVIL'S PARTY, BY BRIAN STABLEFORD

Satan frequently appears in these stories as an urbane and well-dressed man-about-town; it is always taken for granted that he is not to be trusted, but he is nevertheless seen as a person with whom it is a privilege—and sometimes a pleasure—to do business. The human protagonists of most such stories are male, although the advent of feminism brought forth such ironic exceptions as Fay Weldon's *Growing Rich* (1992) and Emma Tennant's *Faustine* (1992). They are usually scholarly magicians using the apparatus of sorcery as a symbolic means to an end, always seeking to take the Devil unawares and exploit him.

The attributes required for this kind of activity have always been seen by almost all writers—including female and feminist writers— as essentially masculine. The species of quasi-Faustian pact-makers, who deal with the devil on more-or-less equal terms, is generally seen as quite distinct from that of female witches, who are simply his minions and his slaves. In this sense, the misogynistic assumptions of the *Malleus Maleficarum* were paralleled and perpetuated in literary witch-images, and underwent relatively slight modification even in the twentieth century. It was noticeable and significant that late-twentieth century scare-stories about the supposed activities of real-world Satanists routinely cast power-hungry men as the prime movers and villains, while their female consorts and accomplices were usually seen as hapless, much-abused victims.

The Effects of the Witch-Panic on the Literary Image of the Witch

The literary images of witches and witchcraft developed by writers who were contemporary with the great panic had little room for the Medean tragic woman whose magic was primarily directed to amatory ends; the majority of images, as might be expected, were of the vile hagwife: ancient, ugly, and motivated by sheer malice.

The archetypal seventeenth-century portrait of the witch is summarized in the melodramatic overture to Shakespeare's *Macbeth* (c1606). Some commentators have suggest that Shakespeare was not responsible for much of the witch-material in the play, and it is possible that a seed he provided was elaborated by other hands to make the most of its audience-gripping potential; wherever the responsibility lies, though the imagery of *Macbeth* has made a deep and lingering impact upon the English imagination. The opening scene, together with the conjuration in Act one, Scene three and the famous "Hubble bubble, toil and trouble" spell in Act four, Scene one may owe some inspiration to the story of the North Berwick witches as well as to Reginald Scot, but Hecate—who appears to congratulate the witches in act four—derives from an older literary tradition.

A similar crew of witches, likewise led by Hecate, appears in the approximately contemporary play *The Witch* by Thomas Middleton (c1620), whose incantations are borrowed wholesale from Scot and whose immediate inspiration was probably the trial of the witches of Pendle in 1612. Middleton's some-time associates William Rowley, Thomas Dekker and John Ford contrived a witch play entitled *The Witch of Edmonton; a known True Story* in 1621, which offers a stereotyped account of the career of a witch in the spirit of modern "drama-documentaries". An old beggar-woman, cursed and reviled by all, is approached by a black dog and signs a contract in blood, then embarks upon a career of vengeful magic, blighting crops, sickening livestock and causing the madness and death of a farmer's wife. Eventually she is charged, tried and hanged at Tyburn.

This vogue continued with several ostensibly-faithful stage adaptations of the 1612 trial, based on a record compiled by the clerk of the court, Thomas Potts. When it released as a pamphlet, with the endorsement of the magistrate, it became a best-seller. The trial had come about through a combination of circumstances that threw two rival families of beggar-women living near Pendle Forest into a fit of vicious mutual denunciation after an itinerant peddler suffered a stroke. The peddler had apparently been cursed volubly by a teenage girl, Alizon Device (pronounced "Davis"), who was charged with witchcraft. Alizon confessed to the crime, and went on to implicate her mother, Elizabeth Device, and her grandmother, Elizabeth Southerne (known as "Old Demdike). These two in turn denounced their rivals, the aged Anne Whittle ("Old Chattox") and her daughter Anne Redfearne. After whipping up a good deal of trouble, the accusers all thought better of it and tried to retract their denunciations, but it was too late; they were brought to trial.

The fate of the supposed witches was sealed by the evidence of two child-witnesses: Alizon's infant sister Jennet, and her cretinous brother James. James backed up an elaborate story told by Jennet, including the casting of spells, the keeping of "familiars" and the use of clay dolls for casting curses. Several other men and women were named by Jennet as having been present at a meeting of witches at Demdike's home, including one woman of some social standing, Alice Nutter. Old Demdike eventually died in jail and ten others were hanged. The 1612 trial gave rise to a sequel of sorts in 1633, when an eleven-year-old boy told a similarly elaborate tale that resulted in the arraignment of seventeen people, including Jennet Device, but the trial was aborted because the judge, dissatisfied with the evidence, sought to have the guilty verdict that the jury returned set aside by officers of the crown. Some of the prisoners were sent to London to be examined, and it was on the crest of the new wave of this publicity that Thomas Heywood and Richard Brome launched their comedy play *The Late Lancashire Witches* (1634).

Unlike the dramatizations of the earlier trial, Heywood and Bome's was a satire against superstition, but literary attention soon returned to the earlier one, which had by far the greater melodramatic potential. In 1681 Thomas Shadwell's *The Lancashire Witches* lifted passages from several classic works on witchcraft and bound them up in a vicious attack on Catholicism and "superstition", as embodied in the character of Teague O'Divelly, an Irish Catholic priest. The play appeared while Protestant lords were attempting to exert strong political pressure on Charles II, using as their battle-cry "No Popery!" and inventing "Popish plots" in order to attack the Catholic nobility; Shadwell's contribution to the political argument was calculatedly inflammatory, but the play owed its sensational popularity to its "special effects", which allowed the witches to "fly" on stage, and to its melodramatic representation of a Sabbat. The 1612 trial was to be milked several more times, most successfully in W. Harrison Ainsworth's lurid historical novel *The Lancashire Witches* (1848)—which tampered extensively with history in order that Ainsworth might make Alizon Device his lovely heroine—and Robert Neill's far less melodramatic *Mist Over Pendle* (1951), which inverts the moral pattern of Ainsworth's dramatization by making Alizon evil (and ugly) while Jennet is heroically innocent (and charming).

British writers began to cash in on the enduring popularity of witch-mythology once the witch-hunt had died away; Daniel Defoe published two quasi-journalistic works, *The History of the Devil* (1726) and *A System of Magick* (1727), both of which drew on witch-mythology. Although Defoe did not make any significant use of the anecdotal material he reproduced in these volumes in his own prose fiction, the books served as source-material for later writers when the Gothic novel became the most popular form of prose fiction in Britain at the end of the eighteenth century. Perhaps surprisingly, the part played by witchcraft and Sabbat imagery in the horrific background of Gothic fiction is not at all conspicuous by comparison with haunted edifices, dark dungeons, lecherous monks and mere banditry. Novels that bring witchcraft into the foreground are relatively rare, and such rare focused examples as James Brewer Norris's *The Witch of Ravensworth* (1808) and Catherine Smith's *Barozzi; or, The Venetian Sorceress* (1815) are content to appropriate the terminology in a cursory manner for application to stereotyped villains.

It was not until after the Gothic craze had evaporated that actual and hypothetical witch-trials became raw material for literary reinterpretation in the same way as the story of Lucifer's fall and the legend of Faust, in such works as William Meinhold's *Maria Schweidler, die Bernsteinhexe* (1843; tr. as *The Amber Witch*) and *Sidonia von Bork, die Klosterhexe* (1847; tr. as *Sidonia the Sorceress*), and Thomas Wright's *The Blue Firedrake* (1892). The tradition then extended throughout the twentieth century in such works as J. W. Brodie-Innes's *The Devil's Mistress* (1915), Edith Pargeter's *By Firelight* (1948), Aldous Huxley's *The Devils of Loudoun* (1952), François Mallet-Joris's *Trois âges de la nuit* (1968; tr. as *The Witches*), and Leslie Wilson's *Malefice* (1992).

The Salem trial was one of the most significant inspirations of this sort to speculative literary analysis, being re-examined in numerous American literary works, ranging from Esther Barstow Hammond's luridly credulous *Yesterday Never Dies* (1941) to Arthur Miller's abrasively skeptical play *The Crucible* (1953)—the latter being intended to make a moral point with respect to the political "witch-hunt" initiated by Joseph McCarthy. Although the trial is not specifically featured, it clearly inspired other painstakingly analytical works such as Nathaniel Hawthorne's short story "Young Goodman Brown" (1835), and Esther Forbes' novel *A Mirror for Witches* (1928).

The literary durability of unsympathetic images of female witches stands in some contrast to the treatment of male magicians—a contrast exemplified by the contrast between Shakespeare's witches in *Macbeth* and his depiction of the male magician Prospero in *The Tempest*. In conventional literary parlance the term "wizard" evolved connotations very different from those of "witch", with the term "warlock" being widely adopted for specific reference to the male equivalent of a witch. The archetypal literary image of the wizard is Merlin, whose character was elaborated in French romances dealing with the *Matière de Bretagne* [Matter of Britain], and who served as tutor to the imaginary King Arthur.

"Wizard" is derived from the Middle English *wysard*, meaning wise man, but wizards cast in Merlin's mould are more imposing figures than "cunning men" who practiced folk medicine, more closely akin to prestigious Magi. Literary wizards are very rarely associated with Satan, even if they are evil, and the wizards of twentieth-century generic fantasy routinely operated in the context of hypothetical Secondary Worlds; the *fin-de-siècle* success of J. K. Rowling's accounts of contemporary wizardly education changed the parameters slightly, most notably in respect of its co-educational concessions, but retained the Merlinian stereotype in the key character of Albus Dumbledore.

Female witches never obtained any significant benefit from this kind of literary aggrandizement, although male makers of Faustian pacts and Gothic villains in general certainly gained some benefit from it. Literary witches are rarely seen to be offering the same defiant challenge to ideological tyranny that is often held to be admirable in clones of Faust, and in some literary representations of Satan himself, even when it is conceded that female witches have more oppressive forces to react against. In works that find it entirely understandable that females suffering social neglect might be glad to make pacts with the devil, such as Sylvia Townsend Warner's proto-feminist allegory *Lolly Willowes; or, The Loving Huntsman* (1926) and John Updike's *The Witches of Eastwick* (1984), the case made on their behalf tends to be rather cravenly apologetic. In the most wholehearted of the rare exceptions to this rule, Marjorie Bowen's *Black Magic* (1909)—which features a female Anti-Christ ambitious to be pope—the sorceress wears male disguise throughout and is continually referred to by the masculine pronoun, even though the reader knows from the start that "he" is really female.

The image of the witch as a Medean erotic enchantress was extensively revived in neo-Classical drama in the eighteenth century, and readily adopted by the Romantic Movements, to the extent that Mario Praz's exhaustive account of *La carne, la morte e il diavolo nella letteratura romantica* (1930; tr. as *The Romantic Agony*) devoted two long chapters to "The Beauty of the Medusa" and "La Belle Dame sans Merci" and only one to "The Metamorphoses of Satan". The vast majority of Romantic *femmes fatales* only qualified as witches in a purely metaphorical sense, but the metaphor continually trespassed in the borderlands of literality. One result of this was the growth of a sturdy twentieth century tradition in which young and beautiful witches under the tutelage of more conventional hag-wives become redeemable by love and domesticity.

Norman Matson's *Flecker's Magic* (1926) goes to some lengths to draw a clear line between a beautiful seeming witch and the hag-wife actually responsible for her enchantment, but Matson exercised a much greater indirect influence via his completion of Thorne Smith's *The Passionate Witch* (1941), whose comprehensively-tenderized spin-off included the René Clair film *I Married a Witch* (1942), which in turn gave birth to the TV series *Bewitched* (1964-71). John Van Druten's play *Bell, Book and Candle* (1956), which also had a successful film version, continued the line of argument, similarly making much of the notion that beautiful female witches may give up their magical powers in order to become conventionally marriageable, and that such a surrender constitutes a kind of salvation. The tradition continued to evolve in such novels as Mary Savage's *A Likeness to Voices* (1963) and Alice Hoffman's *Practical Magic* (1995), and the TV series *Charmed* (1998-2005).

The most abundant repository of literary witches after the end of the witch-hunt was the body of recycled and imitative folktales commonly called "fairy tales". Key features of the witch-image developed by sixteenth- and seventeenth-century witch-hunters were maintained by many such writers, and the illustration of such works soon gave rise to stereotyped images of broomstick-riding hagwives in tall conical black hats, routinely accompanied by familiars in the form of house-cats and equipped with cauldrons in the shape of stewpots. When color illustration became standardized, discolored complexions—often involving a green hue—was often added to the mix.

Because they were ostensibly addressed to children, there is usually no mention in fairy tales of pacts with the devil, and when the mythology of the Sabbat is cited it tends to be somewhat sanitized. Such diplomacy resulted in the term "witch" being removed from some versions of stories in which the stereotype is deployed, reference being made instead to "wicked fairies". In some cases, however, the use of that contrasted term was reflected back into literary distinctions between "wicked witches" and "good witches", after the fashion of L. Frank Baum's *The Wizard of Oz* (1899), whose film version—in which the good witch is, of course, blonde and beautiful, while the wicked witch is green-skinned and ugly—acquired sufficient mythic power of its own to license the tongue-in-cheek analysis of the evolution of malice in Gregory Maguire's *Wicked: The Life and Times of the Wicked Witch of the West* (1995), which gave birth in its turn to a successful Broadway musical.

The confusions generated by the *femme fatale* tradition and the unsteady evolution of witch-images in children's fiction inevitably became topics for literary consideration in themselves, and the twentieth century saw a good deal of calculated recomplication of the traditional imagery. When combined with the increasing influence of lifestyle fantasies involving witchcraft, this recomplication ensured that writers active in the latter decades of the century who were intent on recovering or updating the image of the witch produced by Christian witch-hunters had to work quite hard to do so, as Roald Dahl did in *The Witches* (1983), conscious of the fact that they were facing such determinedly clever ideological opposition as that provided by Terry Pratchett in his depiction of Granny Weatherwax and her associates in such Discworld novels as *Wyrd Sisters* (1988) and *Witches Abroad* (1991).

The persistence of the image of the witch as an embodiment of evil, and the slow but determined growth of a concerted literary opposition to that kind of stigmatization—in contrast to the routine glamorization of the image of the male ritual magician—is highly significant in the context of lifestyle fantasies involving witchcraft, because the continued association of witchcraft with malice and ugliness has helped considerably to sustain an impression of tacit persecution. As the lifestyle fantasies fed back their own influence into literary works, however, the balance of representation shifted so markedly by the end of the twentieth century as to render the witch-hunters' authority obsolete.

Satan and Satanism in Modern Horror Fiction

As the tradition of Romantic *contes philosophiques* in which Satan figures as a sympathetic character continued into the latter part of the twentieth century it became increasingly varied and flagrantly ironic. In Mervyn Wall's novels *The Unfortunate Fursey* (1946) and *The Return of Fursey* (1948) Satan and the accident-prone monk who periodically meets up with him become increasingly confused and desperate. In Mikhail Bulgakov's *Master i Margarita* (written 1938; pub. 1967; tr. as *The Master and Margarita*), the Devil's visit to Stalinist Moscow is a perversely liberating experience for some, though by no means all, of those who encounter him. Satan and Jesus join forces in Bulgakov's novel against a human evil that transcends their age-old rivalry—a theme echoed in such works as Alfred Noyes' *The Devil Takes a Holiday* (1955) and Robert Nathan's *Heaven and Hell and the Megas Factor* (1975). In Jeremy Leven's *Satan* (1982) the eponymous anti-hero, newly incarnate as a sentient computer, goes into psychoanalysis in the hope that he might finally solve the problem of evil and recover his own self-esteem.

THE DEVIL'S PARTY, BY BRIAN STABLEFORD

This ironic tradition was flexible enough to accommodate wryly allegorical works by devout writers, including C. S. Lewis's analysis of the tactics of temptation in *The Screwtape Letters* (1944) and such sophisticated infernal comedies as E. E. Y. Hales' *Chariot of Fire* (1977). Alongside works that deftly combine playfulness and seriousness in this manner, however, the Gothic tradition of Satanic fantasies—in which Satan remains a quintessentially horrific figure embodying all that is evil—continued unabated. It gained a new strength of its own as standards of literary decency were relaxed and the potential scope of the Devil's sadistic depredations was increased.

Although horror fiction, seen as a genre, remained rather esoteric throughout the twentieth century it retained the capacity to produce an unsteady flow of best-sellers, to which Satan and Satanism made a regular contribution in such novels as Denis Wheatley's *The Devil Rides Out* (1934) and *To the Devil—A Daughter* (1953), the latter work being sufficiently graphic to be censored before publication. Wheatley attempted to maximize the shock value of his representations by drawing upon scholarly fantasies regarding the continued existence of Satanism, carrying forward a tradition in which the distinction between fiction and non-fiction was deliberately blurred.

Early examples of this kind of *recherché* fiction had included such quasi-documentary items as Julian Osgood Field's "Aut Diabolos aut Nihil" (1888), published in *Blackwood's Magazine*, which offers a mock-journalistic account of the conjuration of a Satanic spirit by a group of Parisian Satanists, and Joris-Karl Huysmans' *Là-Bas* (1891), in which an account of a scholar's attempts to write a biography of Gilles de Rais is interwoven with a parallel account of his discovery of the exploits of contemporary Satanists. It extended into the late twentieth century in such "case-studies" of diabolical possession as Ray Russell's *The Case Against Satan* (1962)—whose author added an endnote claiming that he had benefited from a minor miracle, which allowed him to finish writing the book in spite of active diabolical opposition—which was reissued for inspirational purposes by the Catholic Book Club, and William Peter Blatty's *The Exorcist* (1971), whose success was ensured by the hugely popular film version made in 1973. Blatty concluded *The Exorcist* with a note thanking the Jesuits for "teaching [the author] to think", and represented the whole enterprise as a gesture of gratitude; the gesture was returned when the novel and film were praised by some Churchmen for reminding people of the real existence of

Satan and helping to alert a complacent public to the danger threatening its members.

The film version of *The Exorcist*, which deployed its special effects spectacularly and ingeniously, helped to initiate a new boom in cinematic horror, which redeemed the film genre from the cheap and camp B-movie vein into which it had fallen. Confident that they once again had the technological means to scare audiences, filmmakers set out to explore the new limits of shock-value. Slickly disturbing films that played teasingly with the idea of modern Satanism—most notably *Rosemary's Baby* (book by Ira Levin 1967; film 1968)—were supplemented and largely replaced by more wholehearted melodramas like the series of Anti-Christ fantasies begun with *The Omen* (1976), continued in *Damien: Omen II* (1978) and concluded in *Omen III: the Final Conflict* (1981).

The wave of fashionability enjoyed by films like *The Exorcist* coincided with an explosion of literature produced by specialist Christian presses, much of it in the form of "confessional autobiographies" by people claiming to have been involved in Satanist cults and covens, which tried very hard to persuade their readers that Satan really is active in the modern world. These kinds of works will be dealt with more fully in a later chapter, but it is worth observing their close relationship—in both timing and substance—with these literary and cinematic fantasies.

It is hardly surprising that modern literary fantasies, scholarly fantasies and lifestyle fantasies feed off one another in a promiscuously uncritical fashion, but it is rather remarkable that some modern Churchmen have so carefully retained the undiscriminating tactics of witch-finders and their scholarly supporters in this respect. The Romantics for whom Satan became a symbol of liberation had no interest whatsoever in pretending that there really had been a war in heaven, or that there really was an actual Satan who might actually be an object of worship, but the other side in the conflict of ideas still has an interest in maintaining that view, and some of its representatives are still prepared to do so by any and all available means.

THE DEVIL'S PARTY, BY BRIAN STABLEFORD

VI.

SCHOLARLY FANTASIES

Reinterpretations of the History of Satanic Abuse

All history contains an element of fantasy, over and above the many relics of the mythic past that continue to pollute the image of the historical past. The fragmentary nature of historical data requires the imagination to be continually invoked to bridge the multitudinous gaps in the partial evidence of documents and artifacts. There is also a significant sense in which historical understanding is necessarily based in an act of the imagination by which the historian and his readers try to "place themselves in the shoes" of the people of the past, in order to see past situations as they appeared to the actors, and thus make sense of what the actors did. "Making sense", as the phrase implies, generally consists of figuring out why it seemed reasonable to the actors to do as they did—why their behavior seemed *rational* to them.

In these kinds of operation, scrupulous historians make every effort to be responsible to the known facts, and to subject the necessary work of the imagination to the strictest possible logical discipline, but the fact remains that all history is, to some degree, the fantasy of scholars. While scrupulous historians are wary of the possible distortions that might be introduced by the imaginative component of their work, however, and try to minimize them, unscrupulous ones—whether their unscrupulousness is accidental or deliberate—often make the most of the opportunity. Fantasy plays a much greater role in the work of some historians than others, and it plays a much greater role in some areas of historical enquiry than others.

Whenever a historian tries to understand behavior that seems puzzling—particularly if it seems dubious in its rationality—the historical imagination must work harder, and is less certain in its results. When a historian attempts to understand the history of an *idea* whose rationality seems dubious, further problems inevitably arise as a result of the entanglement of his own imaginative work with the imaginative adventures of those whose behavior he is trying to understand; the more fantastic the idea in question is, the more hazardous this process of entanglement becomes.

The history of Satanic abuse—which is to say, the history of accusations of sorcery and witchcraft, and of the resultant trials—is perhaps more vulnerable than any other area of historical enquiry to flights of historical fancy. It has attracted numerous historians whose ready-made inclination to such flights of fancy would have prohibited their being taken seriously in any other area of study. It has also seduced some historians whose interpretation of less problematic data is unimpeachable into uncharacteristically eccentric adventures in fantasization.

The more distant in time historians became from the actual events of the great witch-hunt, the greater the leap became that they and their readers had to make in order to place themselves imaginatively in the shoes of witch-accusers and witch-finders. The greater that leap has become, the greater has become the scope for wild and reckless theorizing. The exoticism of some of the theories produced by modern historians to "explain" the great witch-panic is extraordinary—although it might have been even more extraordinary had no such exotica been produced. There is no clear boundary to be drawn between responsible scholarly analyses and scholarly fantasies, especially in terms of the sincerity of their producers, but there can be no doubt that much of what has been written about the supposed history of Satanism and witchcraft, especially for a lay audience, lies well beyond the grey area, in the realm of pure fabulation. The abundant scope that exists for reinterpretation of the great witch-hunt has not only combined its effect with a general hunger for melodrama and various political agendas but with the attractions of magical lifestyle fantasy.

As we have seen, the skeptics who attacked witch-persecution in the late seventeenth century concluded that the gaudier aspects of post-Renaissance witch-mythology were purely and simply the product of the imagination. They mostly asserted that the things witches were said to do—and what they sometimes confessed to doing—were fantasies, and that, while such things might be possible in theory, they almost never happened in reality. There was a margin of caution in most of their writings—many of the skeptics thought that certain magical operations *might* work, either by virtue of some unknown natural principle, or even through the aid of the Devil—but as time went by that margin of caution dwindled away. The eighteenth-century skeptics of the self-proclaimed Age of Enlightenment became increasingly confident that they could declare the entirety of Christian witch-mythology to be imaginary.

One point on which the skeptics of the seventeenth and eighteenth centuries were almost all agreed was that the witch-meetings known as conventicles or Sabbats were entirely imaginary, and that when people sincerely believed that they had attended such meetings their conviction was based in dreams and hallucinations. The skeptics did not deny that there might well have been people who attempted maleficent magic, either formally or simply by ill-wishing their neighbors, but they firmly denied the real existence of any heretical organization or cult of Satanic witchcraft.

This view of the matter was unchallenged throughout the eighteenth century, save for a tiny minority of would-be witch-finders who maintained a rearguard action in favor of witch beliefs. Although the Catholic Church did not give up its demonology, and many Protestant sects remained enthusiastic in preaching about the snares of the devil and the threat of eternal punishment, there was a very widespread reluctance to apply such theories to any actual cases of supposed maleficent magic or demonic possession. The general opinion of the great witch-hunt was that it had been a direly unfortunate series of mistakes entirely based in delusion.

Once it had retreated to a more distant past, however, new suggestions began to be made regarding the witch-hunt. In 1828 Karl Jarcke made some comments on a German witch-trial, expressing the opinion that the witches involved might have been members of a pagan cult whose adherents were attempting to use black magic against good Christians. A similar theory was put forward by Franz Mone in 1839, without attracting much attention. These seem to have been attempts to make the actions of the Church—both Jarcke and Mone were Catholics—seem a little more reasonable, by suggesting that there really had been an enemy at large, although its nature had been somewhat mistaken and the reaction against it somewhat exaggerated. (Some modern commentators have credited similar ideas to Girolama Tartarotti, in a book published in 1749, and to the folklorist Jakob Grimm, but these authors did no more than note that the post-Renaissance witch-image had absorbed some elements from Germanic folklore.) The suggestions made by Jarcke and Mone was largely ignored, and not taken seriously by contemporary historians. Later writers, however, offered similar processes of reinterpretation that proved far more influential.

The Spin-Off of the Occult Revival

In the nineteenth century there was a very considerable revival of interest in the occult and the *outré*, and a marked resurgence of interest in the possible reality of the supernatural, reflected in such movements as Swedenborgianism, Spiritualism and Theosophy. These movements were very various in matters of detail, but they shared a common interest in attempting to recover the essential holism of the occult tradition, employing it in opposition to the "reductionist" tendencies of contemporary science, whose progress had become increasingly rapid as its technological spin-off precipitated the Industrial Revolution.

The perverse relationship between the march of science and the Occult revival is well-illustrated by the Enlightenment-spanning career of Emanuel Swedenborg, who was a convert from science to mysticism, and exhibited all the zeal of the typical convert after making the switch. In 1715 Swedenborg founded Sweden's first scientific periodical, *Daedalus Hyperboreus*, and he subsequently wrote treatises on cosmology, optics and sensory perception before summarizing his endeavors in *Opera Philosophica et Mineralia* [Philosophical and Mineralogical Works] (1734) and *Oeconomia Regni Animalis* (1740-41; tr. as *The Economy of the Animal Kingdom*). He set out to extend this work into a 17-volume encyclopedia of a new human science, but only published three volumes before becoming preoccupied with a "doctrine of correspondence" based on the notion that there is a natural symmetry between propositions in natural science and propositions related to spiritual matters, determined by an innate symbolic aspect of Creation.

In pursuit of such correspondences, Swedenborg began to take an intense interest in his dreams, construing them as visions offering insight into universal patterns of symbolic correspondence. His later works were accounts of his visions, interpreted as communications from and with spirits, and interpretations of the Bible based on his occult theories. Swedenborgian societies began to form in some profusion in the 1780s; his ideas influenced many writers involved in the German and English Romantic movements, whose responses assisted their widespread dissemination. Charles Fourier's *Théories de l'unité universelle* (1822) attempted a similar accommodation of scientific discovery to a holistic philosophy, similarly accumulating numerous disciples, who founded Fourierist communities in the USA and elsewhere.

The upsurge of interest in occult matters exemplified by the proliferation of Swedenborgian organizations was mirrored in an upsurge of antiquarian interest in the history of magic. The members of the German Romantic Movement took a keen interest in folklore, including Christian legendry, and provided the respectable tip of a considerable boom in horror fiction, whose influence in England sparked an equally spectacular boom in "Gothic" fiction. Charles Nodier, the central figure of early French Romanticism, produced an anthology of *Infernaliana* (1822), which he described as a collection of "anecdotes, petit romans, nouvelles et contes", which adds a number of thematic essays to more orthodox recyclings of tales from oral culture, including discourses on diabolical pacts, demonic possession and witches' Sabbats. The text became a rich source of inspiration for subsequent *littérateurs*.

Although increasing interest in Britain was most obvious in the literary field, in connection with analytical commentaries on the sources of Gothic fiction by such "expert practitioners" as Matthew Gregory Lewis and Nathan Drake, it also produced such works as Francis Barrett's *The Magus* (1801), a massive anthology of reprinted magical texts. John Aubrey's *Brief Lives* (1813)—a collection of memoirs originally written in the seventeenth century—repopularized an account of John Dee's experiments in spirit conjuration previously recorded (long after Dee's death) by Meric Casaubon. Walter Scott, who was an avid collector of ballads, issued a series of *Letters on Demonology and Witchcraft* (1830) that served as an important source-book for later writers, although Scott, like Daniel Defoe before him, made relatively little use of such materials in is own fiction. Scott did, however, lay claim to an ancestor who had been a notorious wizard, Michael Scott, and provided an extravagant Faustian representation of him in verse in "The Lay of the Last Minstrel" (1805).

Scott's *Letters* were subsequently singled out for special mention in the introduction to Charles Mackay's *Memoirs of Extraordinary Popular Delusions* (1841), which looked back interestedly on the upsurge of interest in "infernaliana", considering it a key example of his subject-matter. Two of its longest chapters are devoted to "The Alchymists" (covering all reputed magicians, including subsections on John Dee and Rosicrucianism) and "The Witch Mania". The determinedly skeptical Mackay obviously thought that the day of such delusions was finally dead, but he spoke far too soon—

ironically, his adopted (and probably natural) daughter Minnie was to became a highly significant and thoroughly credulous literary popularizer of the occult revival in the hectic *fin-de-siècle*, when she adopted the pseudonym Marie Corelli and briefly became the best-selling writer in the English language.

While the Spiritualist Movement kicked off in the USA by the Fox sisters' mysterious rappings and table-turnings spawned mediums by the hundred, and gained converts by the thousand, some older lifestyle fantasies were revived, including Rosicrucianism. Although Spiritualism achieved sufficient success as a religion to attract charges from orthodox churchmen that it was dabbling in necromancy, it was the literary wing of the Rosicrucian revival that sparked—quite by accident—a renewed interest in Satanism.

The repopularization of Rosicrucianism was greatly assisted by Edward Bulwer-Lytton's depiction of a Rosicrucian sage in his novel *Zanoni* (1842), whose enthusiastic admirers included an unsuccessful French *littérateur* named Alphonse Louis Constant. Constant decided to pose as such a sage, adopting the pseudonym of "Éliphas Lévi" for that purpose. His fanciful account of *Dogme et rituel de la haut magie* (1854-56; tr. as *The Doctrine and Ritual of Transcendental Magic*) was far more successful than his earlier publications, and he followed it up with an equally fanciful and equally successful *Histoire de la magie* (1859; tr. as *The History of Magic*). These became the principal source-books of all subsequent handbooks of "high magic" and prompted the foundation of numerous "Rosicrucian lodges," whose most enthusiastic propagandists included Joséphin Péladan and Édouard Schuré. The upsurge of interest in Satanist lifestyle fantasies chronicled in *fin-de-siècle* literary works by Julian Osgood Field and Joris-Karl Huysmans was an offshoot of this boom, but "Éliphas Lévi" also became a significant influence on scholarly fantasists, one of whom became even more influential in his turn.

The financial rewards reaped by Constant's books excited the interest and envy of Jules Michelet, a poverty-stricken vocational historian. Michelet was inspired by the example of what he knew full well to be a fancifully sensationalized history of magic to produce—in great haste—a sensational history of his own, in order to finance his masterpiece-in-progress: a definitive history of France seen from a radical ideological viewpoint, whose fervent republicanism was intimately connected with anti-clericalism. *La Sorcière* (1862; tr. as *The Witch of the Middle Ages* and *Satanism and Witchcraft*) is not a work of scrupulous history, and makes no real pretence to be—its notes readily admit the extent of its inventions—but its argument is presented with a fine righteous fervor.

Even French witch-finders who were convinced that most witches were female, including Jean Bodin and Henri Boguet, had been content to use the masculine form of the word *sorcier* to describe them, but Michelet preferred the feminine form because his argument include a proto-feminist complaint about the implicit misogyny of the Church; most subsequent writers followed his example. *La Sorcière* includes a series of melodramatic journalistic accounts of witch-trials and similar *causes célèbres*, but it also features a lyrical prologue representing the witches of sixteenth- and seventeenth-century France as an underground movement of social protest and rebellion.

Michelet's manifest primary intention in *La Sorcière* is to assault the ideological tyranny of the Church, and the Church's persecution of witches becomes, in his view, a key symbol of that tyranny, all the more significant for being an inverted reflection of the martyrdom of early Christian saints. In pursuit of this argument he attempts to whip up as much sympathy as possible for the poor witches, who had been abandoned to the pit of legendary contempt by the same literary men who had gone to such lengths to redeem the reputations of Satan and Faustian sorcerers. The text claims that the post-Renaissance witch was actually a friend and protector of ordinary people—in stark contrast to the established Church, which had betrayed its own cause in becoming the ally and accessory of the feudal barons and their successors.

In Michelet's revised image, witches are necessarily female because their gift of "second sight" is quintessentially feminine; the witches of Christendom are represented as the descendants of Circe, the Sibyl and similar enchantresses and prophetesses revered in the ancient world as founts of wisdom and inspiration. That the Church should devalue, blacken the name and burn such individuals at the stake was, in Michelet's argument, the ultimate indictment of clerical evil. Like the skeptics who had come before him, Michelet accepted that the witch had been "invented" by the Church, but he suggested that this invention might have been more literal than previous writers had been prepared to suppose. He argued that the tyranny of the Church might actually have driven healers using folk-remedies, diviners and their followers into a defiant pretence and celebration of diabolical allegiance.

Michelet's text draws a picture of a rebel witch-cult born out of an "age of despair", which had begun when the Church lost contact with the common people and collaborated with a political system that demoted them from the status of vassals to the lowlier rank of serfs. Although he probably did not believe that would-be witches actually did meet at Sabbats, he confidently asserts that they must have done because he believes so strongly that they *ought* to have done, and because it enables him to complain that such meetings were grossly and viciously misrepresented by the Church (unsurprisingly, he finds Pierre de Lancre's accounts the least satisfactory). He goes so far as to produce his own dramatization of a hypothetical Sabbat as a ritual in four acts, entitling it the "Communion of Revolt".

Following his sensationalist account of a series of notorious trials and persecutions, Michelet returns in an epilogue to the moral of his story, declaring that the modern world has been made out of a series of "Satanic" revolutions against the tyrannical and irrational authority of the Church, and that modern "followers" of Satan (by which he means men of science and adherents of political liberalism) must carry forward this long crusade in the name of "Reason, Right, and Nature". His text is thus accommodated to the tradition of literary satanism that had first reached explicit form five years earlier in Baudelaire's *Les Fleurs du mal*.

In order that they be recruited to support and dramatize Michelet's polemic against the Church's ideological imperialism, it was not enough that the victims of the witch-hunt should have been innocent and unjustly maligned; in order to feature as paradigmatic heroes of his long revolution they had to have actually *done something* to strike a blow for the side of "Reason, Right and Nature"—and so he declared that they had. By thus fantasizing the witch-hunt, in the service of his moral propaganda, Michelet was able to exploit not only the cruelty of the witchfinders but also the image of the witch in literary fantasy and orthodox history. He was able to claim that the witch had been maligned and misunderstood in her own day, and still was being maligned and misunderstood by historians and literary men alike.

La Sorcière is a relatively frank and wholly unashamed scholarly fantasy, which casually rewrote history in order to appeal to aesthetic and political sensibilities. In so doing, Michelet constructed an alternative pseudo-history that was more exciting and more interesting than "real" history—which was bound to inspire others, by virtue of its panache as much as its politics.

THE DEVIL'S PARTY, BY BRIAN STABLEFORD

The Progeny of Michelet's Sorceress

Many of the works that took up Michelet's suggestion that the witches burned in the great hunt might have been grossly misunderstood added their own further embellishments to the allegation. One that did so with an unusual enthusiasm was Charles Godfrey Leland's *Aradia: The Gospel of the Witches* (1899). Leland was a dilettante folklorist who was strongly attracted by the supposedly romantic aspects of the life of gypsies. He had written an earlier book on Romany customs and folklore, claiming that everything in it had been gathered first-hand, from the mouths of the gypsies themselves; he made a similar claim in *Aradia*, which is supposedly based on the testimony of an Italian gypsy named Maddalena and offers an elaborate account of the spells and rituals of "la vecchia religione". Leland claimed that this was the ancient gypsy religion, covertly preserved and practiced throughout centuries of Christian persecution, whose secret and harmless rites had been mistaken by witch-finders for Satanist Sabbats, with terrible consequences.

Aradia is an essay in invented mythology, but its real agenda is contained in the poetic form in which the individual elements are cast. It is a literary work masquerading as a "discovery", rather after the fashion of James Macpherson's *Fingal* (1762) and *Temora* (1763), which had been passed off as the work of a third-century Gaelic bard named Ossian in the previous century. The goddess of Leland's imaginary "old religion" is identified as Diana, and her daughter Aradia becomes a kind of messiah-figure. The names are borrowed from the *Canon Episcopi*, the latter being a version of "Herodias", which name was sometimes cited alongside Diana's in copies of the original canon.

Aradia, according to Leland's account, came down from Heaven to establish witchcraft and then returned. Among the rituals and spells is a kind of grace to be said before the wholly innocent "witch-supper". The framework provided by Leland is thus a syncretic compound of feminized Christianity and Graeco-Roman literary paganism. He mentions several antiquarian sources, including Pico's *Strix* and Tertullian, but he also refers to the poetry of Byron and Keats (criticizing the latter because *Endymion* distorts the mythology of *la vecchia religione*). Much of the commentary provided by the "editor" is, in fact, pure literary criticism, slyly denigrating classical works and forms by comparison with verses that are surely his own compositions.

THE DEVIL'S PARTY, BY BRIAN STABLEFORD

Leland finds "a wondrous poetry of thought" in the verses he reproduces, which "far excels the efforts of many modern bards". He complains that modern painters and poets too often fail to perceive or preserve the "real meaning" of the traditions they borrow and adapt, while these supposedly traditional examples retain that meaning in full. The stratagem of "reversed plagiarism"—representing one's own work as that of an ancient and therefore prestigious source—was, of course, already perfectly familiar in connection with magical fantasies. The mythology of Satan was very largely a product of apocryphal writings, and almost all books of black magic had been attributed to real or mythical persons of far greater prestige than their actual authors. (Although we have no idea who actually wrote the book of *Enoch* or the *Key of Solomon,* we can perfectly certain that Enoch and Solomon were uninvolved.) Leland's work is a good-humored literary hoax, written in the full awareness of this great tradition. His historical thesis, presented in the appendix, is very obviously lifted straight out of Michelet.

Neither Michelet nor Leland was taken seriously by scrupulous historians; Leland's work probably passed entirely unnoticed by anyone except a handful of the amateur folklorists at whom it was aimed. Their ideas were, however, to be further developed, and to attain spectacular respectability, in one of the most successful scholarly fantasies of the twentieth century: Margaret Murray's reinterpretation of the witch-persecutions as a Christian crusade against a secret pagan religion. In order to achieve that reinterpretation, however, Murray needed to draw upon the rich legacy of speculative anthropology.

History is, of course, not the only academic discipline to be heavily prone to pollution by scholarly fantasy, and disciplines that attempt to place historical data in a broader theoretical context inevitably multiply its problems. When highly intelligent men make boldly heroic attempts to find theoretical contexts that can make whole tracts of information understandable, they may easily come up with aesthetically-pleasing but wholly mistaken interpretations. The nineteenth-century founding fathers of anthropology, who attempted to build a science out of the uncertain substance of travelers' tales and the often-mysterious relics of the past collected by generations of antiquaries, performed an immensely valuable service in collecting and collating data, and in offering hypotheses regarding possible connective links, but it is not surprising that their hypotheses were often overambitious. The most ambitious of all the early syntheses of anthropological data was James Frazer's *The Golden*

Bough (1890; subsequent editions much expanded), a huge work elaborating the proposition that belief in magic was part of a series of intellectual phases through which all cultures evolved.

In the nineteenth-century infancy of social science it was tacitly assumed that extant human societies were at different stages within a definable evolutionary pattern of progress. This was an aspect of the increasing popularity of evolutionary theory, which seemed to be revolutionizing scientific thought by revealing a new "system" in the life science, much as Newton had earlier revolutionized and systematized physical science. Early anthropologists were also acutely aware of the technological progress that had brought about the industrial revolution, and the dynamic of social progress. August Comte had proposed at the beginning of the century that there was "natural" progression of thought from theology to rationality, which he called the law of the three stages. Comte's law proposed that religion was in the process of being further refined into a "positivist" belief-system celebrating the triumph of science and reason. Frazer adopted the bare bones of Comte's scheme, elaborating it with the aid of ideas adapted from Edward Tylor's analysis of *Primitive Culture* (1871), especially "animism"—a hypothetical ancestor of all subsequent forms of religious belief—and "sympathetic magic": magical practices apparently based on the idea of "natural affinities" between the rituals or the substances used therein and the desired effect or target.

Frazer elaborated the notion of sympathetic magic considerably, proposing that magic must have begun as a kind of proto-science based on two hopeful laws: the principle that "like produces like, or that an effect resembles its cause" and the principle "that things which have once been in contact with each other continue to act on each other at a distance after the physical contact has been severed". Frazer called the first principle the Law of Similarity and the latter the Law of Contact, or Contagion. In his theory of progressive cultural evolution, this kind of magic, having been tried and found wanting, was replaced by primitive religion, whose rites—fundamentally concerned with attempts to ensure agricultural fertility—gradually evolved from animistic roots towards monotheism.

The Golden Bough's account of the "natural" evolutionary pattern followed by all human cultures proposes that magic, initially employed privately in pursuit of individual ends, is taken up institutionally and used publicly for the ends of the community, thus establishing a class of professional magicians. The profession of magic being the most prestigious career available, it attracts the ablest and most ambitious members of society, who soon perceive that it does not work, but support their careers by conscious deception. Eventually, however, the realization becomes general and faith in magic gives way to new ways of thinking as disappointed "primitive philosophers" take refuge in the new hypothesis that unseen beings, like themselves but much more powerful, are the actual arbiters of fate and fortune, requiring propitiation and worship.

The prestigious class of magicians thus becomes the prestigious class of priests, whose world-view passes through various dogmatic metamorphoses and refinement before its final, monotheistic phase is challenged by a new rationalism based on accurate observations and sound theorizing, which permit its superficial dogmas, though not its most basic one, to be replaced by scientific knowledge. The displaced frameworks, however, retain a shadowy presence as "survivals", by virtue of their continued hold over intellects ill-equipped to absorb newer and better ways of thought. In particular, the earliest subspecies of primitive religion—which arise inevitably out of universal magic beliefs and are primarily concerned with community rites intended to assure the fertility of crops—is held to account for a great many survivals preserved as superstitions.

This thesis exerted a powerful aesthetic fascination on many readers and writers—especially those who, repelled in greater or lesser measure by the materialism of modern times, found much to attract them in the notion that humankind once enjoyed a much closer relationship with the natural world and its fertility. Many determinedly anti-progressive thinkers found the notion of "turning back the development clock" very appealing—an aesthetic appeal flamboyantly exemplified by such fantastic extrapolations as Margaret Murray's *The Witch-Cult in Western Europe* (1921).

The Witch-Cult in Western Europe contains no explicit reference to Jules Michelet, Charles Godfrey Leland or James Frazer, although the text is saturated with their ideas. It is conceivable that Murray never read Leland, and reinvented "la vecchia religione" by herself—which would be a remarkable example of imaginative convergence, if it were so—but she was an enthusiastic member of the Folk-Lore Society, at whose meetings she trailed her ideas regarding the witch-cult, and was therefore highly likely to have encountered the ideative substance of *Aradia*, if not the actual text.

Like Michelet, Murray accepts that there really was a secret organization of witches, which really did hold meetings which attracted the hostile attention of the Church. Like Leland, she proposes that these meetings involved the rituals of a pagan fertility religion, whose design closely follows the Frazerian model, which had been superseded—in the natural course of events—by Christianity. In Murray's view, the old religion was not merely a virtually-extinct gypsy religion but the original religion of all Europe, which had persisted far longer in the north than the south, and had survived the conquest of those lands by Christianity, continuing as an "underground movement" covertly supported by many secular leaders. Murray's witches were not rebels against the tyranny of the Church but rather escapists therefrom, quietly attempting to follow their old ways despite the hatred of the representatives of the new mythology. According to Murray, their religion—"the Dianic cult"—was a fertility religion of the kind imagined by Frazer to represent the initial phase of all organized religions.

Unlike Michelet's book, which borrows the tone of sensational journalism, or Leland's, which smacks of literary whimsy, *The Witch-Cult in Western Europe* is a perfect pastiche of scholarly discourse (as befits an academic whose reputation in her own field—Egyptology—remains quite unsullied). It is dry and detailed, with very many references to particular witch-trials, building up the impression of awesomely-scrupulous research and careful analysis. By adding the aura of scholarly exactitude to the aesthetic power of its central thesis the book became widely accepted as the correct "explanation" of the post-Renaissance witch-hunt. Although its spuriousness was appreciated by virtually all contemporary historians who were familiar with the history of witchcraft, it retained its dominance until the Frazerian thesis lost its fashionability, thus robbing Murray's sub-thesis of much of its apparent plausibility.

Apart from its aesthetic qualities and its exploitation of Frazerian mythology, Murray's account had one more factor working in its favor, and that was the fact that it appeared to provide a "rational" account of an episode in history that had come to seemed distinctly irrational. It seemed much easier to many modern readers to believe that the Christian witchfinders had been mistaken than that they had conducted such a long and vicious crusade against an entirely imaginary enemy. Murray's story seemed to make the events of the past more easily comprehensible, in terms of the modern way of thinking. (It is a difficult challenge to the imagination to accept that the people of the past did not share our way of thinking, and that the events which took place then have to be seen to make sense in their terms, not ours.)

How Murray came to concoct such a monumental distortion of history is a minor mystery, but she certainly persuaded herself of its truth. In her first book she was cautious enough to represent all she said as a tentative hypothesis, but by the time she wrote its successor, *The God of the Witches* (1931), and the article on "Witchcraft" that she was invited to write for the *Encyclopaedia Britannica* (editions from 1929-68) she was wholeheartedly committed to it. In her final book, *The Divine King in England* (1952) she extended the exercise in imaginary history to argue that the English Royal Family had been the mainstay of the British witch-cult throughout the Middle Ages, and that the rulers themselves were involved in periodic ritual murder (either as victims or as conspirators in the appointment of surrogate victims).

Murray used a variety of strategies in the attempt to impose her convictions upon the raw material of trial reports and confessions. She began with the bold contention that everyone who had previously written on the subject had been utterly ill-equipped to do so, by virtue of their assumption that the confessions of witches were wholly false. She states (quite wrongly) that contemporary skeptics had no access to first-hand evidence, and that they flatly denied of all statements suggesting supernatural power. In fact, it was Murray who carefully removed from all the confessions she quoted any manifestly fantastic statements that could not be reinterpreted as references to mundane events, calmly stating she had "examined only the recorded facts, without, however, including all the stories of ghosts and other 'occult' phenomena with which all the commentators confuse the subject" and omitting "all reference to charms and spells when performed by one witch alone", thus confining her reportage to "those statements only which show the beliefs, organization, and ritual of a hitherto unrecognized cult.") What this method amounts to is the careful removal from the evidence of everything that conflicts with the theory.

According to Murray, the witch-cult was organized into a series of "covens" (the word is a contraction of "convent", which was sometimes used in Scotland during the period of persecution). Each coven supposedly had thirteen members, led by a male who appeared at the meetings in ceremonial dress, wearing a horned helmet to represent the "horned god". Horned figures had been common in the ancient art of Northern Europe, and had enjoyed a new wave of fashionability in the nineteenth century when numerous *littérateurs* and scholarly fantasies had suggested that they were all avatars of the Great God Pan, the supreme deity of quasi-satanic neo-paganism, but Murray's horned god was recast in a more distinctive mould.

THE DEVIL'S PARTY, BY BRIAN STABLEFORD

Murray drew a great deal of her material from a single set of confessions, offered—allegedly voluntarily—by Isabel Gowdie of Auldearne in 1662. It is in Gowdie's confession, and there alone, that we hear of the rule of thirteen and the male president of the coven (and, for that matter, his female consort, allegedly representative of the Queen of the Fairies). Murray apparently considered Gowdie's confessions—there were four in all—to be especially reliable because they were freely given, although she discounts their more fanciful aspects, which include stories of the metamorphosis of witches into hares, and riding whirlwinds mounted on straws. In fact, Gowdie appears to have been exceptional among accused witches in being literate, and her account includes versions of several well-known tales, including a revision of the legend of Thomas the Rhymer in which she replaces the hero. The formal connection of witch mythology with fairy mythology was not made by anyone else, although there are traces of fairy folklore in many Scottish anecdotes featuring witches, and Diana Purkiss argues in *Troublesome Things: A History of Fairies and Fairy Stories* (2000) that several other Scottish confessions can be read as simple distortions of popular folklore. Murray makes much of this apparent absurdity, proposing that "fairies" might have been relics of a dwarf race driven out of Europe by invaders, surviving in those remote enclaves where Christian witch-finders discovered "witches".

The various chapters of *The Witch-Cult in Western Europe* consist of brief introductory paragraphs baldly stating Murray's position, followed by long catalogues of instances that allegedly "confirm" it. She blithely asserts that here were two kinds of witch-meetings, "Sabbaths" being large-scale convocations, while "Esbats"—a word that occurs only once in the literature, in a confession given in the Basque language to an inquisitor who did not understand that language, although she proposes that it might be derived from the verb "s'esbattre", to frolic—were closed meetings of a inner circle of initiates. The witches' use of "Sabbath", she claims, has no connection with the Jewish term—a blatant falsehood, since the term was obviously borrowed by witch-finders, who also spoke of "witches' synagogues".

The use of speculative etymology to alter the implication of words is a widespread practice among reinterpreters of history; the strategy is used copiously by two of Murray's literary disciples, Michael Harrison and Robert Graves, in works represented as nonfiction. Graves assisted in loading the Anglo-Saxon word *wicca* with hitherto-unsuspected implications, redefining it as "a magician who weakens the power of evil" and thus greatly encouraging its adoption by lifestyle fantasies like Gerald Gardner, who chose the word as the name of his hypothetical Murrayesque witch-religion. The literary influence of Murray's thesis was considerable and swift; it was redeployed in 1927 by no less a writer than John Buchan, in *Witch Wood* (1927), although the arch-conservative Buchan refuses to agree with Murray that cultists of the kind she described could possibly have been harmless, let alone virtuous. Its influence on further scholarly fantasy was similarly significant; although Graves' *The White Goddess* (1948) was by far the most influential book to take its influence aboard it permeated many other texts, including *The Mysteries of Britain* (1928), by the most prolific scholarly fantasist of his era, Lewis Spence.

The popular success of Murray's books distressed many historians, and brought forth a number of vituperative attacks on her work. Some writers took pains to refute the thesis, while others dismissed it with a few choice insults as unworthy of consideration. Few, however, took the trouble to wonder why such a blatantly ill-supported theory should have excited such tremendous popular interest—an interest taken to an unusual extreme by lifestyle fantasists who founded covens of witches in order to act out the Murray thesis. This will be discussed at much greater length in the next chapter, but one can hardly see such a phenomenon as the mere result of unwary belief in a pseudoscholarly thesis. Such inventions obviously answer some kind of psychological need in the people who go in for them, and the utility of Murrayesque mythology in answering this need implies that the success of the thesis was due to factors above and beyond its apparent rational plausibility or the gullibility of the general public.

An Apology for Witch-Hunters

Five years after the appearance of *The Witch-Cult in Western Europe* Montague Summers published *The History of Witchcraft and Demonology* (1926). Like Murray, Summers was an outspoken rebel against traditional skepticism, who chose to accept the substantial truth of the confessions offered by accused witches and who went on to publish several more books in support of his own particular thesis. He too played down the element of the fantastic in the confessions, but not nearly to the same extent, because his contention was that the witches really were exactly what the inquisitors considered them to be—a heretical cult dedicated to the worship of

Satan and the destruction of Christendom—and he was quite prepared to believe that, with Satan's aid, witches really could and did work magic.

Summers was first ordained in the Anglican Church but was subsequently converted to Catholicism, and became possessed of the passionate self-justificatory extremism characteristic of the enthusiastic convert. He associated skepticism with anti-Catholicism (as it was. indeed, associated in the work of such contemporary skeptics as Weyer and Scot and such modern historians as H. C. Lea) and therefore considered it to be virtually blasphemous.

In Summers' eyes. men like Sprenger and Kramer, Bodin, Rémy and Boguet became heroes who had labored to rid the world of a terrible scourge, and had succeeded for a time, although the spread of Protestant heresy and atheism had prevented the completion their work, allowing witchcraft and demonology to resurface again in new disguises; he was even more scathing about spiritualism than the other ideological spin-off of the occult revival. Although he was undoubtedly familiar with much of the scholarly fantasy assembled by antiquarians in connection with that movement, as well as more recent popularizations like Lewis Spence's *Encyclopedia of Occultism* (1920), he was scornful of such work and preferred to hark back to "original sources".

It was not only witchcraft itself that Summers considered to have been a dark and dreadful conspiracy, but the history of witchcraft. He considered that his "correction" of previous misrepresentations amounted to a kind of moral crusade against the "moral cowardice" of his predecessors, whose delicate minds had prevented them from reporting the full horror of witches' rites and depredations. Summers made certain that no one could ever accuse *him* of fearing to dwell at length on the most repulsive and scandalous aspects of witchcraft; his preoccupation with the obscene and horrific aspects of confessions rivals Pierre de Lancre's—de Lancre being, of course, one of the heroes he admired most fervently.

In time, Summers' preoccupation with such imagery extended far beyond the history of witchcraft. He became one of the foremost experts on literary tales of horror, compiling an enormous bibliography of Gothic Novels and editing two anthologies of horror stories (the final chapter of *The History of Witchcraft and Demonology* is a detailed study of the "The Witch in Dramatic Literature"). He also compiled histories of the legends and literature relating to vampires and werewolves. He was a true connoisseur of nightmares, and although it would be unfair to allege that he was unable to distinguish fact from fiction, it is probably not unreasonable to suggest that, in terms of the psychological functions served by his fascination with the morbid and the horrific, the distinction did not much matter to him.

There is a constant prevarication in Summers' pseudoscholarly work between credulity and caution. He recognizes, like Guazzo, that certain aspects of witch-mythology (for instance, broomstick-riding) are hopelessly implausible, and therefore takes pains to establish that his case does not depend on acceptance of such stories. He always takes care, however, to add notes to the effect that he does not consider such things to be impossible in theory. He always wants to have his cake and eat it too: to credit the role of hallucination in order not to alienate the mildly skeptical members of his audience, while also insisting on the very real power and menace of the Devil. He is not overly concerned with what his readers believe with regard to the mythology of the witch-hunt, as long as they can be persuaded to accept the essential claim that there *were* witches, and that they *did* constitute a massive conspiracy dedicated to the overthrow of Christendom.

In this basic contention Summers agrees with Michelet that the witch-cult was a kind of rebellion, but he differs extremely in his moral and political perspective. The fervently anti-clerical radical Michelet took it for granted that all rebels are unsung heroes, while he arch-conservative Catholic convert Summers sees them as double-dyed villains. Seen in this light, the Murray thesis provides an interesting *via media* between Michelet and Summers; Murray is neither a fervent radical nor an arch-conservative but a curious combination of the two, of a kind which has lately become familiar: a nostalgic conservationist. She regrets the passing of the old world, but regards it as sadly inevitable, and therefore makes of witch-persecution neither a vile oppression nor a holy crusade, but a kind of tragedy. Her keen sense of theatre is shown by her determination to absorb into her thesis the dramatic figures and events of history and her exaggerated regard for the importance of fairy mythology. Her nostalgic regard for the past and its legends sits well with her profession of Egyptology, whose focus of concern is the exploration and imaginative reconstruction of a long-lost civilization.

Summers was an idiosyncratic and isolated figure, whose hopeless desire to sell rationalistic audience a set of nightmares three hundred years out of date seems decidedly eccentric. As an unorthodox scholar he found very few disciples—far fewer than Murray—but his labours were not entirely unsupported. Summers' thesis regarding the continuing danger posed by Satanism and black magic was extrapolated by Theda Kenyon's *Witches Still Live* (1927), which carefully takes aboard Margaret Murray's ideas, by the sensationalist popularizer of occult themes Elliott O'Donnell, most notably in *Strange Cults and Secret Societies of Modern London* (1934) and by a third writer heavily influenced by both, William B. Seabrook, author of *Witchcraft: Its Power in the World Today* (1941).

The most elaborate repetition of Summers' thesis was Rollo Ahmed's *The Black Art* (1936), which presumably combined its influence with O'Donnell's to fuel sensationalist British tabloid reportage in the 1940s. The credulous acceptance of this alarmist chain of thought extended far enough to claim the support of a British policeman, Robert Fabian, who published a series of best-selling memoirs that established him as a minor media celebrity, "Fabian of the Yard"; Fabian included a chapter on the threat of black magic in his summary of lessons learned as a member of the Vice Squad..

As might be expected, Summers influence on literature was very considerable; O'Donnell's development of ideas similar to his are more prominent in his fiction—including *The Sorcery Club* (1912), which was published long before Summers' *History*, although Summers influence in clearly manifest in *The Dead Riders* (1952)—than they are in his supposed non-fiction. Far the most successful of Summers' literary acolytes was, however, Dennis Wheatley, who appropriated his mythology lock, stock and barrel into the series begun with *The Devil Rides Out* and deftly combined it with a host of ideas borrowed from Aleister Crowley to create a new brand of thriller fiction. Wheatley's main source of information seems to have been Rollo Ahmed, and he appears to have secured publication for *The Black Art* as a kind of "non-fiction companion" to *The Devil Rides Out*.

Although the books in Wheatley's relevant series celebrate the charisma of the powerful magician, they remain fervently adamant about the anarchic threat posed by contemporary Satanic magic to the social and political order. Wheatley seems to have launched this thread of his literary career in a spirit of total cynicism, but may ultimately have fallen prey to his own inventions; in interviews given shortly before he died in 1977 he claimed to believe sincerely and wholeheartedly that black magic was unutterably dangerous, and that Satan's most devoted modern disciples could be found in Soviet Union, including the Kremlin's corridors of power. In the wide-ranging scholarly fantasy *Le Matin des magiciens* (1960; tr. as *The Morning of the Magicians*), Louis Pauwels and Jacques Bergier took a similarly bold approach to twentieth-century politics when they detailed a conspicuous fondness for pagan mysticism in the upper echelons of the Third Reich.

The scrupulous historians who became angry with Murray simply treated Summers as a joke. No one ever really supposed that his account of the great witch-hunt was a true one, but the account itself, and its concomitant beliefs about Satanism in the contemporary world, still survive and thrive in literary fantasies. Elements of Summers' thesis and aspects of his research were also co-opted, directly or indirectly, into popular journalistic accounts of the history of witchcraft used to support the kinds of scare stories and pornographic gossip that make good tabloid copy.

The Continued Proliferation of Scholarly Fantasies

The three schools of thought embodied by Michelet, Murray and Summers represent the three main varieties of scholarly fantasy that supply unorthodox viewpoints from which to approach the history of witchcraft. Because of their wholeheartedness, they remain more-or-less distinct from scrupulous historical studies, but even the efforts of the most scrupulous historians retain their own elements of bias, their own narrative thrust, and their own idiosyncratic emphases. Henry Charles Lea, who was undoubtedly a scrupulous and assiduous scholar, displays such a keen hostility to Catholicism in his commentaries that he is always disposed to try to prove that all the cruelties of the witch-hunt were invented and initiated by Catholics, and that theirs was the true responsibility, even though Protestants imitated them.

All historians have preconceptions—although the preconceptions of good historians remain malleable and sensitive to the real implications of the data—and these preconceptions inevitably filter the data in order to arrange and organize it, and to make it more coherent. The kind of skepticism that has been taken for granted throughout this study is one such preconception, and there are many people who would considered it excessive or flatly disagree with it. The grey area that exists between conscientious historical works by such writers as Lea, C. Lestrange Ewen, Norman Cohn, and Étienne Delcambre, on the one hand, and such evidently fantastic works as those written by Michelet, Murray and Summers on the other, is very considerable.

Because of the success of Murray's ideas there is an especially numerous group of writers who refuse to accept her theories uncritically, but who nevertheless feel that there "must be something in it". For instance, there is a comprehensive and deadly demolition of the superstructure of Murray's thesis in Elliot Rose's *A Razor for a Goat* (1962). Having pointed out the flaws in Murray's argument, however, Rose builds his own esoteric thesis on the same basic assumption—that there really must have been a witch-cult and that there must be *some* substance of truth in the mythology of the Sabbat. Rose rejects Murray's fertility cult only to reconstitute her secret society of witches as an irreverent opposition to Christianity whose leaders were wandering scholars and strolling players called goliards; he suggests that these men became "witch-masters", organizing anti-Christian ceremonies whose essential appeal was that they were fun, involving sex and the use of hallucinogenic drugs for hedonistic purposes. Rose does not push this hypothesis too hard, and is far from being dogmatic about it; his interest in antiquity is altogether more lively and less nostalgic than Murray's, and this was presumably why he favored a rather different plot for his fanciful narrative.

Other historians who accepted the basic assumption underlying Murray's thesis while rejecting much of its superstructure included Arno Runeberg and Jeffrey Russell. Runeberg, in *Witches, Demons and Fertility Magic* (1947) accepted the fertility-cult thesis in order to account for some elements of Sabbat mythology as "survivals" but rejected the idea that an organized fertility religion still existed in Medieval times. His Sabbats are meetings of magicians who have come to believe that their spells and rituals, preserved by oral tradition, really are empowered by Satan. Russell, in *Witchcraft in the Middle Ages* (1972) also accepted the fertility-cult theory, though he deliberately de-emphasized it, claiming that the witches were primarily an anti-Christian sect in covert but active rebellion. Because of his caution in elaborating this thesis, and his elegant use of the data, his is perhaps the most plausible and persuasive of all the books based on the assumption that there really was a witch-cult; he followed up his first study with a series of volumes tracking the evolution of the Devil from pre-Christian sources to the modern era. The fact remains, however, that the assumption that there ever was any organized witch-cult is extremely dubious, and no such hypothesis is required to explain the pattern of events.

In addition to these serious attempts to argue a case related to the Murray thesis, journalistic accounts draw upon it whenever it seems convenient, just as they draw upon Summers' work. There is a constant market for easy-to-read books about the more sensational aspects of history; the further scholarly fantasies proliferate, the more scope is opened up for pick-and-mix selections of their juicier elements, which can easily muster a veneer of scholarship by the promiscuous citation of secondary sources. One thing that the reader of such works must always bear in mind is that, in connection with this subject, as with any and every subject connected with magic (especially when it goes under new names), there is always a large number of writers who desire to present fantasies as facts, precisely because the fantasies are far more dramatic than the facts, and are made all the more dramatic if one accepts them *as* facts. Many popular "histories of Satanism" have all the virtues of effective fantasy fiction, simply because they *are* works of fantasy fiction, which seek to increase their effect by claming to be true, after the fashion of the folkloristic fantasies out of which the real history of Satanic abuse originally grew.

Many people, for various aesthetic and ideological reasons, prefer the fantastic versions of history to the factual ones even when they know how to tell the difference. It requires a very determined self-discipline to assert that the truth, however complicated or tedious or difficult to understand it may prove to be, is always preferable to a glamorous and seductive lie. That is why there is such an abundance of imaginative space available to be colonized by lifestyle fantasists.

VII.

LIFESTYLE FANTASIES

The Attraction of Fantasized Lifestyles

As with history, all lifestyle is to some extent fantasy; indeed, the very concept of a "lifestyle" is a fantasy of sorts. Although we commonly speak of "fantasy" and "real life" as though they were mutually-exclusive opposites, everyday life actually offers considerable scope for the indulgence of fantasies of various kinds. Private daydreams offer us respite from the stresses and strains of wearisome responsibility, and people act out collective fantasies in conversation and in the context of various kinds of play. Social life requires everyone to maintain an "image" to present in public, which may differ considerably from the private images people have of themselves; the management of both kinds of images is an essentially theatrical business, which involves plotting and presenting narratives in ways that routinely attempt to make them more coherent, more interesting and more dramatic.

There is, therefore, a trivial sense in which everyone is a lifestyle fantasist; although most publicly-presented lifestyle fantasies are thoroughly and determinedly mundane and conventional, it seems probable that many people are more adventurous in constructing private images of themselves, and more adventurous imagery sometimes emerges into public self-representations. Some lifestyle fantasies do, therefore, taken on literal elements of fantasy and the supernatural, and it is fantasies of these kinds that are relevant to the topic of this book,

There is nothing abnormal or unhealthy about fantasizing, but most people guard the secrecy of their daydreams very jealously. It is difficult to imagine life without daydreaming, because such activity provides a means of planning future projects as well as an outlet for frustrations that build up in the course of our everyday routines. Daydreams provide a secure arena for the expression of our wildest hopes of success, and for the venting of our spite in fantasies of revenge. The high value that people place on the collective fantasies of play is evident in the glamour and fame that accrue to skilled sportsmen and actors—far more than ever accrues to the engineers and entrepreneurs whose labor provides us with the material goods we need to sustain our lives.

Just as there is a grey area where authentic scholarship and scholarly fantasies overlap, so there is a grey area where conventional lifestyles and fantasized lifestyles overlap. Just as there are scholarly fantasies which can be clearly recognized for what they are, so there are fantasized lifestyles that can clearly be recognized for what they are. The history and anthropology of such lifestyles is, however, greatly confused by the different degrees to which societies license conventional magical careers. Even in contemporary Western society—where priests are, for the most part, not credited with any special supernatural powers, and where belief in the supernatural is not intellectually respectable—there is no shortage of unorthodox healers and diviners, in whom enough people put their trust to enable them to enjoy highly successful careers, both commercially and in terms of prestige.

Although few people nowadays claim to be alchemists, there was a time when virtually all officially-sanctioned European physicians used alchemical methods of treatment, just as many of them used astrological methods of diagnosis. Such official sanction did not, however, entirely protect them from "persecution by derision" by cynics who believed (correctly) that their methods were not to be trusted—and it is not uncommon for people to think the same of modern physicians, no matter how well-armed they may be with scientifically-credited potions. The history of lifestyle fantasy is intimately entangled with the history of derision, and examples of fantasized lifestyles readily illustrate the fact that derision is a two-edged sword.

The fact that modern astrologers and diviners are routinely subjected to abuse and scorn does not inhibit them from accumulating wealth and prestige, and may actually assist them by supplying a gloss of martyrdom. All showmanship is suspect, but rewards often accrue to those prepared to take it to extremes, as the egregiously overdressed and unashamedly unctuous pianist Liberace cannily observed when he described his reaction to scathing criticism by declaring that he "cried all the way to the bank".

THE DEVIL'S PARTY, BY BRIAN STABLEFORD

The rewards of showmanship not only help to explain why lifestyle fantasies often become fantasized, but also why such fantasization sometimes proceeds to remarkable extremes. Such extremism is rare not because it is so bizarre as to verge on madness, but because it loses its effect entirely when it become commonplace; aspects of lifestyle that are widely adopted become conventional by definition, ceasing to qualify as showmanship and becoming a mere matter of following fashion. This does not prevent fantasized lifestyles from enjoying bouts of fashionability, but the fashionability in question is calculatedly esoteric and the bouts are inevitably short-lived. The determined maintenance of a fantasized lifestyle over a long period of time is, by necessity, practiced by exceptional and dedicated social outsiders. It the essential ambivalence of tolerance and derision that continually attracts people to bid for the particular glamour associated with the inheritors of imaginary age-old traditions of Satanist magic and pagan witchcraft.

The preliterate tribesman who aspires to be a witch-doctor or a shaman is selecting a career recognized by his society as being both possible and legitimate. Not only does he believe in the possibility and propriety of being a magician, but his fellows accept it and confirm his status within the group. Even so, it is not an *entirely* conventional career; even when he obtains the maximum possible social support, the witch-doctor or shaman is always regarded as a man apart, to be regarded with suspicion and anxiety as well as awe and gratitude. No lifestyle that incorporates supernatural aspects can ever be regarded as mundane, because the supernatural is, by definition, that which extends beyond the mundane.

The balance between the likely effects of suspicion and anxiety, on the one hand, and the rewards of awe and gratitude on the other, vary considerably from place to place and from time to time. The former are inevitably exaggerated when orthodoxy is fearful of the corrosions of heresy and willing to subject heretics to extreme penalties. Even so, it is not so very surprising that a man like Marsilio Ficino might attempt to negotiate a path through the hazards of being charged with heresy in order to obtain the rewards of a master magician, nor that others would follow in his footsteps, gladly taking advantage of such apologetic impostures as the Hermetic Tradition.

The *Corpus Hermeticum* that Ficino found so useful and inspiring was exposed as a fraud in 1614 by Isaac Casaubon, who traced many of its sources and identified some of its anachronisms, but Casaubon's skepticism had no more effect than Reginald Scot's.

THE DEVIL'S PARTY, BY BRIAN STABLEFORD

Time had, in any case, moved on; the same year saw the emergence of a new version of Hermetic mythology, which made its debut in a pamphlet generally known as the *Fama Fraternitus*. The pamphlet offered a brief biography of a magician named Christian Rosenkreutz [Christian Rosy-Cross], whose initiation into Hermetic secrets was described in *Confessio Frateritas* (1615) and the ostentatiously allegorical *Chymische Hochzeit Christiani Rosenkreuz* (1616; tr. as *The Heretick Romance; or, the Chymical Wedding*). The third item was signed by Johann Valentin Andreae, who was later to publish the Utopian romance *Christianopolis* (1619); he probably wrote all three.

These "Rosicrucian" pamphlets excited an enormous amount of attention; would-be initiates searched high and low for the mysterious Brotherhood of the Rosy Cross. One early enthusiast was the English philosopher Robert Fludd, who published two apologias for the Brotherhood before setting out to write his own encyclopedia of the macrocosm and microcosm in 1617-26. His account of the macrocosm fused the Aristotelian cosmology of the Church with neo-Platonic ideas and infusions from the Kabbalah, while his account of the human microcosm—which he never completed—attempted to synthesize contemporary anatomy, mystical interpretations of the body's proportions, astrological linkages between various organs and the signs of the zodiac, neo-Pythagorean theories of musical harmony and other mystical correspondences.

A similar spirit of encyclopedic inclusivity was represented in the work of the Jesuit Athanasius Kircher, whose works included two visionary "ecstatic journeys" (1656-7) describing excursions through the heavenly macrocosm and the Earthly microcosm, attempting to bind the entire spectrum of human knowledge into a coherent whole—a whole whose mystical connections, embodied in exotic symbolism and geometrical patterns, seemed increasingly precarious as Classical cosmology was comprehensively devastated by the findings of telescopic astronomy. As we have already seen, however, the Hermetic tradition and its Rosicrucian variant did not disappear entirely, and their eventual resurgence was always inevitable, because rather than in spite of the increasing orthodoxy of its ideological opposition.

Class Divisions in Magical Lifestyle Fantasy

In the days before the great witch-hunt began, healers and diviners working in the lower strata of Christian society were probably able to claim a considerable degree of legitimacy in terms of local custom and tradition, no matter how strongly the Roman Church may have disapproved of them. It seems equally likely that some contrived to continue working during the explosion of full-blooded persecution, in spite of the hazards it posed. These "white witches" and "cunning men" would have represented themselves as entirely benign, and would have been broadly accepted as such by their clients, but they would have continued to suffer the same suspicions and anxieties that afflict all such careers; they must have become favorite targets of accusations and denunciations in consequence, although they must have regarded such accusations and denunciations as horribly unjust and ungrateful. It must have been difficult, even with the aid of torture, to convince such individuals that they really had been willing pawns of Satan.

Michelet's allegation that the existence of widespread belief in the power of Satanic magic would inevitably have encouraged some people to try it is probably true, but there is not an atom of evidence that folk-healers and diviners were any more likely to investigate the possibilities of Satanic magic than anyone else; the logic of their situation suggests that they were less likely to do so, by virtue of their ready-made magical beliefs, and less likely than others to band together for any such purpose. Members of the lower social classes were, in general, probably less inclined to collective activities of that sort than people of higher status who were more conscious of the theatrical aspects of their performances.

The class division that separated highly-placed intellectuals like Marsilio Ficino, J. V. Andreae and Robert Fludd from folk-healers and other kinds of people likely to be accused of witchcraft continued to influence the form of lifestyle fantasies and the likelihood of their adoption long after the witch-hunt had ended. Upper class magicians and would-be witches from humbler backgrounds were mostly content to mimic their equivalent predecessors, but lifestyle fantasy is intrinsically prone to borrowing and adaptation, so there was a cetin amount of ideative transfer—a process assisted by the relative lack of discrimination manifest in some denigratory and derisory accounts of what magicians and witches allegedly did.

This process of appropriation is luridly exemplified by the later evolution of the image of the witches' Sabbat. Although it is highly unlikely that anything remotely similar actually took place during the witch-hunt, Sabbats of a sort subsequently became a key element of lifestyle fantasies involving witchcraft, and the popularity of such scholarly fantasies as Jules Michelet's and Margaret Murray's was greatly assisted by their reconstructions of the idea of the Sabbat. Equally significantly, revised versions of the Sabbat were increasingly incorporated into intrinsically aristocratic lifestyle fantasies, where the Sabbat was gradually transformed—by a strange collaboration of practitioners and their denigrators—into the Black Mass.

The foundations of the mythology of the aristocratic Black Mass were laid by one of the most sensational of all sorcery trials, usually known as the affair of the *Chambre Ardente* after the enquiry that investigated it, which was conducted by officers of Louis XIV of France. The enquiry in question was initiated because of an "epidemic" of poisoning in the highest strata of French society; it opened in 1679 and closed in 1682. In the beginning, the investigators' sole aim was to trace the poisons back to their suppliers, who turned out—according to evidence secured by vigorous interrogation—to be a socially-stratified "crime-ring" including noblemen, professionals and hired agents. The actual distributors of the poisons posed as magicians and fortune-tellers, and were also involved in procuring abortions and similar clandestine "services".

In following through this complex web of criminal activity, the court of enquiry began to extract increasingly bizarre confessions and denunciations. One of the fortune-tellers they tortured, Catherine Deshayes, alias La Voisin, refused to confess and was eventually burned without having admitted anything—but others were willing to talk about her at some length. The enquiry took an unexpected turn when, after various routine allegations of sorcery had been made, allegations were made concerning La Voisin's involvement in pseudo-religious rites addressed to Satan. These were said to take the form of calculated parodies of the Catholic mass, at which renegade priests officiated, using the bodies of naked women as altars. At these "black masses", it was said, babies were sacrificed to Satan and various other atrocities were perpetrated. La Voisin's daughter and an aged hunchback, the Abbé Guibourg, ultimately became the star witnesses in the enquiry, producing ever-more horrible and elaborate tales of obscenity and abomination. Louis XIV's one-time mistress, Madame de Montespan, was implicated by a charge that she had intended to poison the king and the favorite who had displaced her, thus assuring the affair its status as an unprecedented *cause célèbre*.

This trial was the only one of its kind in the seventeenth century, and it is difficult to know exactly what to make of it. It might be simply a rare upper-class version of the standard witch-trial, with the confessions being correspondingly more lurid and blasphemously imaginative but no less imaginary. The descriptions which it produced of the parodic Satanist mass may simply be evidence of the ingenuity and vividness of educated imaginations. Although we cannot know whether the members of La Voisin's circle really did go in for such performances, however, subsequent developments in the use of theatrical black masses suggest that it is not entirely implausible that they might have, given the occasional tendency of aristocrats to think themselves entirely above matters of commonplace morality. If they did, they may not have done so with the intention of attaining any particular worldly ends—or, at least, not wholly for that purpose; they may well have been indulging in blasphemy for blasphemy's sake.

All black masses are more accurately regarded as extreme forms of hedonistic self-indulgence than as exercises in practical sorcery. The concept itself was obviously designed to support its theatrical and sensational aspects, and its central image—the naked woman employed as an altar—is a flamboyant *coup de théâtre*. Something so uniquely shocking and thrilling must have been invented *in order* to be shocking and thrilling, rather than acquiring these properties by accident as the side-effects of some other purpose. Even if we must entertain some doubts as to the possible authenticity of the seventeenth century origins of the black mass, there can be none at all about its later manifestations, which were lifestyle fantasy at its purest, simplest and most extreme.

The black mass as a species of theatrical performance was adopted by several groups of young aristocrats during the eighteenth century, which are generally known by the name of "Hellfire Clubs". The organization that actually adopted that title met at the George and Vulture Inn in London, but the name was borrowed by denigrators of the Friars of St. Francis of Wycombe, established by Sir Francis Dashwood at Medmenham Abbey in 1752. Another Hellfire Club that generated a fine crop of shocking anecdotes was one that met in the Eagle Tavern in Dublin, founded by the Earl of Rosse.

The activities of these groups were play-acting and sensation-seeking, many of the ceremonies being directed to Aphrodite rather than to Satan, but their members had no objection to casual Satanism and parodies of the Catholic mass. Rumor has probably exaggerated them out of all proportion, but the rites in question were essentially orgies. Membership in such organizations did no harm to the orthodox careers of those involved; Dashwood went on to serve as chancellor of the exchequer and became postmaster-general after succeeding to the Lords as Baron le Despencer. This kind of extremism in rebellion against traditional morality was, of course, made possible by the advance of rationalism, although it was usually confined to those whose position in society rendered them immune to criticism and retribution.

The element of Satanism in this kind of fake rite is dispensable, and many similar ceremonies were designed in which the calculatedly blasphemous element was removed in favor of a more scholarly esotericism, but the black mass itself retained a particular status and affection in the fantasies of practitioners as well as commentators who consented to be shocked by it. The horrified reactions of such commentators as Julian Osgood Field and Joris-Karl Huysmans, of course, greatly encouraged further activities of that sort.

Although the scandalous quality of the black mass has ensured its survival as one of the mainstays of lifestyle fantasy, its key elements also spread to other kinds of gathering. The American occultist P. B. Randolph, who was active in the mid-nineteenth century founded a new "esoteric tradition" that cut to the heart of the matter by establishing sexual intercourse as a pseudomagical rite, and many other lifestyle fantasists similarly retained the naked human altar while disposing of Satan; the popularity of Eastern "Tantric magic" in twentieth-century lifestyle fantasy was similarly encouraged by its orgiastic potential.

Aristocratic Lifestyle Fantasies and the Occult Revival

The history of the black mass and its spin-off should not deflect attention away from the fact that there is far more to lifestyle fantasy than mere sensation-seeking. Many would-be scholar-magicians emphasize asceticism rather than elf-indulgence, and Marsilio Ficino's preoccupation with the necessity for magicians to "purify" themselves remains as strong as the fascination of naked human altars. Magicians who rejoice in representing themselves as austere and quietly dignified seekers of wisdom and enlightenment, patiently penetrating ancient mysteries and working slowly towards some ultimate "secret of the universe" also belong to the upper-class intellectual tradition, although that tradition became more democratic in the twentieth century.

The quest of the Medieval alchemists who searched for the elixir of life and a means to turn base metal into gold has been widely reconstrued by scholarly fantasists as a disguised quest for spiritual enlightenment, and a great many modern lifestyle fantasists represent their own magical impostures in exactly that fashion. The presumed nature of such a quest requires long and deep absorption in esoteric texts, and the number of supposedly-esoteric texts released into the mass market by enterprising publishers during the nineteenth-century occult revival multiplied vastly in response, in spite of the implicit paradoxicality of the enterprise. The presumed nature of the task similarly encourages practitioners to represent themselves as members of esoteric organizations; although the logic of the situation favors wholly imaginary organizations (like the original Rosicrucian Brotherhood) over real ones—because any such organization that becomes manifest automatically fails the ultimate test of esotericism—actual Orders similarly began to spring up in considerable profusion during the occult revival.

The principal organizational model of such esoteric orders was provided by the Freemasons. Freemasonry probably originated in Scotland at the end of the sixteenth century, as an evolution of one of the craft guilds that were powerful institutions of the day, many of which had elaborate ritual livery and rites of initiation. While most such guilds became functional professional organizations, however, the Freemasons exaggerated and further elaborated the symbolic aspects of their rituals. In the eighteenth century, when their "secrets" were first "exposed" in a critical tract entitled *The Grand Mystery Laid Open* (1726) they reacted defensively and conservatively, further exaggerating this aspect of their conduct—a move seemingly licensed when the nineteenth-century occult revival gave a new gloss to such "ancient traditions".

Most of the neo-Rosicrucian organizations founded in the nineteenth century—the first in Britain seems to have been a Masonic splinter-group known as the Societas Rosicruciana in Anglia, *circa* 1865—similarly described their units as "lodges" and modelled their ceremonies very closely on Masonic rites. The Masonic habit of describing their rituals as "the Craft"—a hangover from the guild era—was also carried forward by some workers of allegedly-magical rites, preserving that title for widespread adoption by twentieth-century lifestyle fantasists in connection with witchcraft.

The neo-Rosicrucian society that eventually recruited the most members (although that would be the antithesis of success in some eyes) was the acronymic AMORC, founded in the USA by H. Spencer Lewis in 1915, which advertised widely in popular magazines, offering access to the secrets of the universe at very reasonable prices. The hardihood of this particular society was helped by the fact that Spencer Lewis, like Margaret Murray, was invited to contribute to the fourteenth edition of the Encyclopedia Britannica in 1929, on the grounds that he appeared to be the world's leading "expert" on Rosicrucianism. Nineteenth-century European Rosicrucians, however, would have been utterly horrified by this Americanization and commercialization.

The lifestyle fantasies encouraged by the occult novels of Edward Bulwer-Lytton and the scholarly fantasies of Éliphas Lévi had become so widespread even before the advent of Spencer Lewis that the first move made by all ambitious fantasists was to distance themselves from neo-Rosicrucianism, so the latter part of the nineteenth century saw a whole series of "new revelations" channeled from a rich variety of idiosyncratic occult sources. By far the most successful of these new revelations was cobbled together by Helena Blavatsky, whose *The Secret Doctrine: The Synthesis of Science, Religion, and Philosophy*, published in 1888, gave birth to the new religion of Theosophy. Madame Blavatsky's close associate A. P. Sinnett had earlier written a best-selling guide-book to *The Occult World* (1881), which popularized Éliphas Lévi's ideas in England and may have provided the primary inspiration for the founding of the Order of the Golden Dawn, which also became active in 1888 (as did the Society for Psychical Research).

The Order of the Golden Dawn was a direct successor of the Societas Rosicruciana in Anglia; three of its four founders—Samuel Liddell Mathers (who also signed himself S. Macgregor Mathers), W. Wynn Westcott and William Woodman—had been members of the earlier organization and all four of them were freemasons. Although Woodman was the prime mover it was Mathers and Westcott, who had also been members of the Hermetic Society, who became the driving force of the new order, which allegedly resulted from the "discovery" in an antiquarian bookshop of a new set of initiation rituals by means of which its members could set themselves on the ladder of mystical enlightenment. One of the manuscripts in this hoard allegedly put the order in touch with the "original" German Rosicrucian society, with which a postal correspondence was established—although it ceased in 1891 and the order continued its quest for enlightenment by means of its own distinctive path. One of its innovations was the "discovery" in John Dee's "records"—as posthumously issued by Meric Casaubon—of an "Enochian language" used to communicate with the spirit world.

The Golden Dawn was soon split by internal arguments, but the organization retained a crucial significance in the history of lifestyle fantasy by virtue of the number of famous people who passed through it, including such notable literary men as W. B. Yeats, A. E. Waite, Arthur Machen, Edgar Jepson, and J. W. Brodie-Innes, and several individuals who subsequently founded magical societies of their own. The importance of the Golden Dawn was further enhanced by the contribution its members made to the tradition of scholarly fantasy; Mathers and Waite were indefatigable translators of old magical works and theorists of magic. Few of these individuals were authentic aristocrats, but they were all authentic intellectuals, and that only served to emphasize their elitist ambitions.

The most notorious of those who used the Golden Dawn as a springboard for their own lifestyle fantasies was Aleister Crowley, whose aristocratic pretensions carried more weight than most, because rather than in spite of the fact that he frittered away the fortune he inherited. Crowley went on from the Golden Dawn to form the Astrum Argentum, which was little more than a carbon copy, before becoming more interested in sexual magic and founding the Ordo Templi Orientis. Although he was scornful of mere Satanism, preferring—like many other nineteenth-century neo-pagans—to revere the Greek god Pan, Crowley was enthusiastic to court a reputation as "the most evil man in the world" and to wear the nickname the Great Beast, so he became the archetype of the twentieth-century Satanist, the model and inspiration of countless literary representations—most notably those in W. Somerset Maugham's *The Magician* (1908) and Edgar Jepson's *No. 19* (1910).

Another influential "graduate" of one the Golden Dawn's splinter-groups was a former Christian Scientist and Theosophist named Violet Firth, who renamed herself Dion Fortune and founded the Fraternity of the Inner Light. Crowley and Fortune were both prolific writers of fiction themselves, but whereas Firth seemingly used Crowley—along with D. H. Lawrence—as a model to provide counterparts to her female magicians in blatant wish-fulfillment fantasies, Crowley refused to share center-stage in his novels with anyone. His poetry and short fiction were, however, much more wide-ranging than Dion Fortune's, and mostly of higher quality. The literary legacy of the Golden Dawn far outweighed its legacy in lifestyle fantasy, although several other graduates of its splinter-groups incorporated elements of lifestyle fantasy into careers that were primarily literary, including Evelyn Underhill and Charles Williams.

Although Dion Fortune exercised a considerable influence on subsequent lifestyle fantasists it was the exhibitionist Crowley who succeeded in becoming the most important magical legend of his own lifetime, thus ensuring that his posthumous reputation could only grow further by the accretion of rumor and the endeavors of his imitators. He was a great inspiration to other lifestyle fantasists, including many would-be Satanists and—perhaps more significantly, albeit more obliquely—the people primarily responsible for the resurrection of witchcraft as a twentieth-century lifestyle fantasy.

Revisionist Witchcraft

Gerald Brousseau Gardner was born in 1884 and spent the years 1900-37 in the Far East as a rubber planter and customs officer. Following his retirement he returned to England, becoming active in the Folk-Lore Society and joining a pseudo-Rosicrucian organization. It was alleged by others that he was personally acquainted with Aleister Crowley for some years, but the two probably did not meet until 1946. In either case, Gardner obviously took considerable inspiration from Crowley's example; even so, when the time came for him to found his own occult organization, he took great care to distance himself from carbon copy Crowleyites and Fortunesque Kabbalists; instead, he took his inspiration from more recent scholarly fantasy, and "discovered" Murrayite witch-cults still flourishing in rural Britain.

Hypothetical discoveries of this sort had previously been featured in works of fiction, including numerous thrillers about the discovery, often by amateur detectives, of Satanist cults. Examples more closely resembling Murrayesque cults were much rarer, although Edgar Jepson's "The Resurgent Mysteries" (1911) is a remarkable anticipation of Murray's thesis and Signe Toksvig's *The Last Devil* (1927) was a rapid response to its publication. Gardner initially took the same route, publishing a novel called *High Magic's Aid* (1949) under the pseudonym "Scire". The novel was a commercial failure, but Gardner swiftly followed it up with a "non-fiction" book entitled *Witchcraft Today* (1951), which told of his encounter with a modern coven and his initiation into it. The book was equipped with an introduction by Margaret Murray, who appears to have taken it perfectly seriously as a final "proof" of her thesis.

The most notable element introduced into Murray's witch-mythology by Gardner was the "discovery" that witches conducted their rites in the nude. The rites themselves, he claimed, were contained in a grimoire called *The Book of Shadows* which every initiate witch had to copy out by hand, and which was of incalculable antiquity. Gardner presumably intended its text to remain a secret, for the eyes of his new recruits only, but versions of it eventually

193

appeared in print, the first of them issued by Charles Cardell in 1964. The published versions expose *The Book of Shadows* as a blatant fake, which borrows heavily from Leland's *Aradia* and rites invented by Aleister Crowley; it also makes extensive reference to a "ceremonial knife" called an "athamé", a word coined by S. L. Mathers in his translation of the *Key of Solomon* (1888), which is thus entitled to be considered the most ancient element in Gardnerian witch-mythology, dating back all of sixty years.

Gardnerian witch-societies began to appear in some quantity soon after publication of *Witchcraft Today*, most of the new "covens" starting up on their own without bothering to seek affiliation to Gardner's organization. Gardner set up a Museum of Magic and Witchcraft on the Isle of Man which, together with his books, supported him until he died; he maintained his connection with the Folklore Society, although its other members became somewhat embarrassed by the association.

The real appeal of Gardnerian covens, at least so far as Gardner was concerned, appears to have been the element of sexual fantasy associated with the nude rites. Accounts vary as to what these rites actually involved, with the wildest rumors making lavish claims about ritual intercourse and flagellation, but most of the pornographic anecdotes are journalistic inventions. The actuality appears to have been rather mild, certainly not comparable with the exploits of the Hellfire Clubs and other exponents of the black mass. The newspapers, especially the tabloids, consistently confused Gardner's witchcraft with black magic, causing Gardner a certain amount of anguish and calling forth some harsh replies. His cult rejoiced in the kind of nostalgic conservatism that runs through the whole Murrayite fantasy; its key claim was that it was a religion which, although harmless and innocent, had been ruthlessly and unjustly persecuted—a claim rapidly taken up by many other "wiccans".

In Britain, Wiccan lifestyle fantasy remained typically British, pursued by middle-class hobbyists as a form of casual social interaction. When it was exported to the USA, however, it immediately gave rise to commercial enterprises of a much more assertive kind. One of the first people who attempted to turn lifestyle-fantasy witchcraft into a thriving business was Sybil Leek, the high priestess of a Gardnerian coven who used her employment with Southern TV as a springboard to become the first significant "media witch"; she emigrated to the USA in 1964 when her impostures attracted unwelcome hostility, where she found life as a minor celebrity somewhat safer and far more lucrative. The Witchcraft Research Association

THE DEVIL'S PARTY, BY BRIAN STABLEFORD

Leek had funded then came into the custody of Doreen Valiente, author of *Witchcraft Today* (1962), who fared better in becoming the "acceptable face" of British Witchcraft, partly due to taking up residence in Brighton, a town famed for its hospitality to poseurs and eccentrics.

If Sybil Leek's autobiography can be believed, Aleister Crowley was an occasional guest at her parent's home in the 1920s, and she was deeply impressed by him. If this is an invention—as her account of her initiation into the witch-cult by an aged grandmother and a brief episode of gypsy life surely are—the fact that she felt obliged to invent it speaks volumes for Crowley's perceived importance in the twentieth-century extension of the occult tradition. As a US TV personality Leek proudly projected the image of an amiable eccentric, emphasized by the fact that she was usually accompanied by a tame jackdaw named Mr. Hotfoot Jackson. Her books are critical of Gardner's emphasis on nudity and the more bizarre habits of various other lifestyle fantasists; she conducted her own rituals in modest robes. Leek's most significant contribution to the mythology of modern witchcraft was the close association of witchcraft with astrology; it was as an astrological diviner that she made the bulk of her income.

Leek's account of being initiated into the witch-cult by her grandmother became a standard element of twentieth-century witch-mythology; parents tend to be excluded from the story because they are often alive, whereas the initiating grandmothers are invariably safely dead by the time the initiation-story is made public. Alex Sanders, who replaced Sybil Leek after her emigration as the most prominent British "media witch", similarly invented an initiation by his grandmother as well as a meeting with Aleister Crowley to cement his "credentials".

The exact extent of Sybil Leek's influence in prompting the rapid spread of Gardnerian lifestyle fantasies in the USA is difficult to ascertain, but there is little or no evidence of any such phenomenon before she arrived there. What is certain, however, is that Gardnerian lifestyle fantasies made a very considerable appeal in the USA to the burgeoning women's movement, whose members foregrounded its borrowings from Jules Michelet. Michelet's representation of the witch-hunt as an anti-feminist crusade was resurrected in the late 1960s, assertively promoted by such groups as the New York-based WITCH (Women's International Conspiracy from Hell), founded in 1968. WITCH foundered after a matter of months but its manifesto survived, given further endorsement by such influential

US feminists as Mary Daly and Andrea Dworkin, who rediscovered similar arguments in the work of the nineteenth-century American feminist Matilda Jocelyn Gage, whose explicit adaptations of Michelet's argument had fallen on deaf ears at the time.

This feminist argument was converted into full-blooded lifestyle fantasy by numerous individuals and groups, their most influential propagandist being a Californian, Miriam Simos, who adopted the pseudonym Starhawk. Starhawk's energetically poetic and best-selling *The Spiral Dance* (1979) became the most significant handbook of the American Wiccanism, far outshining and largely displacing Gardner's own prospectus. She followed it with *Dreaming the Dark* (1982) and *Truth or Dare* (1987), which stressed the function of magic as a form of consciousness-raising, the ultimate exercise of the power of positive thinking—an exercise that had become vitally necessary by virtue of the long oppression of womankind.

Although Gardner had drawn upon literary precedents in formulating his lifestyle fantasy, his own literary influence was very modest; Starhawk's, by contrast, was immense. She popularized her version of Wiccanism at a time when "fantasy" was first being formulated as a commercial genre in the USA, following the archetypal model of J. R. R. Tolkien's *The Lord of the Rings*, and the 1980s saw a very extensive colonization of the new genre by female writers, many of whom followed a feminist agenda. The best-selling American novel of the last two decades of the century was Marion Zimmer Bradley' *The Mists of Avalon* (1982), which "feminized" Arthurian mythology on lines very similar to Starhawkian lifestyle fantasy. Bradley, who edited a long-running series of *Sword and Sorceress* anthologies and founded her own fantasy magazine, subsequently became something of a guru to numerous writers of a similar stripe, several of whom—including Diana L. Paxson and Gael Baudino—described themselves as priestesses of "Dianic Wicca". Feminized fantasy—including contributions by male writers, such as Sean Stewart's *Mockingbird* (1998)—formed an increasingly significant sector of the commercial genre throughout the 1990s and into the twenty-first century.

Where Gardner and Starhawk led, many others followed—a scrupulously detailed account of the proliferation of modern paganism, together with an elaborate analysis of its ideological borrowings, can be found in Ronald Hutton's monumental *The Triumph of the Moon: A History of Modern Pagan Witchcraft* (1999). The chains of influence are mostly easy to see, because lifestyle fantasists are ruthless plagiarists, although any attempt to record them in detail inevitably becomes tedious. Although new groups of lifestyle fantasists and individuals enthusiastic to kick-start new movements always need to emphasize their distinctness from one another, it also serves their purpose to maintain the fiction that they and their rivals are merely different splinter groups of the same ancient cult, whose legacy of hardship suffering and vilification they are very anxious to possess.

One of the less fortunate corollaries of this necessity is that each individual sect tends to distinguish itself from others, at least in part, by accusing its rivals of having degraded and perverted the age-old tradition, perhaps to the extent of turning to evil. Even witches are perfectly prepared to use Satanic abuse against one another, while posing as martyrs to misunderstanding themselves.

The Experiential Rewards of Magical Lifestyle Fantasy

Many lifestyle fantasists are more than willing to discuss the rewards of their activity, and many of them are quite forthright about the extent to which those rewards are theatrical. Gardner's apologia for witchcraft openly advertises the social aspects of the fantasy—the comfort of being among like-minded friends as well as the sensations of superiority associated with the supposed mastery of occult forces. In the more assertive versions of the fantasy, however, other delusions of grandeur become paramount. Sybil Leek's autobiography includes a chapter entitled "Being a Witch Isn't All Fun" in which she emphasizes that the primary motivation of every witch is "a desire to serve humanity to the best of her ability" but that this is made far more difficult by the necessity of "battl[ing] against ignorance, superstition and unkindness." She points out that his or her situation will inevitably produce "moments of intense loneliness" and that weathering the continuing storm of misunderstanding and abuse will require the sustenance of a "great inner power".

This form of self-representation is useful in two ways. On the one hand, the fact that one's fervent desire to be of service to one's fellow human beings is continually frustrated by the hostility to others provides a perfect excuse for any lack of achievement in that regard, which might otherwise have to be attributed to indolence or incompetence On the other hand, the notion that one has a special inner power to combat loneliness is very convenient if one happens to be prone to moments of intense loneliness, and even the privilege of explaining away such moments as inevitable consequences of a heroic quest, rather than a mere reflection of social incompetence, can be psychologically useful. The greatest utility of witch-mythology, as rewritten by Margaret Murray, is its assertion that persecuted witches were not merely innocent but were better people than their persecutors, because—in spite of their conspicuous lack of acknowledged social status and formal education—they were wiser, kinder, and more tolerant. Unlike initiation into elitist organizations modelled on Rosicrucian lodges, this is a game that almost anyone can play, and one that inevitably became attractive in a historical era when the once-distinctive class-cultures of the upper and lower strata of British society both seemed to be dissolving into middle class values, and in which the particular egalitarian thrust of American society was spreading far and wide by virtue of "coca-colonization".

The aspect of modern witchcraft that involved building a new and better self-image was particularly dear to the heart of the American tradition that was eventually aggrandized by Starhawk. Several of Starhawk's predecessors, in fact, had forsaken feminist propagandizing in favor of producing straightforward "self-help" books. Louise Huebner, for instance, stated in *The Power of Witchcraft* (1969) that "witchcraft is simply a form of self-promotion" and explained the functions of her lifestyle fantasy under the chapter heading "How to concoct a new you—at home in your spare time". Paul Huson was similarly acutely aware of the fact that creating a "new you" is the essence of *Mastering Witchcraft* (1970), whose first chapter recommends chanting the Lord's Prayer backwards, not because it achieves anything in the external world but because it is a vital first step in the process of ideological liberation.

Although Huebner was a typical "white witch" while Huson was an enthusiast for the "Black Arts" their books were in complete agreement in recommending that would-be witches should learn to love themselves and become utterly and unashamedly selfish. That emphasis on rampant egocentricity and winning freedom from the shackles of everyday moral restraint was largely set aside by Starhawk and her followers, but it was taken to its logical extreme by those twentieth-century American lifestyle fantasies who undertook to describe themselves explicitly as Satanists.

This extreme was widely popularized in the late 1960s by the Californian founder of the Church of Satan, Anton LaVey, who appointed himself the heir to a hypothetical "age-old tradition" of Satan-worship, and modestly titled his attempt to popularize his ideas *The Satanic Bible* (1969). LaVey's claims to have ordained 450 ministers of Satan in a single day in 1971, and to have 7,000 members of his church's various branches, may be taken with a pinch of salt, but his organization did enjoy considerable success in the years immediately after its founding, and it endured into the twenty-first century. It was not the first such organization—the Satanic Process Church of the Final Judgment had been founded in London in 1963—but it quickly eclipsed its rivals, to the extent that the Process Church's self-appointed messiah soon moved to the USA in order to take advantage of the publicity that LaVey had generated.

LaVey's *Satanic Bible* explicitly redefines Satanism as "a form of controlled selfishness," and states that the purpose of the Church of Satan is to indulge in, and obtain as much gratification as is humanly possible from the seven deadly sins. Like Anatole France and other conspicuous literary satanists, LaVey and other self-appointed Satan-"worshippers" see themselves as excavators of an escape tunnel, which might and ought to free them from the prison of Christian guilt. Given that the whole purpose of designating pride, avarice, envy, anger, gluttony, lust and sloth as "deadly sins" was to persuade people to be ashamed of their own natural inclinations, the idea of an inverted morality in which all those things would not only be licensed but applauded is understandably tempting.

In its early days LaVey's new Hellfire Club had much the same appeal to the American élite of nearby Hollywood as Dashwood's had had to the aristocratic rakehells of eighteenth-century England. As a former showman (he had worked as a lion-tamer and as a carnival musician in the days when he was plain Howard Levy) LaVey was well equipped to adapt his theatricality to his particular environment. Early enthusiasts for his libertine brand of Satanism included Mick Jagger, Keith Richards and Brian Jones of the Rolling Stones, who attempted to release an album in 1967 called *Their Satanic Majesties Request and Require*, although they compromised with the management of Decca by removing the last two words. Their next album, *Beggar's Banquet*, was spearheaded by a track that they wanted to call "The Devil is my Name", although the powers-that-be at Decca used their veto again to make it "Sympathy for the Devil". Jagger, Richards and Jones were also scheduled to appear in *Lucifer Rising,* a film written and directed by Kenneth Anger—Jagger was to play Lucifer—but the movie was never completed and the Stones settled for a more orthodox career-path. The torch they dropped was, however, immediately picked up by heavy metal pioneers Black Widow and Black Sabbath; Black Widow's album *Sacrifice* (1970) includes several Satanist tracks, including the exhortatory "Come to the Sabbat".

LaVey's Church of Satan spawned several imitations, aided by the inevitable splits in the ranks of its inner circle. The chief splinter groups formed by defection appear to have been Michael Aquino's Temple of Set, which was hived off in the mid-1970s, and the Werewolf Order, established by a one-time boyfriend of LaVey's daughter, Nicholas Schreck. Schreck's attempts to cultivate a Satanic image were more melodramatic than LaVey's, involving combative declarations of admiration for two of the key villains of twentieth century narrative history, Adolf Hitler and Charles Manson.

Manson, the self-appointed head of a small-scale cult, who sent forth members of his "family" to commit a horribly messy murder in Hollywood in 1969, has become particularly significant as a modern icon of evil, and the power that his name has to appall the virtuous is inevitably reflected in the loud approval of some of those who wish to set themselves up in opposition to contemporary ideas of virtue; it was successfully adopted into the pseudonym of the horror-rock musician Marilyn Manson, who eventually cultivated a successful secondary career as a chat show guest. It is frequently alleged that Charles Manson included some sort of explicit Satanism within the ideology which underpinned the killings he ordered, although rumor and the vested interests implicit in Schreck's extensive reportage of Manson's views have undoubtedly exaggerated it. Since the 1969 murders, however, there have been continual attempts by news reporters to link serial killers with Satanist cults, some of which have been enthusiastically aided by the murderers themselves, retrospectively recruited by them to help "explain" their actions.

Expressions of admiration for Charles Manson and other perpetrators of horrific murders are, in some ways, a readier source of notoriety than claims to be literal followers of Satan, given that Manson is indubitably real while Satan is not. One British lifestyle fantasist who made such gestures was the *avant-garde* artist Genesis P. Orridge, who also fronted the rock bands Throbbing Gristle and Psychick TV—which, like many other bands hungry for bad publicity, put on a calculatedly outrageous stage act—and founded Thee Temple of Psychick Youth in Brighton before emigrating to the USA.

In carrying forward the work of the Rolling Stones and Black Widow, Orridge's rock bands further underlined the utility of satanic representations as symbols of rebellion in youth culture, and the particular role of popular music in supplying and supporting such representations. While Throbbing Gristle pioneered "industrial" rock, the Process Church of the Final Judgment promoted its own brand of "dark folk" music. LaVey's most enthusiastic musical supporters and popularizers were, however, The Electric Hell-Fire Club, exponents of electronic disco music, whose first two albums, *Burn, Baby, Burn!* (1993) and *Kiss the Goat* (1995) offered insistent dance beats and lyrics as cheerfully ironic as they were conscientiously blasphemous. Meanwhile, the heavy metal genre continued to entertain the most extravagant Satanist posturing.

A significant landmark in the evolution of Satanist heavy metal music was the release in 1981 of Venom's debut album *Welcome to Hell*. Venom's ostensible Satanism always remained conscientiously tongue-in-cheek, but the extremism of their pose attracted several imitators, the most successful of which was the American "death metal" band Deicide, whose eponymous debut album was released in 1990. The title of Venom's second album, *Black Metal* (1982) was borrowed as a generic description for a cluster of bands that emerged in the early 1990s in Norway. The principal inspiration of Norwegian black metal was Øysten Aarseth, *alias* Euronymous, of the band Mayhem, who ran his own record shop, Helvete [Hell], and his own record label, Deathlike Silence.

The peer-group support offered by habitués of Aarseth's shop and label allowed the Satanist activities of Black Metal musicians to be extrapolated from stage performances and lyric-writing into full-scale lifestyle fantasies. The rivalry between such bands as Darkthrone, Emperor and Burzum resulted in an unfortunate escalation of this collective lifestyle fantasy; rumors of their involvement in arson attacks on churches and the desecration of graveyards gained explosive impetus in August 1993 when Varg Vikernes, *alias* Count Grishnackh of Burzum, stabbed and killed Aarseth/Euronymous. The publicity generated by this affair triggered another in a series of moral panics about the evil effects of heavy metal music, which spread to Britain when a teenager named Paul Timms, who claimed leadership of a black metal band called Necropolis, was convicted of inflicting criminal damage on seven churches and a graveyard.

When he was called upon to justify his Satanist stance following his conviction and imprisonment, Vikernes/Grishnakh proclaimed that he was actually a worshipper of Odin rather than the Christian Satan; other black metal enthusiasts followed suit, transmuting their subgenre into a nostalgic lament for a lost pagan heritage once associated with Viking glory, whose eclipse by Christianity had allegedly reduced Norway from the status of Dark Age superpower to contemporary EC marginality. English and American heavy metal bands usually took the simpler course of denying, if challenged, that their Satanist trappings were anything more than mere theatrics—a strategy successfully followed by the members of Judas Priest when they had to answer the formal allegation that their records had driven two teenagers to suicide by means of subliminal Satanist messages. Satanist posturing by heavy metal headbangers reached its nadir when Ozzy Osbourne of Black Sabbath became the hapless anti-hero of a TV docusoap, and his plaintive protestations that he was "the Prince of Darkness" became an absurd joke.

Anton LaVey's writings, and those of the majority of his followers, are perfectly forthright in stating that there is no such entity as Satan; indeed, the fundamental thrust of libertine Satanist theory is that the non-existence of Satan reflects and re-emphasizes the non-existence of God. Satan, to the Church of Satan and its fellow travelers, is a symbol of proud dissent and a facilitating device of the imagination—and so, by the same token, is all the other apparatus and ritual involved in "magic".

Not all lifestyle fantasists are ready to admit this—especially not those who actually practice as diviners rather than simply holding wild parties—but the more pragmatic handbooks promoting modernized philosophies of witchcraft and magic are similarly open about the fact that they are providing recipes for wholly self-conscious lifestyle fantasies. One thriving Californian group, eschewing all magical impostures, simply styles itself the Society for Creative Anachronism. Even guide-books to lifestyle fantasy that maintain their poses more carefully are very often prepared to let their masks drop occasionally. Aleister Crowley's *Magick in Theory and Practice* (1929) provides a reading-list that features numerous literary fantasies—including Lewis Carroll's *Alice in Wonderland* and *Through the Looking Glass* as well as Maugham's *The Magician* and Jepson's *No. 19*—supplemented with tongue-in-cheek annotations.

Disarming moves of this kind do not, of course, protect lifestyle fantasists from dark suspicion, nor would any serious lifestyle fantasist be content if they did, in spite of the defensive protestations of all modern witches and Satanists that their activities involve no criminal activity whatsoever. The ultimate aims of all lifestyle fantasy are to promote self-esteem and facilitate fun; how effective fantasized lifestyles involving witchcraft and Satanism are, in either respect, is something that only their practitioners can know. One must suspect that the actuality of the experience is as remote from the fantasy as most sexual performance is from most sexual fantasy—but when one considers what most sexual performance would amount to without its fantasy component, that is far from damning criticism.

VIII.

THE RESURGENCE OF SATANIC ABUSE

Domestication and Demonization

The extensive spread of "Wiccan" lifestyle fantasies in Britain and the USA the 1960s and early 1970s brought about a conspicuous domestication of the notions typically embraced by such groups. The tabloid press and popular magazines routinely carried mildly scandalous stories about the alleged activities of witches and Satanists, mostly in a spirit of titillation, employing a familiar combination of pornographic detail and censorious commentary. In Britain such reportage made minor celebrities of Alex and Maxine Sanders, interviews published in *Tit-Bits* in 1966 and *Reveille* in 1969 both being followed up by full-length books by the journalists concerned: *King of the Witches* (1969) and *What Witches Do* (1971). Although Alex Sanders tended to stress the harmless aspects of Gardnerian witchcraft, his wife Maxine was not so diplomatic following their separation. A series of interviews she gave to the *News of the World* in 1975 claimed that rival groups to her own were still engaged in all the activities previously described by Elliott O'Donnell and Rollo Ahmed.

Alongside these straightforward exercises in popular sensationalism more sustained attempts were made to exploit the pornographic potential of the subject-matter in paperback books and periodicals. *Witchcraft*, a magazine launched under the auspices of TNT Publications in 1971, mingled articles on witchcraft and associated subjects (voodoo, secret societies, vampires, and so on) with mildly pornographic fiction. Its illustrations mixed material drawn from antique sources with photographs of naked women, most of which were simply stock pornographic pictures with no manifest connection with witchcraft or the stories in which they were set. Distribution of the periodical was initially confined to outlets specializing in pornography, but it was taken over by New English Library in 1973 and moved up-market. When the magazine failed to capture a mass-market audience NEL dropped it, but it reappeared in 1974 as *New Witchcraft*, with a heavier bias toward conventional sensational journalism, before falling victim to a more generalized economic crisis.

The first issue of *New Witchcraft* showcased David Farrant of the British Occult Society, who offered a thoroughly conventional defense of witchcraft, denying that it had anything to do with Devil-worship (or, for that matter, sex orgies), but he was subsequently charged—amid a blaze of tabloid headlines advertising "black magic" and "voodoo"—with an assortment of crimes, including desecrating graves in Highgate Cemetery. Farrant claimed in his defense that he was the innocent party and was merely trying to repair evil work done by *real* Satanists; he was acquitted of the more serious charges laid against him but eventually convicted of several minor offences, for which he received an excessively punitive sentence of four years' imprisonment. Even this affair, however, seemed merely tawdry, and not to be taken at all seriously; there was no trace of any genuine sense of threat in the coverage of his case.

In the meantime, the colonization of middle-class suburbia by lifestyle-fantasy witchcraft rendered it fit for coverage in such staid lifestyle magazines as *Woman's Own*. In 1977 that magazine featured an interview with two witches named Rusty and Celia Russell-Gough, whose "Temple of the Light of Avalon" was a third-floor flat in Clapham. Their apologia for their pursuit was typically ingenuous: "'Sometimes you do wonder if it's all in your imagination,' said Celia, 'and sometimes you get impatient and angry about it. Once I got fed up because nothing seemed to be happening and I shoved all my robes into a case and put them away. But then a reporter came round the next day, I got them out to show him and I was hooked all over again. That's the thing about witchcraft. It takes hold of you. Once you've had a glimpse of other worlds, this one's not enough.'"

In spite of the lurid copy supplied by the likes of Maxine Sanders and David Farrant, the climate of opinion in the 1970s did not seem conducive to the reinfusion of anxieties about the supposed activities of witches and Satanists with any persecutory force. This appearance was, however, deceptive. The ideological groundwork was already being laid for allegations of "Satanic child abuse" to attract increasing attention in the 1980s, eventually precipitating a moral panic. The panic was soon equipped with its own witch-hunting manuals, replete with fervent argument and horrific reportage, and such propagandistic investigations as Andrew Boyd's *Blasphemous Rumors* (1991).

This new moral panic was not an evolution of the 1970s reportage that had reduced stories about witchcraft and Satanism to the level of flagrant absurdity, nor was it a sudden sidestep in that attitudinal pattern. It was, instead, an extension of conventional ideas relating to the sexual abuse of children. Although this notion had previously been accommodated within a narrative that represented the sexual molestation of children as a series of relatively rare events mostly perpetrated by sociopathic social outsiders, the common opinion changed very markedly in the early 1970s as the notion spread that such crimes were much more widespread than had previously been thought, and mostly involved perpetrators known to, and often closely related to, the victims.

Cases in which small children were kidnapped, raped and then murdered by adults had long been crimes that occasioned a particular horror and vengeful outrage. Such crimes had always generated unusual vituperation in their reportage, and the men convicted of such crimes had routinely attracted such abhorrence as to require segregation in prison lest they be attacked by other prisoners; Ian Brady, the perpetrator of the sickeningly cruel "moors murders" in the 1960s, had become an icon of evil in Britain to rival Charles Manson in the USA. All conscientious parents, therefore, took pains to warn their children of the danger of talking to strangers, especially those who sought to tempted children away from safe havens with offers of sweets or rides in cars.

In the 1960s and early 1970s, when the publicity given to child-murder cases became increasingly extravagant, the impression was created in Britain and the USA that this kind of danger was increasing. The general relaxation of censorship in the 1960s fuelled a great deal of speculative discussion about the effects of pornography on "sex crimes" in general; corollary speculations regarding the effects of pornographic representations of children on the actual sexual molestation of children were seen as particularly crucial. The same decade saw a dramatic increase in public attention to the violence that some children suffered at the hands of their parents—what the British popular press called "baby-battering"—in the context of the frequent failure of social workers to anticipate such incidents and take children into care. Public concern about such issues was further encouraged by feminist crusades to expose the extent to which wives were routinely subjected to domestic violence, and the extent to which women in general were subjected to rape by people they knew.

The frequent use of social workers as scapegoats in baby-battering cases had the effect of making such functionaries far more sensitive to the incidence of all kinds of child abuse, and particularly to the supposed "warning signs" that might allow trouble to be anticipated and averted. Their philosophy of approach shifted markedly; in their own jargon they became more "pro-active". It was in this context that social workers and social scientists in the USA began, in the mid-1970s, stridently to call attention to the domestic sexual molestation of young children as a huge but hidden problem, which would require special inquisitorial techniques if it were to be efficiently detected and countered. In 1977-78 the newly-fashionable "problem" of domestic child abuse was the subject of dozens of articles in American newspapers and magazines, and became a topic for discussion in Congress and in most State Legislatures; as a result, new laws were passed in more than half the states in the Union.

The new wave of concern about domestic child abuse was amplified by the allegation that past complacency had condemned large numbers of victims to the additional indignity of having any complaints they dared to utter disbelieved and condemned as malicious. A tacit but vast "conspiracy of silence" was retrospectively revealed and publicized; this encouraged many adults to come forward with accounts of abuse that they had been forced to suffer in childhood, and had suffered in silence, never realizing that so many others were in the same position.

One effect of this new hindsight was a reappraisal of what had earlier been the conventional wisdom of psychotherapy. Attention was drawn to a change in theoretical direction taken by the father of psychoanalysis, Sigmund Freud. Freud, who had access to data about child sexual abuse provided by a doctor named Tardieu (whose findings were based on post-mortem examinations of children), had initially been inclined to believe stories told by his female patients regarding sexual intercourse with their fathers, but had eventually decided that these accounts must be fantasies, which required explanation in terms of repressed desires. P. M. Masson's *Freud: The Assault on Truth* (1984), argued that this was not merely a mistake but a betrayal, which had condemned many future victims of child sexual abuse to the shame of having their accounts denied and dismissed, and being treated as victims of neurotic delusion.

The Devil's Party, by Brian Stableford

It is, of course, understandable that social workers newly alerted to the possibility of domestic child abuse should wish to "make amends" for their presumed past failure to see the problem at all by bringing a new zeal to their newly-informed perceptions and actions. The publicity given to the problem in the USA was quickly followed by a glut of prosecutions. Although the great majority of these were concerned with single families, the ones which attracted most attention were trials involving "collective abuse" of some kind—particularly cases involving the staff of various institutions to whose care children had been entrusted. Not unnaturally, public outrage was particularly aroused by trials involving the staff of "pre-school" play groups.

The most spectacular case of this kind involved the McMartin preschool in Los Angeles in 1983, where an initial handful of allegations mushroomed on further investigation, somewhat after the fashion of the Blokula scare. More and more children added increasingly bizarre testimony. Although some earlier cases had involved allegations of ritual abuse it was the McMartin trial that gave birth to the idea of *Satanic* ritual child abuse. Child-witnesses in the case offered elaborate accounts of being taken to distant locations in order to be abused, of being forced to drink blood and urine, and of witnessing animal sacrifice. No less than 369 children eventually claimed to have been sexually abused by the teachers at the school; charges relating to forty-one of them were ultimately brought to trial. After hearings lasting more than two years the defendants were found not guilty on most of the counts and the jury were unable to reach a verdict on the remainder. The more bizarre elements of the evidence given by some of the children caused acute problems for the prosecutors, whose attempts to filter them out, so that only mundane evidence was actually brought forward in court, ultimately proved unsuccessful.

The collapse of the McMartin case established a pattern that was to be repeated elsewhere. When subsequent prosecutors brought charges in cases where allegations of ritual abuse had been made, they were extremely reluctant to have reference made in court to black masses or human sacrifice, because they felt—rightly—that such apparently-fanciful material would destroy the credibility of their witnesses. Allegations of human sacrifice proved especially difficult for investigators and juries to swallow, because the physical evidence that such events might be expected to leave behind was never to be found.

THE DEVIL'S PARTY, BY BRIAN STABLEFORD

The Extension of the Moral Panic

The pattern of events that occurred in the USA in the late 1970s and early 1980s was repeated in Britain some ten years later. Public concern about domestic child abuse of all kinds was dramatically raised by a series of TV programs aired in 1986. These were initiated by Esther Rantzen, who first used her *That's Life* program to call for volunteers to provided information about the scope of the problem, and then reported the results of the survey in a special two-part program called *ChildWatch*. A special "Childline" telephone line was set up in order that children suffering abuse might call for help.

Within four months of the *ChildWatch* broadcast, a group of social workers in the county of Cleveland—in association with two doctors using a method of diagnosis known as "reflex anal dilatation"—began a series of investigations that ultimately resulted in 125 children from fifty-seven families being diagnosed as having been sexually abused; sixty-seven were made wards of court and a further twenty-seven were removed from their homes under "place-of-safety" orders.

The Cleveland affair brought public discussion of domestic child abuse to a head in Britain; it seemed to many onlookers that the pendulum had swung from one extreme to the other—from a denial that any problem existed to a conviction that domestic child abuse was rife. Even the tabloid newspapers, in spite of their fondness for sensation, mostly reported the case in terms that were scathingly skeptical about the claims made by the doctors and social workers. Much of the reportage suggested that at least some of the parents had been the victims of a "witch-hunt", and that the hasty removal of children who had not been abused from their homes and families might actually be creating the kind of psychological trauma from which the social workers were ostensibly trying to save the children.

After the matter was raised in parliament, doubts were expressed about the reliability of the test used to prove that the children involved had been subjected to anal intercourse (which many of them denied), and about the techniques of interrogation used by the social workers who had tried to determine whether abuse had taken place and—if so—by whom. Several of the orders making children wards of court were successfully challenged by parents and a judicial enquiry was undertaken, chaired by Lord Justice Butler-Sloss, which reported its findings in June 1988. This report sug-

209

gested new guidelines for the interviewing of children suspected of being victims of sexual molestation and for the implementation of subsequent legal proceedings, but in a much-publicized series of cases of similar mass removals of children from their homes these guidelines did not seem to have been scrupulously followed.

The Cleveland case was quickly followed in 1987 by Britain's first case of alleged ritual abuse, which involved eight children removed from a group of closely-related families in Nottingham. When the case ultimately came to court, in February 1989, ten adults did plead guilty to various charges of incest, cruelty and indecent assault against twenty-three children, but the matter of ritual abuse—though much talked-about—was not officially raised. Because all the people involved were so closely related to one another the case also generated discussion about "generational abuse"—the idea that the sexual molestation of children may become a kind of tradition within extended families, handed on from one generation to the next. The conventional view of domestic child abuse had already accepted that the sons of fathers given to the sexual abuse of their children were highly likely to become abusers themselves, just as the children of violent parents were more likely to treat their own children violently.

Three subsequent cases added fuel to the British debate about ritual abuse. Two that invited a good deal of press coverage—much of it, in the wake of the Cleveland affair, severely skeptical—occurred in Rochdale in 1990 and in South Ronaldsay (in the Orkney islands) in 1991. Both cases collapsed when it was established that the social workers involved had failed to follow the prescriptive guidelines established by the Butler-Sloss enquiry. A further case, on a smaller scale, involving allegations of Satanic rituals conducted in Epping Forest, went to trial in 1991 but the trial was abandoned when the child-witnesses, having produced lurid accounts of human sacrifice at a particular site in the forest, began to vacillate under cross-examination.

Further fuel was added to the British debate in 1990 when the National Society for the Prevention of Cruelty to Children issued a report saying that seven teams of investigators had handled cases of alleged ritual abuse and had concluded, on comparing notes, that the problem was real and widespread. The NSPCC report made much of the allegation that the groups of ritual abusers were also engaged in the systematic production of child pornography.

The idea that the collective abuse of children, ritual or otherwise, was tied in with the production of child pornography had attained a new plausibility by virtue of the availability of "camcorders" enabling anyone make cheap videotapes. Many skeptics were initially unimpressed, on the grounds that physical evidence of this kind was difficult to find, but the march of technology eroded that skepticism considerably when the advent of the internet provided all kinds of pornography with a new and unprecedentedly-hospitable medium of distribution. Amateur videos of all kinds of sexual intercourse, including child pornography, were uploaded to cyberspace on a considerable scale in the 1990s, their sheer profusion encouraging a quest for theatrical variety. No matter how rare "ritual child abuse" had been before 1990, the publicity given to it guaranteed its proliferation thereafter, if only as a matter of theatrical performance.

The extensive publicity given to trials involving collective abuse—and the halo of rumors about Satanism that came to surround them—served to deflect some attention away from what were presumably the more commonplace manifestations of individual child sexual abuse. It is extremely difficult to make any reliable estimate of how extensive this problem really was or is; survey research is a notoriously unreliable instrument when it begins to touch on private matters, especially sexual ones, and it is very difficult indeed to extrapolate from data gained from self-selected samples like the volunteers who wrote in to the *ChildWatch* programs.

If claims by adults to have been abused in childhood are assumed to be reliable (and there may be reasons for doubting some of them, which will be outlined in due course) then surveys whose sample was not self-selected suggest that about three percent of adults might have been subjected to some level of abuse in childhood—although this figure becomes much higher if relatively innocuous forms of "sexual harassment" like exhibitionism are admitted to the definition of sexual abuse. Many of the individuals included in this three per cent figure were, however, in their teens when the abuse occurred, and the abuse of younger children often did not involve actual sexual intercourse of any kind. Any estimate of the number of cases involving the serious abuse of young children obviously depends on what one classifies as "serious" and what one means by "young" but the available survey evidence suggests the possible some-time involvement of tens of thousands of individuals in Britain and the USA.

The publicity given to cases of alleged collective abuse, especially when these were spiced with rumors about Satanic ritual and the mass-production of child pornography, was a natural response to the anxieties awakened by the realization that child sexual abuse is much commoner than had formerly been believed, but a certain caution is necessary in evaluating what *kind* of response it was. Those who believed the more fanciful allegations undoubtedly saw themselves as crusaders against a real evil, but skeptics were surely entitled to wonder whether all the sound and fury might have been a desperate attempt to deny that the problem was inside the everyday moral community, by thrusting it as far outside that community as it could possibly be thrust.

If Satanic ritual child molestation was, in fact, a myth and not a reality, then its psychological function was quite obvious: to defend the increasingly-unlikely thesis that child abuse was something carried out by inhuman perverts for whom *no* vicious behavior was unthinkable. It is hardly surprising that the scapegoats appointed to carry this guilt out of the community and into the desert were accused of being "Satanists", given that this is the central purpose that the idea of Satanism was invented to serve.

It is not difficult to understand why people are reluctant to believe that the sexual molestation of young children is an everyday affair. Such acts are regarded with so much horror that there is an almost universal reluctance to admit that its perpetrators might be ordinary members of the community whose behavior is otherwise acceptable. Give this, it is not entirely to be wondered at that people who find the "perverted stranger" theory of child molestation no longer tenable should feel strongly attracted to other strategies of explanation, which try to accommodate the statistical data about the level of child molestation simply by converting the lone perverts into organized gangs of some kind.

The chief attraction that the idea of collective child molestation—whether or not it is "ritual", and whether or not the rituals are specifically "Satanic"—has for its supporters is that it makes the molesters part of a different community, distinct from our own, and allows the moral boundaries which surround "us" to seem clear again. The idea of collective abuse allows people to separate out a distinct category of "child-molesters" even after they have admitted that the phenomenon is more common and better-concealed than they had previously believed.

In accordance with the customary politics of persecution, it is but a short step from the hypothetical identification of such hidden conspiracies to the supposition that their child-molesting activities are an extension of more general anti-social and anti-human tendencies. Even those who are ready to make such moves, however, ought to remain aware of the danger that if they are made without good grounds, they may succeed only in deflecting attention away from the real nature of the problem and the real possibilities of dealing with it.

Satanism in Modern Confessional Literature

To a large extent, such investigative studies as Andrew Boyd's *Blasphemous Rumors*—subtitled "Is Satanic Ritual Abuse Fact or Fantasy? An Investigation"—duplicate the rhetorical strategies of traditional witch-hunters very closely. Although it maintains a pose of objectivity, Boyd's book is, in fact, a summary of the case for believers in the phenomenon. Its first part—disingenuously titled, "The Making of a Myth?"—reviews cases of alleged ritual abuse from Britain, North America and continental Europe, lists a series of experts convinced of the reality of the problem, categorizing them by profession and then summarizes the "common threads" linking all these various accounts together. All the familiar elements of the Sabbat and the black mass are included in these common threads—animal and human sacrifice, cannibalism, bloody ritual and drug abuse—but they are supplemented with the new feature of pornography-production. This analysis extends into an account of various techniques allegedly used to preserve the secrecy of these activities—threats, blackmail and brainwashing—and a summary of the supposed long-term psychological effects of these kinds of abuse.

Part Two of *Blasphemous Rumors*, "Occult Connections", offers a brief "history" of Satanism, which attempts to establish the continuity of the rituals described in the previous section with the activities of Satanists through the ages; its materials are derived almost entirely from chronicles of lifestyle fantasy, including contemporary tabloid newspaper reportage. Part Three, "A Question of Evidence", addresses the problems of interpretation and proof that arise in connection with allegations of child abuse, and attempts to counter the lack of physical evidence with such arguments as the allegation that Satanists have ways of producing unregistered babies for sacrifice (using coven members and/or prostitutes as "brood mares") and that their "connections in high places" allow them easy access to means of covertly disposing of the remains. All of this echoes tactics used by earlier witchfinders and panic-mongers, but Part Four is more distinctively modern, making use of a kind of evidence that was available in the sixteenth and seventeenth centuries only on a very limited scale and in very primitive forms, but which had become extremely prolific and highly sophisticated by the late twentieth century: confessional memoirs.

Boyd presents a series of "autobiographical case histories" in which four pseudonymous women offer elaborate confessions of having been involved in exactly the kinds of Satanist groups that are described in the earlier part of the book. Two of these are backed up by endorsements from the people to whom they initially made their confessions (one of whom is a psychiatrist, the other a solicitor). At first sight, this might appear to be conclusive evidence of the truth of Boyd's case, but his careful relegation of it to an appendix displays a wise caution. Confessional documents of this general kind had been produced in increasing quantity throughout the century, marketed by Christian publishers as a species of inspirational literature.

The proliferation of confessional literature, especially in the USA, reflect the tendency of Protestant congregations to substitute open admissions for the sealed confessions of the Catholic church; members of a congregation proclaim their sins in order to "testify" to the extent of the redemption that they have now been granted in having "found God", "accepted Jesus" or being "born again". There is an inevitable temptation, in making such confessions, to inflate the relevant sins in order to magnify generosity of Christ's mercy—his "amazing grace", as the hymn puts it.

The fascination of confessional accounts is not restricted to a religious context; various form of psychotherapy have also put a high priority on exhaustive self-revelation, and one of the great successes of twentieth-century popular journalism had been the kind of confessional account that once supported a whole genre of "True Confession" magazines. The contents of such magazines were, as a matter of routine, entirely fictitious, but—like urban legends—the stories relied for their effect on the pretence that they were true. Such items continued to play a significant role in more generalized periodicals until and beyond the turn of the century, and the rapid growth of a *fin-de-siècle* subgenre of "survivor memoirs" was soon confused in the early twenty-first century by a series of scandals in which writers of such memoirs were exposed—surely to no one's surprise—as fakes.

Confessions of having been involved in Satanism and witchcraft were among the most popular narratives of this kind issued by religious publishers for some time before the moral panic regarding Satanic child abuse blew up—they have, of course, a uniquely blatant significance in the context of Christian salvation literature—and the escalation of the panic greatly encouraged their further production. The most popular British example of this kind of testimonial was Doreen Irvine's book *From Witchcraft to Christ* (1973)—from which Boyd quoted extensively, although he refrained from mentioning the explicitly supernatural claims made by the author, and had to concede that Irvine, writing before the panic, made no reference at all to child molestation in her elaborate accounts of modern Satanist ritual.

Doreen Irvine's supposed life-story provides a stereotypical account of a "career of evil" as such a career was likely to be imagined in the early 1970s. It describes her desertion by her mother and neglect by her uncaring stepmother, her acquisition of such bad habits as petty theft and smoking, her abandonment of a dead-end-job in favor of prostitution and strip-tease dancing, and her heroin addiction—all of which is a prelude to her attendance at a Satanist temple, her selection as the favored mistress of the "Chief Satanist", her appointment (by Satan himself) as Queen of the Black Witches, her possession by forty-seven demons, and her eventual decision to take the long hard road to salvation, assisted by charismatic Christian mediators.

The similarly stereotypical account offered in Lauren Stratford's *Satan's Underground* (1988) provides a graphic illustration of lessons learned in the interim. It describes her desertion by her father and neglect by her uncaring mother, who eventually sells her into child prostitution; her exploitation by makers of hard-core child pornography, followed by continued involvement in prostitution and pornography as a young adult; and her selection as the favored mistress of the chief pornographer—all of which is a prelude to her forced induction into Satanic worship and the use of blackmail and terrorization to obtain her participation in human sacrifice, followed by her decision to take the long hard road to salvation.

Both these "autobiographies" present their central characters as victims placed on a slippery slope through no fault of their own, led thereby to the ultimate imaginable depths of degradation. It is noticeable, though, that they both contain an element of sexual self-aggrandizement; "memoirs" of this kind rarely feature mere spear-carriers. Both books contain self-congratulatory prologues by the "carers" primarily responsible for the salvation of the confessors, whose reputations have presumably grown as a result of their having saved the favored mistresses of the most evil men in the world. Irvine's extravagant claims to have acquired considerable magical powers while she was a black witch are only echoed in muted form in Stratford's ambiguous observations about the workability of demonic curses, but Stratford offers a more elaborate account of the supernatural agencies involved in her salvation, which included a quasi-angelic "spirit-guide".

The moral of both these stories—extensively drawn out through several chapters of each book—is that the threat of evil is far greater than ordinary people might ever have supposed, but that God's mercy is equal to the task of saving people from it, no matter how deeply they have become involved, provided that they are truly repentant. It is entirely understandable that devout Christians are interested in accounts of this kind, even setting aside the suspicion that a significant element of their fascination is a kind of prurience not too far removed from that which supports the popular reportage of Satanist lifestyle fantasies.

Documents this kind are not only produced by Christian publishers for the benefit of Christian readers; an early account of Satanist fantasies posing as memories recovered in the course of psychotherapy, *Michelle Remembers* (1981) by Michelle Smith and Lawrence Padzer MD, was issued by mainstream publishers in the USA and UK, although the participants in the recovery took care to obtain support from Roman Catholic clergymen and the services of an exorcist in completing the healing process, and the book is prefaced by a quotation from the pope and a brief statement by the Bishop of Victoria (in British Columbia, Canada). The "memories" the patient "recovered"—in 1976-7—referred back to a time when she was five years old, so the whole story qualifies as a catalogue of child abuse, although its sexual component is carefully muted.

The people who write and read books of this kind are undoubtedly sincere in wishing to alert other people to the perennial dangers of temptation and malice. The authors' ludicrous exaggeration of their own "experiences" is perhaps best understood as a kind of allegory dramatizing a real sense of threat. Like the repentant witches whose confessions were analyzed by Étienne Delcambre, the authors of accounts like these are presumably quite sincere in translating their sense of having been delivered from evil into these terms. This does not mean, however, that we can treat their stories as evidence of the occurrence of real events, even if they are purged of the supernatural element.

Accounts such as these are rarely entirely fanciful. It is part and parcel of their method that they continually come down to earth, intimately interweaving the substance of nightmare and the texture of everyday life. This, after all, is their purpose: to argue that, behind the facades of everyday existence, a cosmic battle between the forces of good and evil is going on. The moral thrust of the arguments put forward by both Irvine and Stratford is that the ordinary, everyday evils that no one takes very seriously are really part and parcel of the much more ominous whole, which only they have had the dubious privilege of seeing in its entirety. When Lauren Stratford finally gets around to spelling out who the members of "Satan's Underground" actually are, we find that it includes players of fantasy role-playing games, bored housewives dabbling in spiritualism, college students interested in parapsychology, professional men interested in the power of positive thinking and anyone at all interested in "New Age" philosophy, UFOs and reincarnation—all of whom, she insists, have unwittingly set foot on the slippery slope that leads directly to damnation. The instant adoption of child sexual abuse into fantasies of this kind, as soon as the issue was brought to the attention of the public, was entirely natural. How could such a horrid gift possibly be left out?

The moral panic that produced so many books like Irvine's, Padzer's, Stratford's and Boyd's can be likened in some ways to the crises of faith that produced the Jewish apocalyptic writings (and hence Christianity itself) and the great witch-hunt. The Christian faith survived the rise of the Newtonian cosmology, which did not obliterate Christian ideas about the nature of man, but in the latter part of the nineteenth century—when organic chemistry brought the human body fully within the scope of scientific inquiry and Darwin's theory of evolution provided a robust alternative to theories of divine Creation—the central tenets of Christian doctrine came into frank conflict with scientific thought. Since then, devout believers have been forced either to acknowledge that the greater part of the Bible has to be construed as an allegory, or to take up arms in order to defend the literal truth of the scriptures against powerfully corrosive arguments. As that defense came ever closer to its last ditch, the desperation of the fight increased accordingly. Given the fundamental nature of Biblical faith, as outlined in chapter 1, it is understandable that this desperation generated attempts to find evidence of the continued existence of dreadful evils, and scapegoats who might be made to bear the moral debits associated with such evils.

We should bear in mind, though, that it is not only people like Doreen Irvine, Michelle Smith and Lauren Stratford who are in the business of reconstructing the narratives of their past lives and celebrating the extent of the personal progress they have made. Whatever else modern psychotherapies may have achieved, they have certainly demonstrated the hunger that we all have for explanations of our present difficulties that will absolve us from blame. Almost everyone feels the need of "salvation" from imperfection and incompetence, and there has always been a healthy market in scapegoats which can take the blame for our incapacities.

It is not merely possible but highly plausible that some of the adults who came forward to tell tales of having been sexually abused as children were desperate to find some such explanation for whatever difficulties they have encountered as adults. Now that having been abused as a child is publicly accepted as an explanation of later failures to form satisfactory relationships, there is an incentive of sorts for people to declare themselves, retrospectively, victims of such abuse. This is one of the factors that may confuse survey research into the extent of the problem, and which certainly confuses all attempts to figure out where, in this context, fantasy ends and truth begins.

The Reliability of Child Witnesses

In the final analysis, as Andrew Boyd observes in *Blasphemous Rumors*, the question of how to interpret the significance of the widespread rumors of ritual child molestation ultimately reduces to the question of how to interpret the evidence of the children who make the allegations. If what they said was not true, then how did they come by the stereotyped imagery that cropped up so frequently and consistently in their testimony, and why on earth did they make such fantastic allegations?

The skeptical account of how children come by the Sabbat-like imagery that forms the core of such allegations makes extensive use of two arguments. On the one hand, skeptics argue that much of this imagery is "put into the mouths" of the child-witnesses by interrogators who employ leading questions to draw it out; this process, of course, is parallel to the process by which men like Pierre de Lancre originally coaxed elaborate fantasies of the Sabbat and its rites from the mouths of little children. On the other hand, skeptics also argue that some of what the child-witnesses recount probably derives from horror films, which—although quite unsuitable for young children—are nowadays readily available in many homes in the form of videotapes.

Although both these arguments are superficially plausible, neither of them is strong enough to be wholly convincing. The former argument certainly helps to explain the spread of bizarre imagery through the testimony of a group of children once it has been introduced, but can hardly account for the origin of such testimony in cases that were not initially suspected to be anything more than ordinary and limited cases of molestation. The latter assumes, rather dubiously, that young children are likely to confuse things viewed on TV with real experience—and even if that were to be accepted, the further problem remains of identifying films that actually do contain this kind of imagery. In fact, the stereotyped imagery of modern horror films makes relatively little use of Sabbat-like imagery; if horror films were the source of the children's tales, one would expect a rather different set of images to have emerged.

The assumption that one needs explanations of these kinds to account for the appearance of Sabbat-like imagery in the testimony of young children might be mistaken. Perhaps adults simply underestimate the extent and complexity of children's oral culture: the culture of ideas and concerns that defines their community as something separate from and independent of the far more elaborate and confusing culture they share with adults, but in which they cannot fully participate. From a much younger age than adults may suppose—certainly at school age and almost certainly at "preschool" age—children begin to construct a social world of their own, which is to a large extent hidden from parents and teachers, having its own customs, rules and folklore. Fantasies of various kinds inevitably play a considerable role in the culture of children, both in their conversation and in their active play, and the attractions of horrific and melodramatic materials are at least as strong in that kind of culture as they are in the culture of adults.

Adults, by and large, have no way of knowing how extensive their children's folklore is, or what forms it takes—and they have no ready way of finding out, because the whole point of that lore is that it is the property of the children, routinely concealed from adults. Perhaps we should not be in the least surprised—however much we may regret it—that small children have some vague knowledge of what witches and Satanists are and what (in terms of our Christian mythology) they are supposed to get up to. Perhaps, too, we should not be surprised that, when small children begin to formulate their own ideas of evil, they can not only aggregate together any ideas of evil they have inherited from adults, but are perfectly capable of reproducing the psychological processes that originally generated those ideas, and of binding them together in much the same way.

It is necessary to remember, in trying to answer the question of how young children came by the imagery deployed in stories of rit-

THE DEVIL'S PARTY, BY BRIAN STABLEFORD

ual abuse, that this is by no means a new phenomenon. It is easy enough to see how the girls who started the Salem witch-scare came by their fantasies, or how some of de Lancre's witnesses developed theirs, but there have been—as for instance, in the Blokula scare—other allegations of a similar kind that were made spontaneously, in much the same fashion as the allegations that started the McMartin scandal and the South Ronaldsay affair. The simple fact is that even very young children do have ready access to ideas of this kind, and the capacity to spin them out very elaborately in response to the right kind of inquisition. The children who began the Blokula scare had never seen a horror movie and were not initially primed by leading questions, but they nevertheless contrived to start a large-scale panic based in extraordinarily colorful and bizarre fantasies. It may be that the more significant question is not *how* children are able to describe events of this kind, which have not really happened, but *why* they should ever want to.

Just as it is much easier to understand how stories of this kind spread like wildfire than it is to understand why they start in the first place, so it is easier to understand why children feel compelled to stick to their guns in defending a lie than it is to understand why they first produced the lie. Everyone knows from experience how difficult it is to come clean once a lie has been told, and how strong the temptation is to produce ever-more elaborate versions of the lie to protect oneself from the ultimate humiliation of exposure; this is a matter of everyday routine. The telling and subsequent defending of "white" lies intended to protect the feelings of others is absolutely necessary to harmonious social existence. "Black" lies, by which we seek to exonerate ourselves from blame by blaming others instead, are less worthy, but they tend to be judged equally necessary by their users whenever things become difficult; the entire history of witch-hunting establishes that beyond the shadow of a doubt.

The moral demands that parents make of their children may vary in content and intensity, but truthfulness is always a cardinal demand—and yet children quickly discover how important it is not to upset or offend their parents, and thus how vital it is that they cultivate, as covertly as they can, the art of lying. It is not at all surprising to find that children are determined, and sometimes very accomplished, liars. It is, therefore, understandable that once a child has produced a particular allegation, which has been taken up by interrogators, the child will not readily recant and may well become increasingly fervent in repeating and elaborating the allegation. If the history of witch-hunts has one central enigma, though, that enigma is why children should ever produce allegations of the particular kind with which we are dealing here.

One possibility worthy of attention is that children's motives for producing such stories may not be so very different from the motives of adults like Doreen Irvine and Lauren Stratford—that is to say, that they constitute a kind of "allegorizing" of experience. In constructing the narratives of our lives we all tend to dramatize; when we tell others about the exciting things that have happened to us we all tend to make small literary adjustments of various kinds. We make the dialogue snappier, the action smoother—and the danger we were in more acute. To have been saved from something dramatically horrible is much more *worthwhile* as an experience than to have been saved from very ordinary hazards. We are all inclined to exaggerate our sense of injury when we are unkindly treated, and to magnify small slights; we should, therefore, be able to understand how these very mundane processes of exaggeration can sometimes be taken to extremes—and how, once having reached those extremes, it is so difficult to reduce the dramatized experience back to its actual proportions.

Children are, for the most part, powerless. The means by which they can exercise power over their parents—begging, wheedling and screaming—are limited, and as often apt to call forth reprisals as to achieve the desired ends. Parents not only have an effective armory to back up their demands that children ought to be good (which sometimes extends to actual violence) but an invincible sense of the moral propriety of that demand. Children have virtually no sanctions to use against parents in pursuit of their own desire to make parents treat them well, and may have little or no confidence in the moral legitimacy of that desire. Occasionally, though, a window of opportunity does appear that might allow this imbalance to be redressed; occasionally, the opportunity arises for children to level accusations against adults *and be heard*.

The vast majority of children do not use such windows of opportunity, partly because they have no real need of them, partly because they fear long-term reprisals, and partly because they can never quite believe that they actually will be believed—all of which reservations are entirely reasonable. But such windows of opportunity do offer the child who—for whatever reason—is thoroughly and desolately miserable an opportunity to make his or her misery manifest; it is not so very difficult to understand how "making misery manifest" may, in some cases, lead to fabulous dramatization.

That, after all, is how most fabulous dramas produced by adults are motivated.

Mot people would prefer to believe that any sexual abuse of small children which does go on is the work of rare inhuman perverts, who only have to be weeded out from the population of the virtuous for the problem to be solved. No doubt small children would prefer to believe it too, and sometimes allow that preference—especially when it is licensed by sympathetic listeners—to confuse their memories of actual events. However, the demonization of child sexual abuse surely does more harm than good. Such demonization does not help us to understand the problem, it does not help us to solve the problem, and it certainly does not help us to deal sensitively and effectively with either the perpetrators or the victims. People aware of the pattern laid out in this history may find it easy enough to understand how a sense of horror and outrage can give rise to the demonization of human behaviors, but that understanding ought to serve to make us even more aware of the fact that demonization is a strategy that is both stupid and dangerous.

The central irony of the whole history of Satanic abuse is, alas, that the melodramatic horror stories people make up about vile conspiracies of Satanists are infinitely more comfortable than the consciousness that all the real horrors of human existence exist within the community and within ourselves, lurking behind the mask of polite behavior. Until we are prepared to recognize that, the prospect of building a better society, in which such horrors are reduced to the attainable minimum, remains remote. In the meantime, Satanic abuse will continue to pour forth from its various fountainheads—not merely literary fantasies. scholarly fantasies, anecdotal rumor and tabloid reportage, but even, alas, the minds and mouths of little children.

SELECTED BIBLIOGRAPHY

Anglo, Sydney, ed. *The Damned Art: Essays in the Literature of Witchcraft*. London: Routledge & Kegan Paul, 1977.
Anon. *Newes from Scotland Declaring the Damnable Life and Death of Doctor Fian, a Notable Sorceror Who Was Burned at Edenbrough in January Last*. London: William Wright, 1591.
Bacon, Francis. *Sylva Sylvarum, or a Naturall Historie*. London: J. H. for W. Lee, 1626 (actually 1627).
Baddeley, Gavin. *Lucifer Rising*. London: Plexus, 1999.
Baroja, Julio Caro. *The World of Witches*, tr. Nigel Glendinning, London: Weidenfeld & Nicolson, 1964.
Baxter, Christopher. "Jean Bodin's *De la Démonomanie des Sorciers*: The Logic of Persecution" in Anglo, *The Damned Art*.
___. "Johann Weyer's *De Praestigiis Daemonum*: Unsystematic Psychopathology" in Anglo, *The Damned Art*.
Bodin, Jean. "Refutation des opinions de Jean Wier" tr. in Monter, *European Witchcraft*.
Boguet, Henri. *An Examen of Witches* tr. E. A. Ashwin, ed. Montague Summers. London: John Rodker, 1929.
Boyd, Andrew. *Blasphemous Rumors*. London: Fount, 1991.
Briggs, Katharine M. *The Witch Figure*. London: Routledge and Kegan Paul, 1973.
Briggs, Robin. *Witches and Neighbors: The Social and Cultural Context of European Witchcraft*. London: HarperCollins, 1996.
Burke, Peter. "Witchcraft and Magic in Renaissance Italy: Gianfrancesco Pico and his *Strix*" in Anglo, ed. *The Damned Art*.
Butler, E. M. *The Myth of the Magus*. Cambridge: Cambridge University Press, 1993.
Charles, R. H., tr. and ed. *The Book of Enoch*. London: SPCK, 1917.
Clark, Stuart. *Thinking with Demons: The Idea of Witchcraft in Early Modern Europe*. Oxford: Clarendon Press, 1997.
Cohn, Norman. *Europe's Inner Demons*. London: Heinemann, 1975.
___. *The Pursuit of the Millennium*. London: Temple Smith, 1970.

Crowley, Aleister. *Magick in Theory and Practice by the Master Therion*. Paris: Lecram, 1929.
Delcambre, Étienne. *Le Concept de la sorcellerie dans le duché de Lorraine au XVIe et XVIIe siècles*. Nancy: Société d'archéologie Lorraine, 1948-51.
___. "The Psychology of Lorraine Witchcraft Suspects" in Monter, ed. *European Witchcraft*.
Eliade, Mircea. *Occultism, Witchcraft and Cultural Fashions*. Chicago: Chicago University Press, 1976.
Ewen, C. L'Estrange. *Witch Hunting and Witch Trials*. London: Kegan Paul, Trench, Trübner & Co, 1929.
___. *Witchcraft and Demonianism*. London: Heath Cranston, 1933.
Fortune, Dion. *The Training and Work of an Initiate*. London: Rider, 1930.
Frazer, James G. *The Golden Bough*. 2 vols. London: Macmillan, 1890. exp 3rd ed. 12 vols. London: Macmillan, 1911-15.
Gardner, Gerald B. *The Meaning of Witchcraft*, Wellingborough: Aquarian Press, 1959.
___. *Witchcraft Today*. London: Rider, 1954.
Ginzburg, Carlo. *The Night Battles: Witchcraft and Agrarian Cults in the Sixteenth and Seventeenth Centuries*. London: Routledge & Kegan Paul, 1983.
___. *Ecstasies: Deciphering the Witches' Sabbat*. London: Hutchinson, 1991.
Glanvill, Joseph. *Saducismus Triumphatus*. London: J. Collins & S. Lowndes, 1681.
Grant, Kenneth. *Magical Revival*. London: Muller, 1972.
Graves, Robert. *The White Goddess*. London: Faber and Faber, 1948.
Grillot de Givry, Emile. *Witchcraft, Magic and Alchemy*. Paris: Librairie de France, 1931.
Guazzo, Francesco Maria. *Compendium Maleficarum*, tr. E. A. Ashwin, ed. Montague Summers. London: John Rodker, 1929.
Harrison, Michael. *The Roots of Witchcraft*. London: Muller, 1973.
Hopkins, Matthew. *The Discovery of Witches*. London: R. Royston, 1647.
Huebner, Louise. *Power Through Witchcraft*. New York: Nash, 1969
Huson, Paul. *Mastering Witchcraft*. London: Hart-Davis, 1970.
Hutton, Ronald. *The Triumph of the Moon: A History of Modern Pagan Witchcraft*. Oxford: Oxford University Press, 1999.
Irvine, Doreen. *From Witchcraft to Christ*. Lutterworth: Concordia Press, 1973.

James I of England. *Daemonologie*, bound with *Newes from Scotland*. London: John Lane, 1924. [1597]

Jennings, Hargrave. *The Rosicrucians: Their Rites and Mysteries*. 2 vols. London: John C. Nimmo, 1887.

Karlsen, Carol F. *The Devil in the Shape of a Woman*. New York: Norton, 1987.

Kelly, Henry Ansgar. *The Devil, Demonology and Witchcraft*. New York: Doubleday, 1968.

Kieckhefer, Richard. *European Witch Trials*. London: Routledge and Kegan Paul, 1976.

King, Francis. *Ritual Magic in England: 1887 to the Present Day*. London: Spearman, 1970.

Kittredge, G. L. *Witchcraft in Old and New England*. Cambridge, Mass: Harvard University Press, 1929.

Kluger, R. S. *Satan in the Old Testament*. Evanston: Northwestern University Press, 1967.

La Fontaine, Jean. *Child Sexual Abuse*. Cambridge: Polity Press, 1990.

Lancre, Pierre de. *Tableau de l'inconstance des mauvais anges et demons*. Paris: Nicolas Buon, 1708. [1610]

Langton, Edward. *Satan, a Portrait: A Study of he Character of Satan Throughout the Ages*. New York: Gordon Press, 1976.

Larner, Christine. *Enemies of God: The Witch-Hunt in Scotland*. London: Chatto & Windus, 1981.

LaVey, Anton Szandor. *The Satanic Bible*. New York: Avon, 1969.

___. *The Satanic Rituals*. New York: Avon, 1972

___. *The Satanic Witch*. Los Angeles: Feral House, 1989.

Lea, Henry Charles. *Materials Towards a History of Witchcraft*. Philadelphia: University of Pennsylvania Press, 1939.

Leek, Sybil. *Diary of a Witch*. London: Leslie Frewin, 1975.

Leland, Charles Godfrey. *Aradia: The Gospel of the Witches*. London: David Nutt, 1899.

___. *Gypsy Sorcery and Fortune Telling*. London: T. Fisher Unwin, 1891.

Levack, Brian P. *The Witch Hunt in Early Modern Europe*. New York: Longman, 1987.

Lévi, Éliphas. *Dogme et rituel de la haute magie*. Paris: Germer Ballière, 1856. Tr. by A. E. Waite as *Transcendental Magic: Its Doctrine and Ritual*. London: Rider, 1896.

___. *Histoire de la magie*. Paris: Germer Ballière, 1860. Tr. by A. E. Waite as *The History of Magic*. London: Rider, 1913.

Macfarlane, Alan. *Witchcraft in Tudor and Stuart England*. London: Routledge & Kegan Paul, 1970.

Macintosh, Christopher. *Eliphas Levi and the French Occult Revival*. London: Rider, 1972.
Mackay, Charles. *Memoirs of Extraordinary Popular Delusions*. London: Richard Bentley, 1841. Revised ed. as *Extraordinary Popular Delusions and the Madness of Crowds*. London: National Illustrated Library, 1852.
Malebranche, Nicolas *De la recherche de la vérité*. Paris: André Pralard, 1674.
Mandrou, Robert. *Magistrats et sorciers en France au XVIIe siècle*. Paris: Plon, 1968.
Martin, Ruth. *Witchcraft and the Inquisition in Venice, 1550-1650*. Oxford: Blackwell, 1989.
Mather, Cotton. *The Wonders of the Invisible World*. London: John Russell Smith, 1862. [1692]
McGowan, Margaret M. "Pierre de Lancre's *Tableau de l'Inconstance des Mauvais Anges et Demons*: The Sabbat Sensationalised" in Anglo, *The Damned Art*
Michelet, Jules. *La Sorcière*. Paris: Dentu, 1862. Tr. by A. R. Allinson as *Satanism and Witchcraft*. New York: Citadel, 1939.
Midelfort, H. C. Erik. *Witch Hunting in Southwestern Germany 1562-1684*. Stanford: Stanford University Press, 1972.
Monter, E. William, ed. *European Witchcraft*. New York: Wiley, 1969.
___. *Witchcraft in France and Switzerland*. Ithaca: Cornell University Press, 1976.
Murray, Margaret. *The God of the Witches*. Oxford: Oxford University Press, 1931.
___. *The Witch-Cult in Western Europe* Oxford: Oxford University Press, 1921.
Notestein, Wallace. *History of Witchcraft in England 1558-1718*. Washington: American Historical Association, 1911.
Oates, Caroline, and Juliette Wood. *A Coven of Scholars: Margaret Murray and her Working Methods*. London: Folk-Lore Society, 1998.
Pagels, Elaine. *The Origin of Satan*. London: Penguin, 1997.
Parrinder, Geoffrey. *Witchcraft, European and African*. London: Faber & Faber, 1958.
Pauwels, Louis, and Jacques Bergier. *Le Matin des magiciens*. Paris: Gallimard, 1930.
Praz, Mario. *La carne, la morte e il diavolo nella letteratura romantica*. Milan: La Cultura, 1930.
Purkiss, Diane. *Troublesome Things: A History of Fairies and Fairy Stories*. London: Penguin, 2000.

___. *The Witch in History: Early Modern and Twentieth Century Representations*. London: Routledge, 1996.
Rémy. Nicholas. *Demonolatry* tr. E. A. Ashwin, ed. Montague Summers. London: John Rodker, 1948.
Rhodes, H. T. F. *The Satanic Mass*. London: Rider, 1954.
Robbins, Rossell Hope. *Encyclopedia of Witchcraft and Demonology*. New York: Crown, 1959.
Rosen, Barbara, ed. *Witchcraft in England 1558-1618*. Amherst: University of Massachusetts Press, 1991.
Rudwin, Maximilian. *The Devil in Legend and Literature*. Chicago: Open Court, 1931.
Russell, Jeffrey Burton. *The Devil: Perceptions of Evil from Antiquity to Primitive Christianity*. Ithaca, N. Y.: Cornell University Press, 1977.
___. *Lucifer: The Devil in the Middle Ages*. Ithaca, N. Y.: Cornell University Press, 1984.
___. *Mephistopheles: The Devil in the Modern World*. Ithaca, N. Y.: Cornell University Press, 1986.
___. *Satan: The Early Christian Tradition*. Ithaca, N. Y.: Cornell University Press, 1981.
___. *Witchcraft in the Middle Ages*. Ithaca, N. Y.: Cornell University Press, 1972.
Scot, Reginald. *The Discoverie of Witchcraft*. London: William Brome, 1584.
Smith, Michele, and Lawrence Padzer, MD. *Michelle Remembers*. London: Michael Joseph, 1981.
Spence, Lewis. *An Encyclopedia of Occultism*. London: Routledge, 1920.
___. *The Mysteries of Britain; or, The Secret Rites and Traditions of Ancient Britain Restored*. London: Rider, 1928.
Sprenger, Jacob and Heinrich Kramer. *Malleus Maleficarum* trans. Montague Summers, London: John Rodker, 1928.
Starhawk. *The Spiral Dance: A Rebirth of the Religion of the Great Goddess*. San Francisco, Cal.: Harper and Row, 1979.
Stratford, Lauren. *Satan's Underground*. Eugene: Harvest House, 1988.
Summers, Montague. *The History of Witchcraft and Demonology*. London: Routledge & Kegan Paul, 1926.
Thomas, K. V. *Religion and the Decline of Magic*. London: Weidenfeld & Nicolson, 1971.
Thomas, M. Wynn. "Cotton Mather's *Wonders of the Invisible World*: Some Metamorphoses of Salem Witchcraft" in Anglo, *The Damned Art*.

Thorndike, Lynn. *The History of Magic and Experimental Science*. 8 vols. New York: Macmillan (vols. 1 & 2), Columbia University Press (vols. 3-8), 1923-58.

Trevor-Roper, Hugh. *The European Witch-Craze of the 16th and 17th Centuries*. Harmondsworth: Pelican, 1969.

___. *Religion, the Reformation and Social Change*. London: Macmillan, 1967.

Valiente, Doreen. *The Rebirth of Witchcraft*. Custer, Wash.: Phoenix, 1989.

Vermes, G. *The Dead Sea Scrolls in English*. London: Penguin, 1962.

Victor, Jeffrey S. *Satanic Panic: The Creation of a Contemporary Legend*. Chicago: Open Court, 1993.

Waite, A. E. *The Book of Ceremonial Magic*. London: Rider, 1911.

___. *The Brotherhood of the Holy Cross*. London: Rider. 1924.

___. *The Occult Sciences*. London: Kegan Paul, Trench and Trübner, 1891.

___. *The Real History of the Rosicrucians*. London: George Redway, 1887.

Webster, John. *The Displaying of Supposed Witchcraft*. London: J. M., 1677.

Wilson, Bryan. *Magic and the Millennium*. London: Heinemann, 1973.

Yates, Frances A. *Giordano Bruno and the Hermetic Tradition*. London: Routledge & Kegan Paul, 1964.

___. *The Rosicrucian Enlightenment*. London: Routledge & Kegan Paul, 1972.

INDEX

Aaron 25
Aarseth, Øysten 201
Abraham 38
Acts of the Apostles 32, 36-37
Adam 22, 27
Ad Extirpanda 56
Agape 48
Ahmed, Rollo 178, 204
Ahriman 28
Ahura Mazda 28
Alain de Lille 57
Albertus Magnus 72, 106
Albigensians 46, 57
Alchemy 36, 39, 64, 72, 189-190
Alexander VI, Pope, see Borgia, Rodrigo
Alice in Wonderland 202
The Alps 85-86
Andreae, Johann Valentin 185-186
Anger, Kenneth 199
Angus, Earl of 116
Anthony, Saint 145
The Anti-Christ 41-42, 155
The Apocalypse 28
Apollonius of Tyana 37
Apologia sine Oratio de Magia 143
Apuleius 143
Aquino, Michael 200
Aradia: The Gospel of the Witches 168, 194
Aristotle 35, 129, 141, 185
Arran, Earl of 92
Arras 86
Asmodeus 147
Astrology 36, 39, 183, 185
Aubrey, John 164
Augustine, Saint 38-39, 42, 68, 73
Austria 90
"Aut Diabolos aut Nihil" 158
Avignon 62

Azazel 21-22
Baal 28
Bacon, Roger, 72
Bacon, Francis 129-130
Bailey, Philip James 150
Balaam 25
Balak 25
Balzac, Honoré de 150
Baphomet 59
Barozzi; or, the Venetian Sorceress 154
Barrett, Francis 164
Baudelaire, Charles 147-148, 167
Baudino, Gael 196
Baum, L. Frank 156
The Beast (of Revelation) 41
Beauvais, Bishop of 63
Beelzebub 28
Beggar's Banquet 199
Bekker, Balthasar 132-134
Belial 27
Bell, Book, and Candle 156
Benedict IX, Pope 60
Benét, Stephen Vincent 150
Bergier, Jacques 178-179
The Berwick witches 115-117, 151
Bewitched 156
The Black Art 178
The Black Death 46
Black Magic 155
Black masses 126, 187-189
Black Metal 201
Black metal music 201-202
Black Sabbath 199, 202
Black Widow 199-200
Blackwood's Magazine 158
Blake, William 146-147
Blasphemous Rumours 206, 213-214, 218
Blatty, William Peter 158
Blavatsky, Helena 191
The Blokula scare 132-134, 208, 220
The Blood libel 44
Bluebeard 63
The Blue Firedrake 154
Bodin, Jean 108-110, 113, 115, 117, 124, 131, 166, 176
Bosch, Hieronymus 145
Boguet, Henri 122-124, 166, 176
Bologna 72
Boniface VIII, Pope, 60, 62
The Book of Shadows 193-194
Borgia, Rodrigo 105
Bowen, Marjorie 155

Boyd, Andrew 206, 213-214, 217-218
Bradley, Marion Zimmer 196
Brady, Ian 206
Brahe, Tyco 129
Brief Lives 164
The British Occult Society 205
Brittany 63
Brittany, Duke of 64
Brodie-Innes, J. W. 154, 192
Brome, Richard 152
Bruno, Giordano 105
Buchan, John 175
Buddhism 38
Bulgakov, Mikhail 157
Bulwer-Lytton, Edward 165, 191
Burgundy, Duke of 63
Burn, Baby, Burn! 201
Burzum 201
Butler-Sloss enquiry 209-210
Butterfield, Herbert 106
By Firelight 154
Byron, Lord 168
Cain 20, 119
Calef, Robert 138
Calvin, John 90
Canon Episcopi 69-70, 75-76, 81, 103, 168
Carcassonne 60, 76
La Carne, la morte e il diavolo 155
Carroll, Lewis 202
Casaubon, Isaac 184
Casaubon, Meric 164, 191
The Case Against Satan 158
Cathars 46, 57
Cautio Criminalis 128
Cazotte, Jacques 147
Le Centenaire ou les deux Behringelds 150
Chariot of Fire 158
Charlemagne 40
Charles I, King of England 120
Charles of Lorraine, Prince 121
Charmed 156
Childline 209
ChildWatch 209, 211
Christ 23, 27, 30, 36-38, 40-41, 47-49, 82, 149
Christliche Erinnerung 128
Christmas 68
Chronicles 20
The Church of Satan 198-199, 202
Chymische Hochzeit Christiani Rosenkreutz 185
Circe 141-142, 166
The City of God 39

Clair, René 156
Clash of Angels 148
Clavicula Salomonis 73, 110, 114, 169, 194
Clement V, Pope 60
Cleveland 209-210
Cohn, Norman 85, 179
Cologne 78
"Come to the Sabbat" 200
Compendium Maleficarum 123-124
Compiègne 63
Comte, Auguste 170
Confessio Frateritas 185
Conrad of Marburg 56-57, 71
Constant, Alphonse-Louis 165
Constantine 50
Constantine, Murray 148
Conventicles, see Sabbats and conventicles
Corelli, Marie 148, 165
Corey, Giles 135
Corinthians 36
Cornelius Agrippa von Nettesheim 106-108
Corpus Hermeticum 105, 184
Cortés 90
The Council of Ancyra 69
The Council of Nicaea 50
The Council of Trent 90
The Covenant 29-30, 32
Covens 173-174
Crowley, Aleister 178, 192-195, 202
The Crucible 154
The Crusades 40
Cunningham, John 116-117
Daedalus Hyperboreus 163
Daemonologie 117-119, 131
Dahl, Roald 157
Dalton, James 150
Daly, Mary 196
Damien: Omen II 159
Daniels, Jonathan 148
Darkthrone 201
Darwin, Charles 32, 217
Dashwood, Sir Fredrick (Baron le Despencer) 188-189
Dauphiné 85
Davenport, Basil 150
David 20, 30
Day of Judgment 32-33, 41
The Dead Riders 178
The Dead Sea Scrolls 27
A Deal with the Devil 150
Deals with the Devil 150
Deathlike Silence 201

De Betoverde Weereld 132-133
De Civitate Dei 39, 42
Dee, John 114, 129, 164, 191
A Defense of Poetry 147
Defoe, Daniel 153, 164
Deicide 201
Dekker, Thomas 152
De la démonomanie des sorciers 108-110
Delcambre, Étienne 95-100, 179, 216
Demonolatria 121-123
Denmark 90, 116
De Occulta Philosophia 107-108
De Praestigiis Daemonum 106
Descartes, René 129-131
Deshayes, Catherine (La Voisin) 187-188
Deuteronomy 21, 23-24
Device, Alizon 152-153
Device, Elizabeth 152
Device, Jennet 152-153
Devil, The 20, 42, 57, 63, 69-71, 73-74, 77, 84, 85, 89, 105, 110-112, 114, 117-118, 121, 123, 127, 132, 135-138, 147, 149-151, 158, 162, 177, 180
"The Devil and Daniel Webster" 150
The Devil and the Doctor 148
"The Devil Is My Name" 199
The Devil, Poor Devil! 148
The Devil Rides Out 158, 178
The Devil's Mistress 154
The Devils of Loudoun 154
The Devil Takes a Holiday 157
Le Diable amoureux 147
Le Diable boiteux 147
Diana 69, 75, 142, 168
The Diet of Speyer 90
The Diet of Wurms 90
Digges, Thomas 111, 114, 129
Discours des sorciers 122-123
The Discoverie of Witchcraft 24, 110-115
The Discovery of Witches 119-120
The Divine King in England 173
Doctor Faustus 150
Dogme et ritual de la haut magie 165
Dominican Order 55, 60, 69, 75, 77-78, 81
Drake, Nathan 164
Dreaming the Dark 196
Dublin 62
Dumas, Alexandre 150
Duncan, Geillis 115
Dworkin, Andrea 196
Egypt 33
The Electric Hell-Fire Club 201
Elizabeth I, Queen of England 90, 92, 110, 115

Elymas 37
Emperor 201
Encyclopaedia Britannica 173, 191
Encyclopedia of Occultism 176
Endymion 168
England 90, 92, 100, 112-113, 119-120
England, Church of 90, 134, 176
Enneads 35
Enoch 22, 26-27, 29-30, 33, 169
Epping Forest 210
Erasmus 89-90
Essex 100, 117, 119
Euripides 142
Euronymous 201
The European Witch-Craze of the 16th and 17th Centuries 86
Europe's Inner Demons 85
Eve 27, 82
Everyday witchcraft 67-68, 85, 142
Ewen, C. L'Estrange 93, 179
Exodus 24-25
The Exorcist 158-159
Fabian, Robert 178
Fairy tales 156-157
Fama Fraternitas 185
Farrant, David 205
Faust 149-150, 153, 155, 166
Faust (Nye) 150
Faust (Spies) 149
Faustbuch 149-150
Faustine 151
Faustus 149
Femmes fatales 155-157
Festus 150
Ficino, Marsilio 105, 107-108, 184, 186, 189
Field, Julian Osgood 158, 165, 189
Fingal 168
Finland 133
Firth, Violet 192
Flaubert, Gustave 148, 150
Flecker's Magic 155
Fleurs du mal, Les 147-148, 167
Florence 105
Fludd, Robert 185-186
Forbes, Esther 154
Ford, John 152
Formicarius 74-76, 86
Fortune, Dion 192-193
Fourier, Charles 163
The Fox sisters 165
France 58-61, 86, 88, 91, 94, 147, 187
France, Anatole 148, 199

Franciscan Order 55, 58, 60, 62, 69
Fraticelli 58
Frazer, James 169-172
Frederick I, Emperor 53-54
Freemasons 190-191
Freud, Sigmund 207
The Freud: The Assault on Truth 207
The Friars of St. Francis of Wycombe 188
From Witchcraft to Christ 215
Galileo 129
Gardner, Gerald Brousseau 175, 193-197
Gaule, John 119-120
Gawaine and the Green Knight 74
Genesis 19-22, 26
The Gentleman in Black 150
Gerhardie, William 148
Germany 56, 86, 90-91, 94, 127, 162
Gilles de Rais 63-64, 86, 158
Glanvill, Joseph 131-133
Gnosticism 35-39, 107
God 19-22, 24-26, 28-29, 32-33, 41-42, 70, 79, 82, 89, 96-97, 110-112, 134, 146, 202
The God of the Witches 173
Goethe, J. W. 149
The Golden Ass 143
The Golden Bough 169-171
Gomorrah 37
Good, Sarah 135
Gotthelf, Jeremias 150
Gowdie, Isabel 174
The Grand Grimoire 73
The Grand Mystery Laid Open 190
Graves, Robert 174-175
Greek and Roman literature 140-144
Greek Orthodox Church 51
Gregory I, Pope, 40
Gregory IX, Pope 55, 57, 71
Grimm, Jakob 162
Growing Rich 151
Grimoires 73-74, 110
Guazzo, Francesco Maria 123-124, 131, 177
Guibourg, Abbé 187
Guichard, Bishop of Troyes 60, 62
Hales, E. E. Y. 158
Hammond, Esther Barstow 154
Handbook for the Christian Warrior 89
Harrison, Michael 174
Harvillier, Jeanne 108-109
Hawthorne, Nathaniel 154
Heaven and Hell and the Megas Factor 157
Hecate 142, 152

Heidelberg 149
Hellfire Clubs 188-189, 194, 199
Helvete 201
Henry VIII, King of England 90, 92
Hermes Trismegistus 39
The Hermetic Tradition 39, 105, 184-185, 191
Heywood, Thomas 153
Highgate Cemetery 205
High Magic's Aid 193
Histoire de la magie 165
The History of the Devil 153
The History of Witchcraft and Demonology 175
Hitler, Adolf 200
Hjarne, Urban 133-134
Hobbes, Thomas 129
Hoffman, Alice 156
Holland 90
The Holy Office 56
Hopkins, Matthew 118-120, 138
Horace 142
Huebner, Louise 198
Huson, Paul 198
Hutton, Ronald 196
Huxley, Aldous 154
Huygens, Christian 129
Huysmans, Joris-Karl 158, 165, 189
Iamblichus 35-36
Iceland 144
I Married a Witch 156
Incubi and succubi 74-75, 77, 109
Infernaliana 164
Innocent IV, Pope 56
Innocent VIII, Pope 77, 105
The Inquisition 54-58, 76-78
Iranaeus 34
Ireland 62
Irvine, Doreen 215, 217, 220
Isaiah 19, 21, 34
Islam 43, 51, 147
Israel 20, 23, 25, 32, 111
Italy 85, 124
Jack Faust 150
Jagger, Mick 199
James I, King of England (and VI of Scotland) 21, 115-120, 124, 127, 131
James II, King of England 134
James V, King of Scotland 92
Jarcke, Karl 162
Jason 141-142
Jeanne d'Arc 63
Jehovah 19, 22, 25, 27, 32, 148
Jepson, Edgar 192-193, 202

Jerusalem 31, 58
Jesuits 88, 90, 185
Jesus 32, 49, 148
Joan of Arc, see Jeanne d'Arc
Job 19-20
John 41
Jones, Brian 199
Jovian 50
Jubilees 27
Judas Priest 202
Jude 37
Judea 30-31
Julian (the Apostate), Roman Emperor 38, 50
Justin Martyr 34
The Kabbalah 39, 105, 185, 193
Keats, John 168
Keller, David H. 148
Kelley, Edward 114
Kenyon, Theda 178
Kepler, John 129
Kerr, John 116
The Key of Solomon, see *Clavicula Salomonis*
Khomeini, Ayatollah 147
Kilkenny, 61-62
King of the Witches 204
Kings 20
Kircher, Athanasius 185
Kiss the Goat 201
Knights Templar see Templars, The
Knox, John 92
Kramer, Heinrich 77-82, 86, 109-110, 176
Kyteler, Lady Alice 61-62, 85
Là-bas 158
Labourd 100, 124
Lamiarum sive Striarum opusculum 77
The Lancashire witches 120, 152-3
The Lancashire Witches (Ainsworth) 153
The Lancashire Witches (Shadwell) 153
Lancre, Pierre de 81, 100, 124-126, 167, 176, 218, 200
The Last Devil 193
The Late Lancashire Witches 153
LaVey, Anton 198-202
Lawrence, D. H. 192
"The Lay of the Last Minstrel" 164
Lea, Henry Charles 76, 85, 176, 179
Ledrede, Richard de, Bishop of Ossory 61-62
Leek, Sybil 194-195, 197
Leland, Charles Godfrey 168-169, 171-172, 194
Le Sage, Alain René 147
Letters on Demonology and Witchcraft 164
Leven, Jeremy 157

Lévi, Éliphas 165, 191
Levin, Ira 159
Leviathan 34
Leviticus 21, 24
Lewis, C. S. 158
Lewis, H. Spencer 190-191
Lewis, Matthew Gregory 150, 164
Liberace 183
Liber Sacer 73
Liber Sacratus 73
A Likeness to Voices 156
Lilith 21-22
"Les Litanies de Satan" 147
Lolly Willowes; or, The Loving Huntsman 155
The Lord of the Rings 196
Lorraine 95, 100, 121
Louis XIV, King of France 187
Loyola, Ignatius 90
Lucan 142
Lucian 143
Lucifer 28, 146, 153, 199
Lucifer 146
"Lucifer" 148
Lucifer Rising 199
Lucius III, Pope 53-54
Lunn, Brian 148
Luther, Martin 89-90
Macbeth 111, 151, 154
Macfarlane, Alan 100, 117, 119
Machen, Arthur 192
Mackay, Charles 164-165
Macpherson, James 168
Magi 38, 155
The Magician 192, 202
Magick in Theory and Practice 202
Maguire, Gregory 156
The Magus 164
Malebranche, Nicholas 129-131
Malefice 154
Mallet-Joris, Françoise 154
Malleus Maleficarum 77-82, 86-87, 94, 107, 109, 151
Mandrou, Robert 87-88, 101
Mani 38
Manicheism 38, 57, 147
Mann, Thomas 150
Manson, Charles 200, 206
Manson, Marilyn 200
Marcus Aurelius, Roman Emperor 48
Maria Schweidler, die Bernsteinhexe 154
Marlowe, Christopher 149
Mastering Witchcraft 198

Marx, Karl 51
Masson, P. M. 207
Mastema 27
Master i Margarita 157
Materials Towards a History of Witchcraft 85
Mather, Cotton 134, 136-138
Mather, Increase 134
Mathers, Samuel Liddell 191, 194
Maturin, Charles 150
Le Matière de Bretagne 154
Les Matin des magiciens 178-179
Matson, Norman 155-156
Matthew 28
Maugham, W. Somerset 192, 202
Mayhem 201
Mayfarth, Johann 128
McCarthy, Joseph 154
McMartin Preschool 208
Medea 141-142, 151, 155
Medea 142
Medici, Cosimo de 105
Medici, Lorenzo de 105
Meinhold, William 154
Mekilresha' 27
"Melmoth reconcilié" 150
Melmoth the Wanderer 150
Memoirs of Extraordinary Popular Delusions 164
The Memoirs of Satan 148
Memorable Providences Relating to Witchcraft and Possessions 136
Le Meneur de loups 150
Merlin 154-155
México 90
Michael 27, 34
Michelet, Jules 165-169, 171-172, 177, 179, 186, 195
Michelle Remembers 216
Middleton, Thomas 152
Midelfort, H. C. Erik 83, 100
Milan 77, 124
Millenarianism 41, 58
The Millennium 40-42
Miller, Arthur 154
Milton, John 146-147
Minucius, Felix 48
A Mirror for Witches 154
Mist over Pendle 153
The Mists of Avalon 196
Mithraism 38
Mockingbird 196
Mone, Franz 162
Monter, E. W. 87-89, 101
The Monk 150

Montespan, Madame de 187
Montfort, Simon de 57
Mora 132-133
More, Henry 133
More Wonders of the Invisible World 138
Murray, Margaret 169, 171-175, 177, 179-180, 186, 190, 193, 198
The Mysteries of Britain 175
Mysticism 36, 39, 185
Nantes 64
Napoléon I, Emperor of the French 56
Nathan, Robert 157
The National Society for the Prevention of Cruelty to Children 210
Navarre 91-92
Necropolis 201
Neill, Robert 153
Neo-Platonism 35-37, 39, 50, 73, 105, 107
Neo-Pythagoreanism 35, 37, 39, 185
Nero 41
New English Library 205
Newes from Scotland 115-116
The News of the World 204
The New Testament 19, 27, 33, 41, 145
Newton, Isaac 170
Nider, Johannes 74-76, 81, 86
Nightmares witches 66-68, 74, 142
No. 19 192, 202
Noah 38
Nodier, Charles 164
Nogaret, Guillaume de 60, 62
Norris, James Brewer 154
Norway 116, 201
Nottingham 210
Noyes, Alfred 157
Numbers 25
Nutter, Alice 152
Nye, Robert 150
Occult Science 39, 72, 163-167, 191
The Occult Tradition 39
The Occult World 191
Odin 201
O'Donnell, Elliott 178, 204
Odyssey 142
Odysseus 141-142
Oeconomia Regni Animalis 163
O fiscio prodigioso 150
The Old Testament 19-27, 32, 42, 139
The Omen 159
Omen II: The Final Conflict 159
On Imagination 106
Opera Philosophica et Mineralia 163
The Order of the Golden Dawn 191-192

Origen 34
Orleans 52-53, 63
Orridge, Genesis P. 200
Osbourne, Ozzy 202
Osbourne, Sarah 135
Ossian 168
Ovid 143
Oxford 72
Pacts, Diabolical 71-74, 79-80, 148-150, 155, 164
Padzer, Lawrence 216-217
Pan 173, 192
Paracelsus 107
Paradise Lost 146-147
Pargeter, Edith 154
Paris 72, 86
Parris, Samuel 135
The Passionate Witch 156
Paul, Saint 32, 34, 36, 38, 75
Pauwels, Louis 178-179
Paxson, Diana L. 196
La Peau de chagrin 150
Péladan, Joséphin 165
Pentagram 73-74
Persia 33, 38, 50
Peru 90
Peter of Berne 86
Petronilla of Meath 61-62
Pharsalia 142
Philip the Fair, see Philippe IV
Philippe IV (le Bel), King of France 58-62, 88
Philistines, 25
Phillpotts, Eden 150
Philostratus 37
Phips, Governor (of New England) 136
Pico della Mirandola, Gianfrancesco 104-106, 117, 139, 168
Pico della Mirandola, Giovanni 105
Pistis Sophia 36
Pius IX, Pope 149
Pizarro 90
Plato 35, 129, 141
Plotinus 35
Pompey 31
Porphyry 35
Potts, Thomas 152
The Power of Witchcraft 198
Practical Magic 156
Pratchett, Terry 157
Praz, Mario 155
Primitive Culture 170
Prometheus Unbound 147
The Promised Land 23, 28-29, 31

Prose Edda 144
Psychick TV 200
Le Puits de Sainte-Claire 148
Purkiss, Diana 174
The Pyrenees 86, 126
Pythagoras 35
Qumran 27, 30
Randolph, P. B. 189
Rantzen, Esther 209
A Razor for a Goat 180
Recherche de la vérité 131
Redfearne, Anne 152
The Reformation 65, 88-90, 93, 101, 106
Regino, Abbot of Prum 69
Rémy, Nicholas 100, 121-124, 176
The Renaissance 36, 38-39, 52, 64, 67, 72, 81, 89, 97, 100, 105, 110, 140, 144, 149, 161, 166
"The Resurgent Mysteries" 193
The Return of Fursey 157
Reveille 204
The Revelation of St John the Divine 33, 41-42, 58
La Révolte des anges 148
Richard, Keith 199
Robin Artisson 61
Rochdale 210
The Rolling Stones 199-200
Roman literature, see Greek and Roman literature
Romanticism 147-149, 155, 157, 159, 163-164
Rome, fall of 50
Rose, Elliot 180
Rosemary's Baby 159
Rosicrucianism 164-165, 185, 190-191, 198
Rowley, William 152
Rowling, J. K. 155
Runeberg, Arno 180
Rushdie, Salman 147
Russell, Jeffrey 180
Russell, Ray 158
Russell-Gough, Rusty and Celia 205
Sabbats and conventicles 71, 75, 77, 81, 85, 98, 105, 109, 121-122, 125-127, 130, 132-133, 153, 162, 164, 167-168, 174, 180, 186-187, 218-219
Sacrifice 200
Sadducism 114, 131
Saducismus Triumphatus 131-133
Sade, Marquis de 95
Salazar y Frias, Alonso de 126-128
Salem 93, 100, 134-138, 154, 220
Samuel 20, 25
Sanders, Alex 195, 204
Sanders, Maxine 204-205

Satan 19-20, 23, 26-28, 32-34, 38-42, 52-53, 64, 69-71, 73-74, 79, 81-82, 89, 97, 103, 114, 123, 133-134, 145-151, 155, 157-159, 166-167, 169, 178, 186-187, 189, 200-202, 215
Satan 157
The Satanic Bible 198-199
The Satanic Process Church of the Final Judgment 199, 201
The Satanic Verses 147
Satan's Underground 215
Saul 25
Savage, Mary 156
Savonarola, Girolamo 105
Savoy 76
Scandinavia 90
Schmalkaldic League 90
Schreck, Nicholas 200
Schuré, Édouard 165
Die Schwartze Spinne 150
Scot, Reginald 24, 110-115, 117-118, 121, 124, 129, 134, 176, 184
Scotland 90, 92-94, 97, 119, 152
Scott, Michael 164
Scott, Sir Thomas 111
Scott, Sir Walter 164
The Screwtape Letters 158
Seabrook, William B. 178
Secretain, Françoise 122-123
The Secret Doctrine 191
Sefer Yetzirah 39
Select Cases of Conscience 119
Selene 142
Semiazaz 27
Sena, Jorge de 150
Seneca 82
Septuagint 20-21
Serpent (in Eden) 19-21, 33-34
Shadwell, Thomas 153
Shakespeare, William 111, 151, 154
Shelley, Percy 147
Show trials 45
Sibyl, The 166
Sidonia von Bork, die Klosterhexe 154
Simon Magus 37
Simos, Miriam see Starhawk
Sinnett, A. P. 191
Smith, Catherine 154
Smith, Michelle 216-217
Smith, Thorne 156
The Society for Creative Anachronism 202
Sodom 37
Solomon 21, 30
The Sorcery Club 178
La Sorcière 165-168

The Sorrows of Satan 148
Southerne, Elizabeth 152
South Ronaldsay 210
Spain 51, 91, 124, 127
The Spanish Inquisition 56, 91-92, 126-127
Spee, Friedrich von 127-128
Spence, Lewis 175-176
Spengler, Oswald 150
Spies, Johann 149
The Spiral Dance 196
Spiritualism 163, 165
Sprenger, Jacob 77-82, 86, 109-110, 176
Stalin 46
Starhawk 196, 198
Stewart, Sean 196
Stockholm 133
Strange Cults and Secret Societies of Modern London 178
Stratford, Lauren 215-217, 220
Strix 104-105, 117, 168
Sturlasson, Snorri 144
Succubi, see Incubi and succubi
Summers, Montague 119, 175-179
Swanwick, Michael 150
Swedenborg, Emanuel 163
Swedenborgianism 163-164
Switzerland 90, 94
Sword and Sorceress 196
"Sympathy for the Devil" 199
A System of Magick 153
Tableau de l'inconstance des mauvais anges et demons 124-125
Tableau de l'inconstance et instabilité des choses 124
The Talmud 21, 39
Tardieu, Dr. 207
Tartarotti, Girolamo 162
Temora 168
The Tempest 154
The Templars 58-61, 85
The Temple of Set 200
Tennant, Emma 151
Les Tentations de Saint-Antoine 148, 150
Tertullian 34, 48, 168
Testaments of the Twelve Patriarchs 27
Teutonic mythology 144
That's Life 209
Thee Temple of Psychick Youth 200
Their Satanic Majesties Request and Require 199
Theocritus 142
Theodosius 50
Theophilus 149
Théories de l'unité universelle 163
Theosophy 163

THE DEVIL'S PARTY, BY BRIAN STABLEFORD

The Thirty Years War 101
Thomas Aquinas 52, 73
Thomas the Rhymer 174
Thompson, Agnes 116
Throbbing Gristle 200-201
Through the Looking-Glass 202
Timms, Paul 201
Tit-Bits 204
Titus 31
Toksvig, Signe 193
Tolkien, J. R. R. 196
The Torah 21
Torquemada, Tomas de 56
To the Devil—a Daughter 158
Toulouse 85
Tractatus contra daemonum invocatores 76
"Le Tragédie humaine" 148
The Tragical History of Dr. Faustus 149
Trevor-Roper, Hugh 86-88, 101
The Triumph of the Moon 196
Trois âges de la nuit 154
Troublesome Things: A History of Fairies and Fairy Stories 174
Truth or Dare 196
Tylor, Edward 170
Tyndale, William 21
Underhill, Evelyn 192
The Unfortunate Fursey 157
Der Untergang des Abendlandes 150
Updike, John 155
Urban IV, Pope 56
Urban legends 80, 139
Utlagh, Roger 62
Utlagh William 61-62
Valais 85
Valiente, Doreen 195
Vallin, Pierre 85
Van Druten, John 156
Venom 201
Victoria (BC), Bishop of 216
Vikernes, Varg 201
Vineti, Jean 76
The Virgin Mary 149
Visconti, Girolamo 77
Vondel, Joost van den 146
Wagnerbuch 149
Waite, A. E. 192
Waldensians 57-58, 86
Wales 93
Wall, Mervyn 157
The War in Heaven 26-29, 33
Warner, Sylvia Townsend 155

Warren, Mary 135
Warzburg, or Wurtzburg 127-128
Weir, Thomas 97
Welcome to Hell 201
Weldon, Fay 151
The Werewolf Order 200
Wesley, John 24, 93
Westcott, W. Wynne 191
Weyer, Johann 106-108, 110, 114, 117, 121, 124, 176
What Witches Do 204
Wheatley, Dennis 158, 178
The White Goddess 175
Whittle, Anne 152
The Whore of Babylon 58
Wicked: The Life and Times of the Wicked Witch of the West 156
Willard, Samuel 135-136
William of Auvergne 73
William III (of Orange), King of England 134
William of Paris 73
Williams, Charles 192
Wilson, Leslie 154
The Wisdom of Solomon 20
WITCH (Women's International Conspiracy from Hell) 195
The Witch 152
Witchcraft 204
Witchcraft in the Middle Ages 180
Witchcraft: Its Power in the World Today 178
The Witchcraft Research Association 194-195
Witchcraft Today 193
The Witch-Cult in Western Europe 171-173
The Witches 157
Witches Abroad 157
Witches, Demons and Fertility Magic 180
The Witches of Eastwick 155
Witches Still Live 178
Witch Hunting in Southwestern Germany 1562-1684 83
The Witch of Edmonton 152
The Witch of Endor 25
The Witch of Ravensworth 154
Witch Wood 175
The Wizard of Oz 156
Woman's Own 205
Wonders of the Invisible World 136-137
Woodman, William 191
Wright, Thomas 154
Wyrd Sisters 157
Yeats, W. B. 192
Yesterday Never Dies 154
"Young Goodman Brown" 154
Yule 68
Zanoni 165

Zend-Avestra 28
Ziarnko, Jan 125
Zohar 39
Zoroastrianism 28, 38
Zugarramundi 126
Zurich 90
Zwingli, Ulrich 90

www.ingramcontent.com/pod-product-compliance
Lightning Source LLC
LaVergne TN
LVHW041613070426
835507LV00008B/206